RAVENSCRAG
The Allan Royal Mail Line

RAVEN

The Allan Ro

SCRAG

yal Mail Line

Thomas E. Appleton

McClelland and Stewart Limited

To my wife

0-7710-0720-5

The Canadian Publishers
McClelland and Stewart Limited
25 Hollinger Road, Toronto

CONTENTS

ACKNOWLEDGEMENTS

I am deeply grateful to the Allan descendants who most generously placed personal records and recollections at my disposal. For my wife and me their friendship and hospitality, equally warm on both sides of the Atlantic, is the outstanding memory of a delightful research tour. This rewarding experience brought life and colour to faded historical documents in scattered places which are otherwise all that remain to piece together a tale of enterprise and courage on the sea, a legend which lies behind the growth of Canada and links it with the Scottish heritage.

My warmest thanks are due to Lord Allan of Kilmahew, Richard Allan at Moreton-in-the-Marsh, Miss Jean C. Allan and her sister Elspeth at Hunter's Quay on the Firth of Clyde, A.H. Allan at Tobermory in the Island of Mull, Mrs. May M. Last and Mrs. Christopher Jennings; in Canada I must thank James C. Routledge at Belmere, Que., and at Montreal Mrs. Sydney Dawes, Miss Phoebe Campbell, and Duncan McEachran.

In Ayrshire I would like to thank especially Robert and Inez Kirk of the Dundonald Burns Club, and Mrs. Ingrid Pillans of Fairlie House, who took us over the ground of the early Allan history where lay the footprints of James Allan and Robert Burns.

In other areas of research my appreciation is due to George Ayoub, Edward F. Bush, Emery Nagy and J.W. O'Brien in Ottawa; from Montreal I am indebted for assistance from Dr. R.A. Cleghorn and Dorothy Trainor of the Allan Memorial Institute, Edgar Andrew Collard. Editor *Emeritus* of the *Montreal Gazette,* Captain W.P. Embleton of C.P. Ships, Ernest Rolland, and Miss Annette R. Wolff.

Much historical material was brought to my attention as a result of correspondence and personal contact with old and new friends. Among these are Basil Greenhill, Director of the National Maritime Museum at Greenwich, Captain E.F. Aikman at St. Andrews, Captain J.F. Aspin of the Shipping Federation of Canada, Miss Ishbel D. Crawford of Glasgow who generously permitted me to select from her collection of Allan Line memorabilia Neils W. Jannasch of the Maritime Museum of Nova Scotia, William Lind the prominent Scottish marine archivist, C.H. Milsom of the *Journal of Commerce* in Liverpool, David Moore of the Vickers Experimental Tank in London, George Musk, late of C.P. Ships in Trafalgar Square, and Miss Agnes C. O'Dea of the Centre for Newfoundland Studies at Memorial University. To Mrs. Nellie Glen Shaw of Burford, Ont., and Arthur Bruce of Ottawa, I am grateful for permission to quote from family diaries.

My thanks for valuable information from Britain go also to J. Percival Agnew in Glasgow; Ivor C. Borland, Erith; Charles A. Chalmers, Glasgow; Bryan Edwards, Liverpool; John Graham, Troon; S.F. Hunt, Pinner; Mrs. Eva W. Davies, Liverpool; R. Kellock, Greenock; Mrs. Miriam Langdon, Liverpool; Hugh McCallum of the *Greenock Telegraph;* R.G. Olsen, Wirral; Ernest P. Owen, Liverpool; Arthur Page, Liverpool; A.N. Ramsay, Liverpool; A.M.M. Stephen of Alexander Stephen & Sons Ltd., in Glasgow; H.E. Waller, Wirral; and to the staff of the Liverpool Museum.

In Canada I also thank Lionel Duhamel, Montreal; John Corby of the National

Museum of Science and Technology in Ottawa, Dr. C.T. Fitzgerald of Ottawa, J. Stephenson Fry, Montreal; C.W. Harris, Vice-President of the Bank of Montreal; Paul P. Hutcheson of Montreal; Rober Mainwaring, Brockville; J.W. McGiffin, President of Canada Steamship Lines; Ronald Metcalfe, Montreal; F. Stockton of the Royal Trust Company; G.W. Thornhill, Montreal; Miss Constance Troy of Ottawa, and Montagu Yates of Baie d'Urfe, Que. If I have inadvertently omitted to thank others of the many people who gave of their time and knowledge to put me in touch with valuable information, I can only apologize, coupled with the explanation that letter files have been voluminous.

My appreciation for the Public Archives of Canada has a special place, based on many years of experience; the staff are always helpful, the material is encyclopedic and I would particularly mention the newspaper room where a century and more of periodicals is available. For shipping research the sailing notices in the *Glasgow Herald* and *Montreal Gazette,* appearing almost daily, are a priceless source of information, particularly with the aid of microfilm.

In a work of this nature it is essential for the author to have critical and informed advice. In this connection I must record my gratitude to Dr. W. Kaye Lamb, formerly the Dominion Archivist of Canada, who encouraged me throughout, to Eric Reford of Montreal, who very kindly read my drafts with infinite patience and a knowledge of the St. Lawrence shipping trade based on five generations of family involvement; to Douglas J. Williams of Victoria who, for the second time, kindly responded to my request for literary guidance. There are errors and omissions, of course; for these my mentors are in no way responsible, being mine alone.

My appreciation goes also to the Canada Council whose help made it easier to cover research which might otherwise have been missed. The publishers have my sympathy; theirs is a difficult trade in which the waywardness of authors is but one of many hazards.

Finally, and with affection, I commend my wife, Vi, for her professional editorial help and, more especially, for her unfailing support. She has made many friends for both of us during four fascinating years with *Ravenscrag* and the Allan Royal Mail Line.

Thomas E. Appleton,
Ottawa.

Ravenscrag, Sir Hugh Allan's Montreal mansion, about 1902, now the Allan Memorial Institute. (Courtesy, Notman)

PROLOGUE

RAVENSCRAG

"For gold the merchant ploughs the main,
The farmer ploughs the manor;"

Robert Burns
When wild War's deadly Blast was blawn

It was near midnight when a light phaeton drawn by a pair of matched thoroughbreds swung carefully off Pine Avenue through the ornamental iron gates of *Ravenscrag*. As gravel gritted under hoof and wheel, not even the old coachman could smarten the pace to enter the grounds with a flourish, for the horses were blown. Far behind and below, in the velvety darkness of a mild evening in May 1881, the lights of Montreal receded gently to middle distance where Victoria Bridge triumphantly spanned the River St. Lawrence, leading to the plains of the south shore which, all but unseen, merged into the distant hills of Vermont.

Turning left and then right the carriage followed a circular driveway, halting abruptly with a jingle of bits and tossing of heads as the groom leapt down to hold his horses. From the grey limestone portico with its massive columns a servant hurried from the light of the entrance hall. From the darkness outside, the interior could be seen for a moment in all its classic proportion like a brilliant stage setting. At the apex of the portico, unseen but emblematic of the Allan House, the family crest was carved in stone, surmounting the motto *Spero*, "I Hope."

The carriage swayed as the owner of this mansion emerged in an unpretentious way to help his lady, for Sir Hugh Allan was nothing if not a devoted husband and family man, and they entered their home together.

For Sir Hugh it had been a triumphal evening in his honour, a dinner given in tribute from the citizens of Montreal, the culmination of several similar occasions which, perhaps not entirely to his surprise, had been held elsewhere in Canada and the United States. Tonight, in Montreal which he loved so much, it had been especially gratifying, even touching at times, in memories of the past and hopes for the future; " . . . a splendid ovation to the pioneers of our commercial greatness" ran the headlines in the *Montreal Gazette*, coupling Sir Hugh with his younger brother Andrew. Everyone who was anyone had been there and, joined by their ladies, row upon row of elegant figures in starched linen or décolletage were esconced among flowers and crystal beneath a vaulted ceiling rich in moulding and fresco. There they all were, friends and associates, competitors and rivals and some shadowy figures which the old man for all his vitality could scarcely remember – a few he had never met and never would. Eloquent over nine or ten courses of a relentless Victorian dinner, speaker after speaker gave round upon round of toasts and speeches to four hundred and fifty guests, an impressive tribute to a lifetime of purposeful activity. Unspoken amidst the hubbub of conversation and applause in the fragrance of port and cigars, undercurrents of more personal feelings swirled in undisguised admiration of their guest of honour for the most part, through placid reaches of indifference to a towering but remote public figure, to whirlpools of envy and perhaps malice towards the "Prince of Ravenscrag."

It was over now. Saying goodnight to his family, Sir Hugh closed the door behind him as he entered the library, savouring a nightly ritual of reflection in solitude. For a while he browsed around his favourite room turning over familiar books and papers under soft lamplight glowing on brass fireplace ornaments and mahogany panelling. He sunk into his leather armchair by the fender, reaching for a decanter and tray left by the butler. He had never been a drinking man, indeed he was opposed to it, for too many of his compatriots had gone the way of 'John Barleycorn'; but, now turned seventy, he had accepted medical opinion that a glass of brandy would settle the events of the day. Perhaps it would.

"The Prince of Ravenscrag" someone had called him. What nonsense he thought, what arrant nonsense. Certainly his was a fine house, the realisation of boyhood dreams after a lifetime of toil and struggle. He could remember shaking down for the night as a young clerk on a pallet in the attic of his employer's office on St. Paul Street. But "Princely"? In a way perhaps the description fitted, for in the rough and tumble of mid-nineteenth century Canada not even the Governor General was more splendidly housed. Those were far-off days when he had landed on the waterfront from his father's brig after a month and a half from Scotland, a passage which he and his brothers had reduced to a week-and-a-half by their magnificent liner *Parisian* which now lay for all to see and admire alongside her berth at the crowded docks below *Ravenscrag*.

The *Parisian* had made a hit; how right they had been to spend money on a very large steamer of latest design for the Montreal trade – how right and how typical. What an unusual family they were, he mused. He was the second son of old Captain Alexander Allan, "patriarch" of the Line and long dead, and he remembered how his father had started in 1819 with small sailing ships running from Greenock to Quebec. How fortunate it had been that the five brothers, working from both sides of the Atlantic, had built on their father's foundation until they now owned one of the great shipping companies of the age. James and Bryce had followed their father to sea in his ships, Bryce now running affairs in Liverpool where Allan Line mailboats left the Landing Stage every Wednesday as regular as clockwork. James, who was the eldest son and the first to become a master mariner, was ensconced in Glasgow, where with his youngest brother, Alexander, to run the freight and passenger side, the business went by the name of J & A Allan, Shipowners. But the financial impetus had come from Montreal where Hugh Allan had succeeded in bringing ocean steamships to the St. Lawrence trade when others had failed, steamships which now served the principal ports of eastern Canada and the United States. The old wooden sailing ships had gone but the Allan Line flag was still carried in full-rigged iron clippers which made handsome profits as they tramped the Seven Seas in much the same way as of old.

But the *Parisian!* There was the ship that would make their name! At dinner in the Windsor Hotel Sir Hugh had been delighted to find that Captain Wylie, commander of the new ship, had also been invited. The sense of occasion had been heightened by a sheer extravaganza, a floral model of the *Parisian* suspended by festoons of smilax from the enormous central chandelier, which the *Montreal Gazette* described in detail. Floating above the guests on a sea of exotica, the flagship of the Line was formed from white and carmine pinks propelled by a screw of white eucharis. Twin funnels of immortelle in red, white and blue sported the Allan colours under their inevitable smoke, represented for the occasion by billowings of dark feathery grass. With the Canadian Ensign fluttering at the fore and the Union Jack at the stemhead, the pride of the Allan fleet had satisfied the artistic, maritime and patriotic instincts of the entire gathering.

And what a gathering it had been. With the Mayor of Montreal in the chair, the civic rulers of Halifax, Boston, Portland and Baltimore had placed their names on the subscription list, as had the presidents of half the chambers of commerce in eastern North America. But both in civic and commercial interests one city was most noticeably unrepresented – Toronto. Old rivalries between Montreal, which since the days of the fur trade had dominated Canada, and the brash western City of Toronto which had more recent ambitions in the same direction, were accentuated at this gathering. Toronto had finally lost out on the biggest contract in the history of the Dominion – the biggest gamble according to many – the building of the Canadian Pacific Railway which had held its first directors' meeting less than three months previously in Montreal.

The CPR; if ever there was a 'might have been' in Sir Hugh Allan's makeup it must have floated into his awareness that night, if indeed it ever completely left him. But he was stoical and reserved in this, as he was in business affairs in general; and although he had tried and failed to bring the Pacific Railway to Montreal ten years before the group now in control, certain prominent figures testified by their absence from this dinner that the great railway rumpus was not forgotten. Government House was represented by an ADC, but where was the greatest of them all, Sir John A. Macdonald, the enigmatic Prime Minister who now more than ever spoke for Canada? Railways with their vast territorial appetites and political involvements had brought little but trouble to Sir Hugh, whereas ships on the trackless ocean had left a wake of prosperity and satisfaction. It had been a difficult period, now almost a decade ago, and how strange that the man who precipitated the row, Lucius Seth Huntingdon, was there in person as the local member of Parliament; even stranger, after all that had occurred, he was an Opposition Liberal representing a predominantly Conservative House of Commons at this testimonial dinner to Sir Hugh Allan who had been the central figure in a notoriously distressing episode. The "Pacific Scandal" they had called it; Sir Hugh had no qualms.

And then there were the Americans. Often Sir Hugh Allan had been accused of an American bias. Responding to the toast of the President of the United States, the American consul at Montreal had replied that:

. . . trade will eventually go by the cheapest route. This no law can change, and no law ought to change if it could. If we can put wheat from Manitoba into Liverpool by way of New York cheaper than you can by way of Montreal, no man in Canada will have the right to

12

complain. If you should finally be able to put wheat from Kansas into Liverpool by way of Montreal cheaper than we can by way of New York, or New Orleans, our mouths ought to be closed. We welcome you to the competition. But at whatever point the product of the west reaches the coast, one thing is certain; exactly at that point the Allans will load their ships.

He had been right of course. Trade brought prosperity although not everyone could see that, especially the politicians. Politics was no trade for a shipowner but there had been times when it had been necessary to go round by the back door. In railways there was no other way, for railways and politics were so inextricably mixed that they were impossible to separate. What a poker game it all was – and what players! Many of them had been at dinner in the Windsor Hotel, but some were missing. Sir John Abbott, for years the trusted lawyer of the Allans and now counsel for the newly formed CPR, was there. Sir George Etienne Cartier was dead; the fiery Frenchman who had been 'out' in the Rebellion of 1837, when young Hugh Allan had tramped the province in his red coat with the militia, had ended up as one of the key figures of the Confederation of Canada. But in the surge and sway of political life in Quebec he and Sir Hugh had been at the vortex of many a whirlwind. Sir George had died while travelling in England and his body had been returned to Canada in the *Prussian,* one of Sir Hugh's steamships. That had been eight years ago, but in his mind's eye Sir Hugh could still see the *Prussian* as she lay in the stream off Quebec City of a summer's night in 1873 to land the body. By the light of hurricane lamps the case containing the heavy casket was lifted by main derrick and lowered to the deck of the waiting tender, the government steamer *Druid,* for conveyance ashore for requiem high mass at the Cathedral. The old *Druid,* how often he had seen her paddling her way to supply the lighthouses in the Gulf of St. Lawrence. There were never enough lighthouses, there was never enough money in the young Dominion of Canada to do the things which needed to be done.

As he savoured these memories from the chair in his library, the focal point of the house, the open fireplace with its glowing embers brought his mind back to *Ravenscrag.* He was fond of the name, always had been, and in 1866 he had bestowed it also on a fine full-rigged clipper ship built on the Clyde. But it was the house itself which had given so much pleasure since 1860 when he and Matilda bought the site, the choicest place for miles around. There was a history of course, as there was to everything in the Old Province, a history dating back to 1800 when Simon McTavish of the North West Company bought the land. They knew what they were about, the Nor'Westers, but McTavish had the ill fortune to die in 1804 before he could finish a mansion which would house his French wife in a chateau of imposing proportions. It had lain half-finished, for years, the haunt of vandals and others to whom the weatherbeaten, tenantless walls afforded an irresistable attraction. Some said it was more than a haunt for ne'er-do-wells, it was haunted; at full moon, when windy clouds scattered shafts of eerie light, there had been reports of ghostlike glints which fluttered into the features of the old fur trader. Sceptics said that an unfinished tin roof on the weird deserted walls reflected the moonlight. Hugh Allan was not put off by this nonsense about a fellow Scot. He paid cash and took over the property from McMartin the farmer who was then the tenant. McTavish never left the place even in death; his body rests in a vaulted limestone mausoleum nearby.

The McTavish ruins were demolished some time before 1862 when the building of *Ravenscrag* began. Three years later the house was finished, Italian Renaissance of course, an imposing structure with walls of enormous thickness, gabled, columned and porticoed, the whole finished off with a square tower from which windows on all sides opened on a panorama of Montreal and the River. Here on many an occasion Hugh Allan would train his telescope eastwards towards Longue Point where the silvery ribbon of the St. Lawrence was interrupted by a moving dot which grew quickly in size until it could be recognised as an inward ship with the Allan colours at the main. Nothing missed his eye and he could tell at once whether all was ready for a quick start at discharging cargo in the morning. He even knew what cargo she had brought because the manifest, which had been sent by rail from Rimouski ahead of the ship, was already on his desk at the office of the Montreal Ocean Steamship Company, Messrs. Hugh & Andrew Allan, at the corner of Youville and Common Streets.

And then there was *Belmere*. *Ravenscrag* was the place in winter when the snowshoe clubs gathered at McGill for a scramble up Mount Royal and in the evening the house would ring with laughter. Sir Hugh and Lady Allan had a round dozen in their family, four boys and eight girls, ranging from schoolroom age through emerging independence to young matrons already married. In summer when the entire city baked under a blanket of humid heat, the whole family would bundle into the train for a quick run south to Lake Memphremagog where cool waters and wooded slopes wandered across the border into Vermont. It was scenery which had inspired Kreighoff, from that very site before *Belmere* was built, to paint the majestic profile of the Owl's Head which is the highest peak for miles around – not that the man was worth collecting, but he did have an eye for the Quebec scene in all its blaze of colour. As he thought of his summer home at *Belmere,* Sir Hugh turned to the table where a leather-bound album lay open at the title page. On a sheet of notepaper, ruled faintly in pencil to guide a formal hand, instructions for the dedication of a very special gift had been given to Notman, the photographer whose work filled the album from cover to cover:

To His Royal Highness
Prince Arthur etc. etc.
In memory of his cherished visit to Belmere,
From Hugh Allan,
Montreal, June 1870

What a time that had been. The young Prince Arthur, a boyish subaltern of the Rifle Brigade who was combining regimental duties with the grand tour of the New Dominion, had been engagingly interested in everything he was shown, especially by the young ladies. What a pity the Governor General had been such a bore; surely they could have arranged for a more lively entourage than that of Sir John Young for a week in the country! But everything passed off without a hitch and His Excellency was raised to the peerage as Baron Lisgar that year. The private telegraph line had made an impression, though – specially wired from Montreal where it connected with the trans-Atlantic cable, Hugh Allan's electric telegraph was used to produce a daily summary of the world's news, written out each morning and placed respectfully beside the royal plate at breakfast. As he turned the pages of Mr. Notman's album, alternating tastefully between groups and views connected vaguely by a sepia wash montage of rustic scenery, Hugh Allan once more beheld his family and guests. They were grouped nonchalantly around the Prince at croquet on the lawn, at tea on the verandah or in basket chairs under the awning of the steam yacht *Ormond* as it glided away from the boathouse on Lake Memphremagog, with the Royal Standard waving lazily from the masthead.

The girls had enjoyed the visit, for Prince Arthur was an attractive young man. From the time that he arrived in Montreal in September 1869, invitations to dinners and dances had made for a season of pleasurable excitement, including a trip to Ottawa for a private and very select party at Rideau Hall. What fun it had been; the whole affair culminated in a splendid military revue at Quebec where HRH had presented colours to the 69th Regiment before joining them for return to England in HMS *Crocodile.* He would have been faster and more comfortable in the Allan Royal Mail Line, but there it was. Thirty years ago, at the time of the Crimea, the War Office had been glad enough to charter the fast Allan Liners *Canadian* and *Indian* (and a profitable transaction it had been too); but in peacetime nothing would do but that

15

the entire battalion of the *Prince Consort's Own,* at heaven knows what outrageous cost, must cross the Atlantic in an unwieldy government troopship.

Perhaps it was all for the best – certainly his efforts had not gone un-noticed. A faded cutting from the *Montreal Gazette* of 28 July, 1871, summed it up nicely:

> . . . that his eminent services in connection with steam navigation have been recognised, is a matter for sincere congratulation among all classes of the people of Canada. It is a subject of highest pride to Canadians that one who has done so much to develop the great interest of the St. Lawrence route has not only reaped the pecuniary awards which enterprise and indomitable pluck, such as he has shown, richly deserves, but has also been honoured with well merited distinction by his Sovereign.

He had chosen to be known as "Sir Hugh Allan of Ravenscrag", a style which sat easily on plain Hugh Allan, for the past forty years an increasingly familiar figure on the board of some of the most famous business corporations in Canada. The Bank of Montreal, the Merchant's Bank and a host of other companies financing telegraphs, cotton, coal and iron, sewing machine factories, rolling mills, paper production and many other industries had known his tireless energy and shrewd judgement.

What of " . . . enterprise and indomitable pluck," as the *Gazette* called it? It was all very well for those newspaper fellows to write that way, but he seldom thought of life like that. There had been bad times, of course; times when ruin lurked just around the corner. On top of this, disaster had come when it was least expected, sometimes with a persistence which defied the laws of chance. Telegrams from outlandish places announcing shipwreck, loss of life and heartrending suffering had never been easy to bear. They were never far from his mind on sailing day, when the Blue Peter whipped at the halliards in a rising wind and a wisp of steam from a whimpering safety valve showed that yet another Allan Liner was ready to face the sea.

Burns had put it rather well: " . . . the best laid schemes o' mice and men gang aft agley." Not that he had much to say in favour of that erratic genius – too unreliable by far – but in this at least the poet had been right. The great thing was to persevere in life: and if one scheme failed another must be ready; there must be no going back. This was his heritage from generations of Ayrshire forbears whose lives had been ruled by the stark necessities of survival.

16

CHAPTER ONE

The Ayrshire Allans

"An honest man's the noblest work of God"

Alexander Pope, as quoted by R.B.
in *The Cotter's Saturday Night*

The modern traveller from Montreal to Scotland will more than likely arrive at Prestwick Airport about breakfast-time. As the undercarriage comes down with a slight bump and the muffled greyness of sea and sand gives way to Ayrshire pasture, it is less likely that he will have time to view in all its glory the gateway to the Clyde. But striding across the tarmac in the snell breeze of morning he may see for a passing moment the jagged profile of the Arran mountains to the westward, known locally as the 'Sleeping Warrior' from its resemblance to a recumbent knight in effigy; and he will glimpse the unmistakable hummock of Ailsa Craig – "Paddy's Milestone" – rising from the sea.

In the eighteenth century Ayrshire had nothing like its lush appearance of today, which includes some of the finest farmland in all Britain. Colonel William Fullarton, an enlightened agriculturist of the time, left a vivid description of his county in 1793 when he wrote:

A stranger passing through these districts must be surprised to observe such a multitude of agricultural defects still existing. But his applause could undeniably be excited when he understood the great

17

difference between the present management and that which took place forty years ago. At that period there was hardly a practicable road in the country . . . the farmhouses were mere hovels, moted with clay, having an open hearth or fireplace in the middle, the dunghill at the door, the cattle starving and the people wretched. The few ditches which existed were ill constructed and the hedges worse preserved . . . no fallows . . . no green crops . . . no sown grass – no carts or wagons – no straw yards; hardly a potato or any other esculent root and indeed no garden vegetables unless a few Scotch kail which, with milk and oatmeal, formed the diet of the people. There was little straw, and no hay except a scanty portion of the poorest quality collected from the bogs . . . The ground was scourged with a succession of oats after oats as long as they would pay for seed and labour and afford a small surplus of oatmeal for the family, and then remained in a state of absolute sterility or over-run with thistles till rest again persuaded it to reproduce a scanty crop.

This description, perhaps something of a surprise to modern ears, came from someone who knew what he was talking about. William Fullarton (1754-1808) was an educated man who had travelled widely; he had served in India as a colonel in the 98th Regiment of the Honourable East India Company's army, and also in their diplomatic service, before returning for a period to his native Ayrshire where he did much to advance farming. Fullarton's career, which culminated in the Governorship of Trinidad before he finally retired to Scotland, was typical of many at a time when that country was emerging from centuries of strife, poverty and isolation. Before the Union with England in 1707 there had been little choice for the sons of gentlemen; they could risk their honour as mercenary soldiers in the service of some European prince, or their fortunes as merchants in a highly partisan country divided by the Jacobean struggle. By mid-eighteenth century, with growing peace and stability after the 1745 rebellion had been digested at home but with the prospect of interminable wars abroad, there were new opportunities for soldiers, administrators and traders in the expanding British Empire. It was a world in which the Scottish character found a ready acceptance, a development which men of ambition were not slow to exploit. But the dawn of the Scottish Renaissance, rosy enough for those with means and education, was hardly to be appreciated by the toiling majority of the rural population.

With the limited opportunities open to ordinary people it was small wonder that service in landed families and great houses provided some variety in the struggle for existence, and sometimes attracted men of character and ability. Among these were William Burns† and James

Allan. They were both at various times employed on Fairlie Estate, a property belonging to Colonel Fullarton which he had purchased from the Fairlie family – factors to the Earl of Eglinton and Winton – about 1780 or so.

William Burns had been a gardener at Fairlie before branching out as a tenant farmer at Alloway, near Ayr. He was a dark-eyed, sensitive man with a taste for reading and a passion for education, a passion which not even the fluttering light of a tallow candle could dim. His wife was almost illiterate, but made up for this by a remarkable memory for Scottish songs and an enthusiasm for country lore. Their son Robert, "Robin" to the family, and first of seven children, was born after the Fairlie interlude; he inherited his father's literary bent and his mother's poetic instincts. By the time that he was twenty-one he was recognised generally as a young man of talent – which some thought genius – and a magnetic personality which most people of warmth and sensibility found irresistible.

James Allan, who lived near Fairlie and was well known to Burns the gardener, was a joiner or carpenter by trade. He was employed with his father and brother, who were masons, at the building of a fine new mansion, completed on the estate about 1776. Fairlie House, one of many handsome stone residences designed by Robert Adam (then the most sought-after architect in Britain – and a Scot) is a noble house, simply proportioned, with porticoed entrance and radial fanlight in unmistakable Adam tradition. Its classic stone frontage and elegant windows are surmounted by five prominent chimney stacks, which have stood unabashed for nearly two hundred years. Not surprisingly, in the heart of a vocal and expressive community, it was promptly nick-named "Fairlie five-lums," an undeniably accurate description which remains to this day. Fairlie House is a beautiful and gracious private home, little changed since it was built.

In 1775 James Allan married Jean Brown, a younger sister of Mrs. Burns the gardener's wife, and the two men became better acquainted as "guid-brothers." The Browns came of a tenant farming family in the Parish of Kirkoswald, a fair way from the Burns at Alloway, and farther still from Fairlie House and Kilmarnock. But despite the discomforts of long journeys on horseback over rutted cart tracks, family ties were strong. Sometimes young Robert Burns, an interesting relative to say the least, would visit the Allans. Not only Uncle James and Aunt Jean but a thriving circle of younger cousins welcomed his arrival and the fun which went with it. James Allan had prospered at his trade, or at least succeeded in earning a steady living, an achievement which was then

† William spelt his name "Burnes," but for simplicity the style 'Burns' is used throughout.

hard enough, while his family grew. There were four boys in a row, beginning with James and Andrew, then Alexander in 1780, and John two years later. The boys were followed by three girls, Fairley who was named in the spelling of the period to commemorate their happy home, then Janet and Margaret.

Colonel Fullarton was, of course, well acquainted with both families. As a judge of character and a fair-minded man, his opinions of them are interesting. On one occasion when he was about to leave home for an extended period, he called the entire staff into the panelled library – which may have been Allan's own work – to hear instructions which would keep them fully employed and out of mischief in his absence. After a brief harangue in clipped military fashion he turned to his carpenter, who in working homespun and Kilmarnock bonnet stood apart from the liveried footmen and house servants, with a telling remark: "As for you James Allan, I never saw you idle and you may do just as you like." Clearly, James Allan was a reliable type, with a natural appeal to a regimental officer – an appeal which not all of his kind extended to the nephew. But it is also to Colonel Fullarton that we are indebted for a rare tribute to young Burns the farmer, for he too had succumbed for a time to the urge to farm his own place. In Fullarton's *General View of the Agriculture of the County of Ayr*, published in 1793, the author acknowledges a good method for removing the horns of cattle to " . . . Mr Robert Burns, whose general talents are no less conspicuous than the poetic powers which have done honour to the county of his birth."

Whatever talents Burns may have had as a farmer in 1793, he had no success back in 1786 when he was close to the Allans. His poetic genius was beginning to promise something by way of making a living, however, and he resolved to publish a collection of his poems, and to use the proceeds for a passage to Jamaica, where he planned a new life overseeing in the plantations. While all this was turning over in his mind, the Allans found him on the doorstep of their Fairlie cottage one evening in July of that year, urgently seeking shelter and seclusion. As always, Robin was irresistable: by now estranged from his mother – for his amorous adventures had been the talk of Ayrshire – and with his father dead of disappointment and hardship these last two years, the errant nephew found a soft spot with Aunt Jean and Uncle James, who made him welcome as usual. One can imagine the commotion and excitement among the small boys as they peered from the "ingle neuk" when their much talked of cousin stepped into the firelight. It was an event which wee Sandy – the name Alexander was too stiff except for the flyleaf of the family Bible – would remember for the rest of his life.

There was more to "Robin's" visit than the convenience of a bed and board although he was within reach of Wilson's the Kilmarnock printer, a bare five miles away, where he must now correct proofs. He was on the run from arrest, under a warrant taken out by James Armour. This sturdy fellow considered that his daughter must be shielded at all costs from marriage with a wayward poet, who had already announced his intentions in the most embarassing way. By no means the first crisis in Burns' life, the humiliation of this was probably the hardest to bear. Jean Armour, the longest lasting love of his life and the girl whom he did eventually marry, had been bullied by her father. He refused his consent to the marriage when Jean was expecting Burn's child, and resorted to action at law for paternal support – hence Robin's flight to the Allans' cottage, sheltered in the grounds of Fairlie House and well back from the high road and the prying eyes of "Holy Willies."

Sandy was too young at the time to understand the meaning of these events, realising only that cousin Robin would soon be off to Jamaica, a romantic place very different to homely Ayrshire. But it might have stuck in his boyish mind that Burns had deferred this adventure, originally from Greenock to Jamaica in a ship called the *Nancy,* in favour of a later sailing in a ship with an odd name for a West Indiaman, the *Bell.* If so, it was a boyhood memory which would pop up with a singular interest later in his life.

Before long the success of the Kilmarnock Edition of *Poems, Chiefly in the Scottish Dialect* by Robert Burns encouraged a change of plan. All but 13 copies of the 612 volumes printed by Wilson were sold within a month and Scotland was not denied her National Bard. No doubt in later years, when reading in his cabin on long voyages under sail, Sandy Allan reflected that this strange episode gave rise to yet another romantic interlude, Burns' affair with Mary Campbell, immortalised as "Highland Mary."

Meanwhile, in the steady round of country life, the Allans continued at Fairlie until 1792 when James Allan died. We know how highly his employer valued him – but before long the estate cottage, possibly one of those still standing, was needed for his successor. Doubtless Colonel Fullarton did all he could to ease the blow, and the widow joined her husband's family in their two-storied stone house in the village of Old Rome, adjoining the Fairlie Estate. Old Rome has long since been absorbed by farm land – the Allan family home to which Jean and her seven children moved was demolished about 1920 – and the only remaining link there is a cottage on the main road which was once the schoolhouse attended by the Allan children.

Robin mourned the death of his uncle along with the rest of the family. It has been said that Burns may have had James Allan in mind in 1785 when he quoted Pope's line " . . . an honest man's the noblest work of God." If so, it would have been an apt tribute – certainly Fairlie Cottage with its warm family life might well have inspired the setting for *The Cotter's Saturday Night.*

Jean Allan had now to bring up her family. About a year later, when Sandy was thirteen or fourteen, it was time for him to help his mother directly in her efforts to keep the young ones at school until the boys could go out to work and the girls were marriageable. His older brothers were already at work when Sandy was apprenticed to James Cunningham, a Kilmarnock shoemaker. The move to Old Rome had shortened the journey into "Killie," but even so it was three miles from his mother's house to the workshop in College Wynd, a daily walk which was nothing "by-ordinar" for an Ayrshire lad. A chronicler of the time, John Kelso Hunter, relates a story of the shoemaker and his apprentice in *Retrospect of an Artist's Life,* first published in 1867.

The story goes that Sandy was both mischievous and industrious, a healthy combination which occasionally got him into a scrape. The apprentices, who by this time were living in the garret above their master, had got into the habit of tapping on the floor with one foot as a reminder to those below that mealtime was approaching. One of the journeymen dared young Allan to keep up this tapping, or "happing," while Cunningham was at his supper in solitary state. Before long the old man could stand it no longer and came roaring up the stairs in a great to-do, shouting that " . . . Sawn'y Allan would hap t'Hell for a penny loaf."

In the shoemaking trade, as in most others, it was the custom for young journeymen to seek a change from the scenes of their apprenticeship and start their adult career in fresh surroundings under a new employer. On receiving his coveted "lines" (the colloquial term for a certificate of apprenticeship) from old Cunningham, Sandy Allan was employed by James Nisbet, a master shoemaker at Loudenskirk near Galston. Sandy was a likeable lad who got on well with Nisbet and might in time have risen to mundane prosperity as a manufacturer of footwear, had it not been for an illness. We do not know exactly what this was – accounts of the period mention trouble with an arm or leg, probably the latter – but it might have been polio. At any rate, Sandy Allan was advised to go to the coast for a change of air and off he went to Saltcoats, pronounced "Sal'c'ts," probably about 1800.

The little seaports of Ayrshire, Ayr itself, Troon, Irvine, Saltcoats and Ardrossan, spaced northwards at intervals along the glorious beaches and dunes of the County (fine golf courses all) have had their ups and downs with the peaks and valleys of the Scottish economy, be it the West Indian trade, the export of coal from local pits, or the herring fisheries. As salt fish was then a staple diet for sailors and soldiers – and indeed for the general population in winter – the fishing industry was encouraged by a government bounty to ensure a continuing reserve of men for the Royal Navy. There was also a considerable shipbuilding industry – not that Ayrshire launched the great 100-gun ships and stately 74's of the period, but rather the auxiliary vessels needed for their sustenance, almost as essential but long forgotten.

Even in the eighteenth century, when the sailing navy was independent of the shore to a degree never matched until the advent of the nuclear submarine, it relied whenever possible on foreign bases such as Gibraltar, the Mediterranean, the West Indies, and Portugal. These were convenient anchorages for periodic replenishment of food, men, naval stores and ammunition. Ayrshire shipowners, many of whom built owned and sailed their own vessels, were very much alive to this specialised aspect of the shipping business, ideally suited to their temperament and environment. One interesting memento has survived to illustrate this period: a presentation piece of pottery badged on one side with an Irvine-built supply sloop in full sail, and on the other with a flowery dedication to Sir George Brydges Rodney, who as Rear Admiral of England from 1771-4 was responsible to the Board of Admiralty for shipbuilding. Apart from transports built in this manner or hired to supply the Navy, the British Army maintained garrisons or field forces the world over. To feed them, fresh meat on the hoof was shipped from the nearest market when conditions warranted.

At that period the harbours of Saltcoats and Irvine, barely three miles or so apart, were characterised by fleets of small wooden ships which, with their interesting sights, sounds and smells, were a heady elixir to the youth of the period. At low water the homely, round-bilged vessels, brigs and schooners with a few barques among the larger – and of course local sloops among the smaller known in the west of Scotland as "gabberts" – would lie against stone piers, their masts slanting inwards with yards cockbilled to clear adjacent buildings. As the tide rose over the sandy bottom, lapped by sea and and seaweed, shipwrights (or carpenters as they were known in Scotland) would work with maul and oakum to caulk some damaged plank or wale. With high water the vessels floated and straightened up and they would shift their berth as occasion demanded, perhaps by tarry-breeked seamen at winch or capstan, perhaps by horses which were everywhere. It was a cheerful and unhurried scene, typical of hundreds of other busy little ports, where sea-air enlivened by a whiff of Stockholm tar and oak shavings was guaranteed to put ideas into the head of any youngster of spirit.

Whatever his illness might have been – and there is no further reference to it – Sandy Allan benefited from the change by which the stuffy air of a cottage workshop was replaced by the invigorating atmosphere of Saltcoats. But cured of one disease it is hardly surprising that he was not immune from another – a sharp and more permanent attack of "sea fever," that incurable longing which throughout history has lured men to the ends of the earth. Nor was a young shoemaker as far removed from the realities of shipboard life as might have been imagined. Shoemaking was then a skilled trade at which a man might make anything from a gentleman's riding boots or a lady's shoe to the common clogs of the country people, an activity far removed from mere cobbling. With his heritage of woodworking from the carpenter's shop at Fairlie-five-lums, we can be certain that Allan was a good man with tools, in or out of his own trade. Also leather was then used in ships for many purposes from valves in wooden bilge-pumps to chafing gear in the rigging aloft, and a lad with this background would have no difficulty in finding a berth in some local ship.

Thus, at the age of twenty or twenty-one, Sandy Allan went to sea; he was much older than the ordinary run of ship's boys, and with a tradesman's skill was probably signed on as carpenter, soaking up meantime the business of a seaman and the practice of ship husbandry under masters of the art. In small traders of this kind, advancement from foremast hand to mate and master was by opportunity and merit as owners might decide. Not till 1854 would the law of the sea require formal examination and certificates of competency for officers in the merchant service. Some canny shipowner recognised a promising young man in Saw'ny Allan the ship's carpenter, for before long there is a reference to Captain Alexander Allan as master of the *Bell,* then engaged in the coasting trade, which was probably the former West India trader in which Robin had thought to leave Scotland for ever in 1786.

Whether or not the association of his first command with Burns, Bonnie Jean and Highland Mary ever came to mind we do not know. But it was about this time that the young shipmaster, who boarded in Saltcoats when his ship was in, would find his way of an evening from bachelor lodgings to a warmer welcome at the fireside of the Crawfords of Windmill Street, in the Castleweerock. His courtship of the daughter of the house blossomed and on 24th November 1806 Captain Allan and Jean Crawford were married. They set up their first house around the corner in Hamilton Street, which was a step nearer the harbour. Doubtless Jean learned, if she did not already know, that however much in love, some corner of a seaman's mind is thinking of his ship. The actual cottage cannot now be identified, and it is unlikely that it still stands, but the atmosphere of Saltcoats is recognisable. One can easily picture the little building with its dormer windows fronting on a cobbled street within sound of the sea. Rain or shine, fair weather or foul, Hamilton Street in Saltcoats was a snug berth for a sailor.

The young Allans prospered as their family arrived. The captain most probably held some of the sixty-four shares into which the law divided his vessel, and certainly he was a man of promise, well able to sail his ship and make a profit. In November 1807, with the birth of baby James, the house in Hamilton Street became a family home. But a sailor must keep the sea and before Hugh was born three years later his father was working the Bay of Biscay. Here Ayrshire ships were snapped up by government as hired transports in the last and bitter phase of the Napoleonic war. By this time Sandy was master of the *Hero,* a brigantine of 175 tons, just right for running supplies to Wellington's army, which had been sent to the Iberian Peninsula in 1808. She may have been employed in the first place as a trooper, for many similar vessels served as "Lobster-smacks," as ribald seamen called them when crowded with scarlet-coated regiments of the line. Certainly the *Hero* supported the first expeditionary force as a transport for military supplies and beef-cattle.

In the Peninsula War, as in all other wars involving merchant shipping, masters were placed in an unusually difficult position. The normal mercantile procedures of peacetime were invariably upset by the demands of the convoy system, which caused immense delay. For a profit-conscious shipmaster accustomed to using his own independent judgement, it was galling to waste a fair wind while slow-moving convoys assembled or to find that the speed of his vessel must correspond to that of the slowest sailer. In a popular nautical text-book of the period, The *Seamen's Vade-Mecum,* merchant ships are advised to make the best of their way from an enemy:

> . . . a merchant commander is not obliged to fight if he can with safety shun it; for a merchant ship is not sent to sea to annoy the enemy by venturing his cargo, but to increase the trade of the Nation, the Publick Revenues, and employ the poor. Therefore, whenever he can depart from an enemy without the hazard of battle, it is prudence to do so.

Sandy Allan was not the man to "venture his cargo" unnecessarily; and although it was heresy, then as since, to leave the protection of escorting frigates without good reason, ships must "increase the trade of the Nation and employ the poor." French or no French, Captain Allan soon decided that he could avoid contact with the enemy more easily by depending on his own judgement and seamanship rather than by keeping his telescope glued to the Commodore in some wagon of a seventy-four which sailed about as well as Fairlie-five-lums. With night coming on and the escort chasing to windward, flag signals could easily be misunderstood and it was a simple matter to up with the helm and slip off into the murk to leeward. Thereafter the *Hero* would crack on sail and make the best of her way keeping a sharp lookout.

Once at anchor in the Tagus the frustrations of the voyage were forgotten. Commissary officers of the British Army were glad enough to get supplies, however shipped. As the hatches came off and the mate discharged shot, powder or beef for the ragged regiments entrenched at Torres Vedras, the captain would welcome a stroll in unfamiliar sun-drenched streets and would have no trouble in supplementing his government charter with a profitable return freight if need be – port or sherry in the wood found a ready sale to the wine merchants of Ayr and Greenock.

By the time that the weary outward convoy had straggled into Lisbon the *Hero* would be off again for the English Channel under a press of sail, ready enough to dodge French privateers but equally watchful for the menace of British frigates cruising in the approaches to home. The Royal Navy must be manned, and although hired transports were theoretically protected against the system of impressment, zealous frigate commanders would board them in case they harboured naval deserters, a practice which was not uncommon. Avoiding friend and foe alike, the *Hero* would land her military cargo at Plymouth or Portsmouth before returning to the Firth of Clyde with a profitable share for her owners.

In this way, making perhaps three voyages to the convoy's two, Captain Allan pleased charterer, owners and crew alike. Dependent families in Saltcoats could look forward to something more than "champit tatties" on the dinner table. As for the captain himself, always sure of a loving welcome at Hamilton Street, he would be none the less pleasing with a Spanish mantilla for Jean and perhaps a dress length of black silk which would enhance the joy of a young matron on the arm of her sailor husband to the Parish Kirk.

As the war with Napoleon ground slowly on, Sandy Allan became one of a small circle of shipping men to be reckoned with in Ayrshire business circles. In those days life was more leisurely, and there were long spells in port to make up for hardships at sea. Usually ships underwent a refit in winter months when gales were bad and the Narrow Seas were strewn with the wreckage of less fortunate vessels. Meantime the family circle widened. With James and Hugh barely out of the baby stage Jean had twins in 1812 – both boys, Alexander and Bryce – and then, following the parental pattern at Fairlie cottage, three girls, Jean, Janet and Margaret who were born between 1812 and 1819.

When peace came, Alexander Allan was thirty-five, a prime seaman thoroughly experienced in business, part-owner of a ship, and owner of a modest capital from his exertions. The question was, what to do now? The Old World of the eighteenth century with its leisurely ways and interminable struggles had been shattered by the French Revolution, but at long last there was hope that Europe might settle down. In Scotland, which had made great strides in Allan's lifetime, people were beginning to look across the Atlantic where many of their sons had fought in Mr. Pitt's highland regiments in the American wars. Some had settled in the remote half-continent of Canada, won from the French and delivered from the Yankees. Already Quebec and New Brunswick or Nova Scotian ships were to be seen in the Clyde taking lumber or with molasses from the West Indies to the growing sugar refineries at Greenock. They would take emigrants on the return trip to Canada if nothing better offered. Some British ships, or rather ships owned in Britain (for all were then British by registry) were trying their luck in this Atlantic trade with its promise of hard-won profits in the face of a windward passage and unknown dangers on the other side. Was there a chance here for a resolute Scots shipowner with a reputation for initiative?

By 1818, with thoughts of this kind running in his head, Captain Allan had joined with others of like mind and a decision had been taken: they would order a ship, especially built for the Quebec trade, of which Allan would be master. The order was placed with Gilkison, Thomson & Company of Irvine, whose yard near Harbour Street was afterwards taken over by the Ayrshire Dockyard Company. Alexander Allan held eight of the sixty-four shares. Eight more were held by Alexander Harvey another local shipmaster, four each by James Gilkison the builder, Samuel Paterson and John Wilson, with the remainder being taken up by Ayrshire lawyers and merchants.

In the early spring of 1819 the new vessel was launched. It was a cheerful little ceremony at which townspeople gathered round. The foreman carpenter shouted hoarsely to keep his men hammering in unison as wedges were knocked from beneath the sliding ways. When the hull started to move, imperceptibly at first, there was a breathless moment of suspense. Flags and bunting fell aside to reveal the name *Jean* carved and gilded on trailboard and transom, with Irvine as the port of registry. Once safely in the water the bows dipped momentarily, in that unmistakable curtsey which marks successful launching. It was a graceful salutation which was shared by the lady sponsor and her Sandy, the more intimate from their secret hopes and fears: Jean was pregnant with Margaret. The Atlantic must be crossed and re-crossed before the expected child was born.

Meantime, fitting-out went ahead quickly, for every rigger and shipfitter knew exactly how to carry on his trade without the aid of drawings or supporting office work.

The *Jean* was a brigantine, that is, two-masted with square rig on the fore, fore-and-aft on the main; she was about the same size as the *Hero*,

170 tons or so, and was carvel built with a wide square transom, in general appearance not unlike the typical British coaster which would survive for a century yet to come. A model of the *Jean* is believed to have featured in a "Warship Week" display at the Ayrshire Dockyard in May 1942 but it cannot now be traced although a photograph remains.

In a few weeks a crew was signed on and the *Jean* made sail for the first time on her trial run up Firth to Greenock and her loading berth. Alexander Allan had gone the rounds of exporting houses in Glasgow and Greenock as the ship neared completion, and had appointed agents who ran the following advertisement in the *Glasgow Herald* of 24th May in a column of shipping announcements:

> Notice to Shippers and Passengers for Canada: the *Jean*, Allan master, at Greenock for Quebec, will clear on Tuesday 1st. of June, and proceed to sea at first favourable opportunity thereafter. For freight or passengers apply to Messrs. Alan Kerr & Co. Greenock, or John Parker, Wallace Court, Glasgow.

Jean Allan might have sailed round in the ship, or possibly taken the pleasant coast road for Greenock, but with her family to look after it is more probable that farewells were said in Saltcoats. When sailing day came the master loosed his topsails at first light, and the *Jean* was warped out of harbour as the heavy mainsail was sweated up. With prevailing winds a vessel would reach out through the Cumbrae Heads at the Gate of the Clyde, settling to her stride off the Ayrshire coast from whence she would be plainly visible at Saltcoats. Did she close her home port for a final wave? Probably not, for a leading wind would fetch her past Holy Island on the starboard tack and a prudent seaman would be loth to drop to leeward. Yet prudence must have been tinged with longing, and perhaps the master rationalised that he would ease sheets to avoid a capful of wind from the Sleeping Warrior as Saltcoats with its slate roofs dropped astern and finally sank into the haze.

A week later, when her maid brought the *Herald* with an early cup of tea, Mrs. Allan would see the brief notice in the departure column of 11th June: "Sailed, June 5th, *Jean*, Allan master, for Quebec."

CHAPTER TWO

Square Sail to Quebec

"Nightly thoughts and dreams by day
Are ay with him that's far away"

R.B.
On the seas and far away

C aptain Allan had a good season in 1819, making two
trips to the St. Lawrence "between the ice," as the saying was. From his
first departure on 5th June he was back at Greenock on 4th August, after
discharging at Quebec and loading a return cargo of lumber. With little
more than two weeks at home, he was off again on 21st August by way
of Dublin, where he picked up a few passengers for Canada before
returning to the Clyde on 11th October.

This was by no means bad going for an 80-foot sailing ship on her
maiden voyage, the more so as Sandy Allan had never previously
crossed the Atlantic. The ocean passage presented no difficulty on this
occasion, and he was never far from the great circle track which is the
shortest distance. Landfall and navigation on the Canadian side were
another matter, however. The only lighthouses on the coasts of Newfoundland and Nova Scotia were then at St. John's and Louisbourg, and
of course at Halifax – none of them of much help in finding the Cabot

Strait. There were a number of general charts of the Canadian coast but those of the Gulf of St. Lawrence were sparse in important detail. It was known that the complete lack of aids to navigation compounded natural dangers, with rocks and shoals washed by uncertain tides and currents. To make matters worse, the primitive magnetic compass of the day was not always to be relied on and unexpected deviations had been observed. The approaches to Quebec had been surveyed in detail by James Cook, who had sounded ahead of the British fleet carrying Wolfe's army sixty years previously; but here, in any case, Allan could expect to find pilotage, an advantage denied to Admiral Saunders in 1759. The fact was that despite the work of brilliant hydrographers such as Jolliet in the days of New France, and Cook and Desbarres in the British North American Colonies, ordinary merchant ships had little enough to guide them in the Gulf of St. Lawrence. The Gulf was recognised among shipowners as the most dangerous part of the trans-Atlantic trade, a traffic with more than its share of natural hazard by ice and fog.

On leaving the Gulf in September after sleepless nights in narrow waters, sometimes lying precariously to a single anchor in some awkward spot where he would pace the deck uneasily to await daylight, often making short tacks of exacting pilotage in the swift-running channels below Quebec, it was a relief for Captain Allan to take his departure from the rocky lump of St. Paul's Island and square his yards to a fair wind through the Cabot Strait for the broad Atlantic. For the first time in a couple of weeks he could now relax and go below to the cramped comfort of his transom berth where a quick glance through the cabin skylight would suffice to re-assure that all was well on deck. Above his berth the swinging card of a tell-tale compass would show that the mate on watch was steering the course ordered, while the lurch and sway of the *Jean* would infallibly tell of a change in wind or weather. There was time to think as the mind reacted to the homely domestic rhythm of creaking bulkheads, the tick of the cabin clock, and the familiar pattern of sea routine in which watch followed watch in a system as old as time itself.

The captain had plenty to think about as he wrote up the log. He did this in a wonderfully fair hand at noon each day while the steward laid dinner in a cabin where neither could stand upright except between the beams or in the companion. The old Port of Quebec had made a great impression with its stimulating scenes and had been surprisingly busy. He had found that twenty-five new ships would be launched that year before freeze-up, ten of them exceeding 500 tons. His mind went back to anchoring on arrival: lying in the stream, the little *Jean* was in company with dozens of other brigs, barques and ships awaiting their turn to load or working cargo at the timber berths which lined the river below Cape Diamond from Spencer Cove to the crowded wharves of lower Quebec.

It was a change from the grey buildings and slate roofs of Greenock, and yet not unfamiliar. Along waterfront streets where stone houses of unmistakably Gallic style were brightened by green shutters, the entire marine community of agents, merchants, chandlers, coopers, shipbuilders and boarding-house keepers clustered in surroundings which had changed but little since Wolfe and Montcalm. They had died on the heights above in a battle then within living memory. The old fortress of St. Louis sprawled behind a projecting wooden balcony, crowning the rocky promontory above a sheer drop to the chimneys below. Here the society of Quebec and the officers in garrison would stroll of a summer's evening as bugles rang and the British flag was lowered serenely to fife and drum and to the distant wail of the bo'sun's call from warships far below. It was the finest view in all the British North American Colonies, a panorama stretching from the shining spires of Isle d'Orleans to the east, through the heights of Levis opposite, westward over the shimmering waters of the St. Lawrence, a route by which men could reach eventually the limitless prairies of an empty half-continent.

As the little brigantine ran her latitude across the Western Ocean, thoughts like these were running in Sandy Allan's head, always occupied with hopes for a promising business in which he had a commanding stake, and the necessity of providing for a healthy young family. With sons to follow his example, who might one day be taught to sail a ship and manage affairs, certainly there were possibilities in this new trade.

When the *Jean* made her landfall off the North of Ireland after a fast passage, and swept into the Clyde before the boisterous winds of autumn, Captain Allan's satisfaction on the outcome of his first season turned to more personal thoughts. The rough realities of loneliness at sea would soon be behind for that year, to be compensated for by the joys of family life. His parting with Jean in August had been more than usually poignant, but each was in tune with the other and separation was a fact of life. If a sailor's wife could hardly expect to have the comfort of her husband at childbirth, there is no doubt that Jean and Sandy Allan made up for absence by an abiding faith, which sustained them far beyond the restraints of time and distance. On arrival at Greenock first words were reassuring: their seventh child, Margaret, had been born on 6th September, mother and daughter both well.

As the Allan family were reunited at Hamilton Street in Saltcoats, the shipping agents arranged for discharge of cargo at Greenock. The *Glasgow Herald* of 22nd October noted that Alan Kerr & Co. had parcels of timber, board, staves, barrel heads, handspikes, casks, oars, spars and sundry other lots for various consignees. When all had been landed, the *Jean* sailed for her home port of Irvine and the Allans settled in for the winter.

Because of his knowledge and experience in the Quebec trade Captain Allan was now in a leading position among the *Jean*'s shareholders, and he began to buy them out. Shares in a vessel were portable; they could be bought and sold at will, unknown to all except the parties to the sale. Before long Sandy Allan was the principal owner. Alan Kerr & Co. of Greenock and John Parker of Glasgow had no direct interest in the vessel. They were employed on commission advertising sailings, arranging for the receipt of cargo as wharfingers and for its loading and discharge as stevedores. They were agents for many Irvine shipowners, in whose absence at sea they would settle voyage accounts, arrange for customs clearance, and conduct the hundreds of individual transactions which collectively make up the great business of shipping.

But the judgement behind these activities, both in Scotland and in Canada where similar agents worked in every port of consequence, was a matter on which Captain Allan had the last word. Indeed, from his first sailing the *Jean* was identified, not only by a flag carrying her name in bold letters, but also by her owner's private signal or houseflag representing Allan himself. Contrary to the usual custom by which the houseflag has pride of place at the main topmast head, the *Jean* wore her name flag at the main and the Allan signal at the fore. There was good reason for this reversal of precedence for Alexander Allan, with memories of his part in the Peninsula campaign, had chosen as his emblem the *tricoleur* of France. To avoid confusion with his national colours as a British ship, the blue, white and red was therefore relegated to the fore topmast. It was an odd choice, and perhaps a bold one, for there was a notorious impact in the popular jingle "blue to the mast, bloody to the last," the seaman's *aide memoire* for the banner of the French revolution. For countless thousands the *tricoleur* invoked memories, glorious or miserable as the case might be. Even the peaceful farmers of the St. Lawrence nourished a secret pride in the colours of a regime which, renouncing old ways for new, had lost sight of kinsmen in the seigneuries of New France. For Sandy Allan himself, with a quaint sense of humour inherited from Ayrshire forbears, his houseflag was nothing more nor less than recognition of profits made in Napoleon's war, profits which kept the house in Hamilton Street, built the *Jean,* and were well on the way to founding a dynasty. Given the circumstances of a new trader breaking into the heart of French Canada, a modern advertising executive could hardly have done better.

For Captain and Mrs. Allan these were the founding years, well-knit at home, prospering at sea. Andrew was born to them in 1822, a welcome addition to the family circle which now numbered five boys and three girls. Their warm family life in Saltcoats was complemented by fireside talk of an evening when the children were in bed. Spring and fall voyages were then the subject of discussion between Captain Allan and his business associates. The *Jean*'s growing reputation had attracted shippers, always appreciative of dry cargoes and fast passages. Other enterprising masters and mates went into the same trade, some from Saltcoats, others from farther afield. In 1822 Alan Kerr & Co. advertised the brig *Robert,* John Neal master, to follow the *Jean* on the Quebec berth, a trade which attracted a third ship by 1824 when Captain John McAlpine was announced in the *Glasgow Herald* as closing for Canada in the "fine new brig *Corsair*" under the same agency. These were ships operated in much the same way as the *Jean,* owned in ones or twos at the most, and while trade was sufficient for all, there was as yet nothing to fear from larger groups with more capital.

By this time it was clear that the centre of gravity had shifted from Irvine and Saltcoats where the shipowners lived, to Greenock where the agency business, on which cargoes depended, was concentrated, and there the Allan family went in 1824. The eldest son James, who was then 17, had almost certainly gone to sea with his father before this. The time had now arrived when Hugh must follow his brother in some form of training likely to bear fruit in the family business. At the age of 13, having completed his education in the Kirk of Scotland parish school at Saltcoats, Hugh Allan was therefore put into the counting house of Alan Kerr & Co. who handled the *Jean*'s affairs. Captain Allan had decided that Hugh was bright at figures and that the second son had better master the business from the financial side. It was a far-sighted move at a time when the Scottish educational system was in advance of the village schools elsewhere in Britain. A boy reared in a God-fearing home could then be introduced to the ways of the world under competent employers who had earned the family trust.

Greenock was then a leading port in Scotland. Although Glasgow was the source of much of the outward cargo, the River Clyde was shallow. Cargoes such as coal, iron and manufactured goods were lightered downstream to Greenock and Port Glasgow, where processed sugar and other West Indian products were assembled for shipment to Canada. Greenock was also a distribution centre for inward cargoes such as lumber, potash and wheat which found a ready sale in the town itself or at Port Glasgow for lightering upstream. Buyers from Paisley, Helensburgh and Largs were among those from other west of Scotland towns which looked to Greenock for supplies from overseas.

In this way 1824 was a busy year for Captain Alexander Allan, ending up with a flourish. His response to changing patterns of trade by moving to Greenock was matched by the decision to place an order in Canada for a new ship. The old established yards at Quebec were busy. Allan's order went to Montreal, then at the start of a brief flurry of wooden shipbuilding and already the final port of discharge for the *Jean*. As the future depended on keeping his good reputation with shippers, the new vessel was built to a high specification. It combined the best work of Canada, where timber was plentiful and labour cheap, with an outfit of sails and equipment from Greenock shipsmiths, ropemakers and sailmakers whose products had been tested by personal experience. Included in this outfit were copper fastenings and copper sheathing. An obscure reference notes that the designer was paid five pounds for his services, a fee most probably earned by some Scots shipwright who had emigrated to Montreal to try his luck at lofting to his own ideas.

But with all this flourish of business activity, as 1824 closed, fate had a cruel blow for Jean and Sandy. When the Captain arrived home after laying down his new ship while in Canada on the fall voyage, it was to find that his third son, Alexander, one of twin boys then aged 12, had died on 14 November. Looking back from today, and as they then had eight children, perhaps the loss of one was the least to be expected in conditions of their time. But this sadness, then inseparable from the lives of most families, was mixed with a strong and enduring sense of heritage, for the last child to be born to them, already on the way, arrived in May 1825 and succeeded to the name Alexander.

In the spring of 1825 Captain Allan set off once more for Montreal in the *Jean*, his last voyage in command of that redoubtable little vessel. In recognition of the move from Irvine and Saltcoats the *Jean* had been registered *de novo* at the port of Greenock on 4th March, breaking the last link with Ayrshire. The surviving twin, Bryce, was taken to sea for a change of air and an introduction to the ways of a ship. From such a family, and at such a time, it is unlikely that he waited to be asked twice.

Sandy and young Bryce arrived at Montreal to find their new ship ready for sea, and command of the *Jean* passed to Captain Currie, formerly the mate, who took over as master and sailed for Scotland as usual. Sandy Allan, anxious to put his new investment to profitable use, and perhaps to show Currie what was expected of him, cleared from the St. Lawrence within a few days of the *Jean* and made a good passage to Greenock with a cargo of wheat, ashes and lumber – including a lone bale of bearskins among odds and ends – to arrive on 4th August 1825, the same day as Currie in the *Jean*. One thing was clear, masters in the Allan ships were expected to make passages.

The new brig, which was called the *Favourite*, was greatly admired by Mrs. Allan and family. Two oil paintings, commissioned by Captain

34

Allan, have survived to record his satisfaction with this aptly-named vessel. Bigger than the *Jean* and with her high topsides painted black and white with simulated gunports in 'Nelson' fashion, a style which the Allans and other leading shipowners retained until the end of sail, the *Favourite* had no difficulty in finding a cargo for her fall voyage. She returned in December. Now that he was regularly established in the St. Lawrence trade with two vessels, Captain Allan flew his houseflag boldly at the main as senior master of the fleet. The *Jean* and later ships commanded by others continued for some years to wear it at the fore.

Alan Kerr & Co. lost no time in advertising the merits of the new brig. Inserts in the *Glasgow Herald,* most probably the work of young Hugh, were careful to advise intending travellers that " . . . the *Favourite,* being six feet between decks, affords ample room for steerage passengers and she has good accommodation in the cabin." The paintings of the *Favourite* show her to have been powerfully rigged and well-masted, as befits an Atlantic packet of sturdy build and heavy displacement. It is interesting to note that her fore and aft mainsail was carried on a separate "try" mast stepped immediately aft of the lower mainmast and attached to it, an arrangement which enabled the gaff jaws and sail hoops to run up and down freely above the height of the mainyard. Vessels rigged like this, called "snows," were among many variations on the brig theme. The *Favourite* was perhaps unusual in that she carried a similar arrangement on the foremast. With this impressive outfit of fore and aft canvas, the *Favourite* combined the advantages of a square-rigger in strong fair winds with the ability of a schooner at turning to windward in narrow waters. At the same time this handy storm rig, well reefed down, could be used in hurricanes or when icing made it virtually impossible to work aloft on the yards. Her square canvas, with royals on both masts, was complemented by a full outfit of studdingsails for light weather, but in the winter months Captain Allan sailed his ships with nothing above t'gallants on shortened spars.

Whatever the weather, Allan knew that success on the North Atlantic demanded from him staying power in the business sense. While at sea he must have officers who could be relied on to sail a ship to the limits of common sense and safety. Any fool could crack on, but torn sails and broken spars would eat up hard-won profits. The trend was already set: Currie of the *Jean* had been trained by the "Old Man" himself, James and Bryce were standing watches under the eagle eye of one or the other, Hugh was being introduced to the ledgers from his high stool in the Greenock office of his trusted agents, while the child Andrew and baby Alexander would be given their chance when the time came.

For Hugh and Bryce the apprenticeship stage was already running out and opportunities were opening fast. In the log of the brig *Favourite,*

Alexander Allan master, for her voyage of 1826 appears a pencilled list of some half-dozen passengers, the last name being Hugh Allan, then aged 16. The second mate on this occasion was Bryce who was only 14. Boys went to sea early in those days and many a naval midshipman and merchant service apprentice was already a useful hand even earlier. Of one thing we may be sure: with their father in command, Hugh would be no mere passenger. He would be soaking up the ways of a ship. Bryce, young as he was, would be in charge of his watch, even if he only had to tap on the companion to bring the ever-watchful master on deck. On arrival at Montreal Hugh walked ashore to continue his mercantile career by learning the business there. The Allan family now had a foot in Canada.

The log books of the *Favourite,* of which several have survived, provide an excellent window on the period. All were carefully written in a firm legible hand, usually the master's, sometimes with a footnote initialled "B.A." by his second mate son. The heading was always short and to the point: "Brig *Favourite,* on a voyage from Quebec towards Greenock, June 1829." It was traditional, and well-founded amidst the uncertainties of the sea, that the log must not appear presumptious in forecasting arrival at one place from another by recording progress from Quebec "to" Greenock. It should circumspectly note only the day's run "towards" the desired haven. From the first entry of the log proper, *"23rd June,* at 1 a.m. got underway with the last of the flood and set all sails" to the last line which reads, *"Monday 20th July,* arrived at Greenock in 27 days" the entire voyage is carefully documented on one page only, a line for each day. Vertical columns are ruled with headings for distance made, latitude by observation, and "longitude in." As the longitude column omits the phrase, "by observation," it must have been derived from dead reckoning. In any case chronometers were not then common in small merchant ships. The term "dead" reckoning is a corruption of the phrase "deduced" reckoning. Each voyage was remarkably consistent, this one winding up with the typical notation of landfall: *"Saturday, July 18th,* at noon Aranmore Island bore South 12 miles."

Westward passages were much longer and the fall voyage of that year may be regarded as typical. Despite the careful daily notations one must keep in mind much that is not recorded – the wearying and exhausting motion of a small sailing ship beating endlessly against the grain of the North Atlantic, and the skill, judgement and courage required to keep going with maximum result day after day, week after week, and indeed year after year. Some ships may have blown about the ocean but never Alexander Allan's, which were forced to their limit for every mile of the way.

36

Wednesday 19th August, left the wharf in tow of a steamboat with a smart breeze from the Eastward, 8 p.m. abreast of the Craig.
Thursday 21st at 4 p.m. Tory Island bore SW 8 miles, wind N b E, from which I take my departure.

On Friday 11th September, after a single page of curt notation in which his best day's run was 150 miles and his worst 63, landfall in Canada is noted as Cape Chapeau Rouge, which was sighted at a distance of 25 miles about noon. It would be another sixteen days of frustration in the Gulf before he could write:

Sept 27th, arrived at Quebec all well, in 38 days.

In the next few years the Allan fleet expanded. In 1830 the *Canada,* their first full-rigged ship, came from the yard of Steele of Greenock, a firm which later turned out some of the finest clipper ships ever built. When Captain Allan took over the *Canada,* James moved up to command the *Favourite,* thus becoming a shipmaster in his own right at 23. He was by now an experienced officer with his feet firmly on deck and a sound knowledge of all that concerned the family business.

The sailings for 1831, announcing the "Fine newly-built coppered ship *Canada,* Alexander Allan master," and the "Well-known coppered brig *Favourite,* James Allan master," set a pattern which appears year after year in the *Glasgow Herald.* Both vessels advertised that they would send steerage passengers free of charge from Montreal to Quebec should the sailing ships be unable to get up river, always a possibility at a time long before the St. Lawrence was dredged and when the depth might be as low as 10 feet in a dry season. Sailings were remarkably regular and, although two voyages were all that could be accomplished in a season at that time, some very good passages were made – including one by James Allan in the *Favourite* when he made the remarkable time of 19 days from Quebec to Greenock in 1832. It was in the months of November and December, and the little brig must have been driven as never before. James was an apt pupil.

Although the Allans faced competition in the Canadian trade, for every year brought a fresh quota of "Fast-sailing brigs" and "Fine new ships," they had not been seriously challenged since 1825, when the appearance of the *Favourite* had been enough to counter opposition from an Aberdeen group, headed by George Thompson. Thompson eventually made his name in the Australian trade with the Aberdeen Line, which for a spell put the Allans on their mettle. The Allan Line was now the only fleet to have sailed annually since 1819, a confident trading position which was reflected in the tone of their advertisements. In 1833, for example, with the *Canada* still at sea on her eastbound voyage from Quebec, she was listed in the *Glasgow Herald* of 24th July as "Daily expected, to sail about 20 August," a canny forecast which was not far out as she did indeed leave again for Canada on the 28th of the month. Faith was a pre-requisite of success in business in those days before rapid communications, for how otherwise could the agents make the arrangements necessary for a quick turn-round after immediate discharge and a waiting cargo?

In 1834, after some forty years at sea of which fifteen had been on the North Atlantic commanding his own ships, Alexander Allan "swallowed the anchor," and came ashore to manage affairs from his agent's office at Greenock. James succeeded his father as master of the ship *Canada,* while Gavin Burns, an up-and-coming mate, relieved James in the little *Favourite.* The days of the two-masted brigs and brigantines were about over. Soon it was Bryce's turn to show what he could do: his chance came in 1837 when he followed his brother in the *Canada* to become master of this fine full-rigged ship in his twenty-fourth year.

Meantime, with the popularity of the Clyde-built *Canada* among passengers – hardwood ships built in Scotland had the edge on pine construction in the Colonies – the Allans went to Steele of Greenock for their next ship, the barque *Arabian.* It was a fine command for the eldest son and an occasion not to be overlooked in the sailing notices that year. In the *Glasgow Herald* of 1838, among vessels advertised as "First spring traders," appears the *Arabian,* "First-class fast-sailing barque, James Allan commander." The expression "Commander," in place of the precise but more prosaic term "Master," was gaining favour among advertisers as being good for business. Trade followed the flag, and nowhere did the flag have more appeal than in the Royal Navy and the Honorable East India Company – or their descendants the Blackwall frigates, where officers had rank and prestige already spilling over to the better class of ordinary merchant ships. The well-run Allan packets, with their confident air and homely Scots economy, were slowly becoming "liners," a description already changing from its original meaning "line-of-battle ship" to merchantmen on regular routes. The term "Allan Line," although not an official title, began to be used in conversation about this time.

One other custom originated with the barque *Arabian*; it was the first of the fleet to be named with the suffix *-ian,* a style of nomenclature which later became distinctive in the Allan Line steamers. The *Arabian,* which was shallower in draft than the *Canada,* marked a more significant development by opening up regular sailings direct from Glasgow. This avoided costly lightering of cargo to Greenock and subsequent transhipment. A few of the smaller vessels in the Canadian trade had made occasional sailings from the Broomielaw, Glasgow's first ocean terminal, as conditions permitted. With the channel now dredged to a minimum depth of 15 feet at spring tide, the way was open for the phenomenal period of growth in which Glasgow became known as the "second city of the Empire." After commanding the *Arabian* for a year, James Allan came ashore to manage the Glasgow end of the business, opening the first permanent office there in 1842. Shippers and passengers were invited to apply to "James Allan, 87 Union Street, Glasgow, or Alexander Allan Esq., at Greenock."

These were years when the Allans again added to their fleet. In 1841 the Allan advertisement was headed for the first time with "Line of Packets to Canada," a description which was not out of place with the addition of the barque *Blonde* in 1840 and the *Caledonia* a year later. Alexander Crawford was master of the *Blonde,* advertisements of the period making a point of emphasizing that he was " . . . well acquainted with the navigation of the Gulf and River of St. Lawrence." Bryce Allan became master of the ship *Caledonia,* a command which he held in the best family tradition.

The "Old Man" himself, a seaman above all else to the end of his days, was unable to resist one final trip in command of his own ship in 1839. A replacement was already ordered from Montreal for the brig *Favourite*, now past her prime and in any case too small. Taking passage in the fall of that year, he sailed his new vessel back to Scotland in time to supervise finishing touches during the winter. The name *Favourite* was too precious to let go: it was transferred to the newcomer, which took up regular sailings in 1840. As early as February that year, in plenty of time to attract passengers for the spring voyage, Alexander Allan, Esq., of Greenock invited freight or passage in very superior accommodation in the "New splendid fast-sailing barque *Favourite,* George Bannerman master."

These were the years of achievement for Sandy Allan. In business, his unremitting energy and complete mastery of sailing ship management had transformed a loose grouping of individual ships into a cohesive fleet with well-established headquarters ashore. Through his sons he had endowed it with operational initiative at sea and in Canada. His portrait, painted about this time, is redolent of the qualities which had brought him thus far: the expression is one of openness, health, and moderation, the dark hair unmarked with grey except for a becoming touch at the temples. Prosperity had not damaged his naturally buoyant outlook. The steady gaze of a master seaman and shipowner, well able to hail the royal yard on the wildest night or make up a balance sheet of his voyage accounts, is relieved by the beginnings of a smile. It was a long time since Sawn'y Allan the shoemaker's apprentice had " . . . happed t'Hell for a penny loaf" but the mischievous youth is not entirely lost in the man of action and affairs.

The portrait of Jean Allan, a companion-piece, shows him to have been equally fortunate in private life. With her clear Ayrshire complexion and dark hair she looks a happy woman, well able to cope with life and to advance with her husband from their first house in Hamilton Street by the Saltcoats seashore to the solid comfort of a shipowner's home in Greenock, while retaining the simple dignity of Scottish life which she and Sandy typified. Like all her family, she loved the sea. In the fall voyage of the ship *Canada* in 1834 Mrs. Allan had taken passage to Montreal with James, a compliment alike to her eldest son, who must have enjoyed having his mother on board the pride of the fleet, and to Hugh, with whom she spent barely a month in Montreal. It was a short enough interlude, which none but a natural traveller would feel worth the duration of ten weeks at sea on the North Atlantic.

By this time the Allan ships were in the van of the trans-Atlantic passenger fleet from Scotland. From a few cabin passengers in the days of the *Jean* and *Favourite* the Allan packets were now attracting steerage passengers from among the better type of emigrant. In April 1843 an advertisement for the *Blonde* reads:

Emigration to Canada . . . this well known ship presents to persons about to emigrate a most desirable opportunity, and such as is seldom met with, of which the high econiums passed on her and her captain by the large and respectable body of passengers who went out last year, is a most convincing proof. Her height between decks is fully seven feet and she is fitted up in the most comfortable and convenient manner. Passengers supplied with stores free of duty.

James Allan, 87 Union Street, Glasgow."

But despite the very evident attention paid to passenger's comfort, an attention which was sadly lacking in many emigrant ships of the time, Atlantic travel was seldom routine. Sometimes it was adventurous in the extreme, occasionally it was an exercise in survival. Such was the spring voyage of the ship *Albion* under the command of Captain Bryce Allan in 1847.

The *Albion,* built at Greenock in 1845, was one of the best and longest-lived of the wooden fleet and was still sailing, cut down to a barque, thirty years later. Ships like this were as good as anything afloat. Their appearance, performance and general standard more nearly approached the Blackwall frigates than the ordinary run of Atlantic traders. A painting of the time shows the *Albion* in the familiar black and white port-painted colour scheme, the *tricoleur* flying bravely at the fore truck, the name flag at the main. She carries royals and t'gallants above the classic deep topsail of the period and stuns'ls on both fore and main. Like the first *Favourite,* gaff trysails are fitted for extreme conditions when everything must be snugged down and within reach of the deck. The poop is protected from the bitter cold of the North American coast by a half-round shelter across the taffrail; with her quarter-boat swung out ready for use in naval fashion, the *Albion* faces the sea with all the confidence of a well-dressed matron at a charity ball.

On Thursday 25th March 1847 the *Albion* cleared the Tail of the Bank off Greenock in tow of the tug *Defiance* to the Gate of the Clyde at Cumbrae Heads. Always a moment to savour, final parting was signified by a toot from the steamer and an answering curtsey from the stately square-rigger as topsails were sheeted home and she dipped to the open sea. The tug circled for last-minute letters, ranging under the lee quarter at full speed as the *Albion,* with everything drawing aloft, heeled to her stride in the freshening breeze. By noon on the following day Bryce had logged his departure from Tory Island bearing SW b S, distant 7 miles.

They had a good passage across the Atlantic with strong fair winds until 10th April when they ran into loose ice about 40 miles from Cape Ray, that formidable inner gatepost to the Cabot Strait. Sometimes grinding through the pack, sometimes sailing freely in areas of open water they struggled on. In a letter home Bryce Allan gave a vivid account of this interminable voyage.

Tuesday, 13th April. For two days we continued boring through it with a fair wind but last night a gale from the East springing up with snow caused us to lay the ship and furl all sail. Today the wind is right ahead, blowing a gale, and we are still drifting in the ice without a stitch of canvas set. We are all heartily sick of it and would be thankful for a glimpse of clear water. Four of us entered the ice in company, the *Great Britain, Eromanga* and *St. Andrew.* I hope, if we all get out safe, this will be a warning not to dispatch ships so early in the Spring.

Wednesday 14th April. This voyage hitherto has been one full of adventure. On Monday night we succeeded in getting the good ship into clear water. About 40 miles from Cape Ray we found a clear passage of 30 miles between the ice and Newfoundland, but as we approached the Cape the passage became narrower until I scarcely found room to work the ship, and had last night not been calm, I do not know what we would have done as the land being white with snow it is very difficult to ascertain our distance off at night. We therefore this morning came in here, Port-aux-Basques, where we now lie at anchor. This afternoon I went to the top of a high hill where I had a view of the Gulf and found, by the aid of a good glass, that there was nothing to be seen but ice, ice as far as the eye could see.

Thursday 15th. Here we are still lying in Port-aux-Basques harbour, although I would much rather be again at sea if the ice is cleared away, but as I see that there is some slight damage to the vessel, I am afraid to attempt the ice until I see a prospect of getting through. Oh that the Great God who has hitherto been so kind as to take me out of my difficulties may yet carry me in safety to my place of destination.

Friday 16th. I am afraid my troubles are not yet at an end. Last night it came on a strong gale from the east which brought in a large body of ice into the harbour and caused our anchor to drag, and the ship took the ground by the heel. I assure you I spent a very miserable night; it rained a great deal and I was on deck until three o'clock this morning. The ship floated whenever the tide rose and came off herself the wind having changed, but today we are hemmed in on all sides with ice, and we can neither move the ship one way or another, nor communicate with the shore. I have now made up my mind to leave this place as soon as I can get out for I would rather be in the ice than here.

The ensuing period was the most miserable in Bryce Allan's life at sea. He was able to get ashore occasionally but his climb to the hilltop brought only the sight of other ships driving about in the ice outside with the unsettling thought that they might get out while he remained safe but imprisoned. Meanwhile the passengers amused themselves as best they could. There were six men, eight women and two children at the cabin table and one servant. The gentlemen of the party caught trout, speared flounders and shot ducks, none of which was of much comfort to the anxious captain, except to liven up the menu as supplies ran lower and lower. With the need to conserve food and candles, life on board was becoming cold and dark.

Ten days later the mate made the daily trip to the observation point ashore and hurried back with the news of clear water outside. All hands were called on deck, the topsails were loosed. Manning the capstan with a will after eleven days at anchor, the crew of the *Albion* toiled at halliards and braces as they made sail and tacked out to the Cabot Strait, only to find that they had joined the ships *Eromanga* and *Belleisle* to form a captive trio in heavy ice and bitter cold – all very discouraging.

Tuesday 27th. I daresay you will be calculating that I am by this time safe in Quebec, but we are still some 600 miles from it and no prospect of getting there for some time to come. We are only 100 miles nearer than we were on the 8th. I feel very dull at our long detention. We are already 32 days out and very little prospect of getting out of this ice. We were trying today to cut it with an axe but could make no progress and had to give up in despair. The steward is already telling me that his stores are nearly out. I was obliged to tell the passengers last night to be more careful of candles. One great blessing is we have plenty of water having filled six casks at Port-aux-Basques where we had little else to do.

By this time the passengers were walking on the ice for their daily constitutional, visiting the imprisoned *Belleisle* for a couple of hours and the *Albion* in turn was boarded by two men from Cape Breton who had come from a sealing schooner on the ice edge, not much more than a mile distant. They brought news which was hopeful but exasperating – the Gulf was clear of ice.

We have only about a mile to go but that mile will cost us some trouble and we must have a fair wind. We are farther from Quebec now than we were on Sabbath last. I am getting more dispirited every day but am confident that it is very sinful as I ought to put my trust in God . . . who afflicteth not willingly, and I have no doubt that my trials and detention are sent to try my faith. O that they may produce a more beneficial effect and, instead of despairing, may my faith become stronger and stronger. Tomorrow will be the 1st of May, a day of enjoyment to many thousands in Scotland. God grant that it may be a day of enjoyment for me but if we are still in the ice I am afraid that there will be very little to remind me of May Day.

In a few days the three ships were seriously short of provisions. Always willing to help those worse off than himself, Captain Allan sent 100 pounds of beef across to the *Belleisle,* all that could be spared. On 5th May the wind came on to blow from the west, the ice drifting remorselessly under enormous pressure towards a lee shore on the west coast of Newfoundland:

At 9 o'clock I ordered all hands to be called and the boats to be got ready and in the meantime made the steward fill some bags with biscuit, and the passengers to put on warm clothing. It was a fearful time of excitement, expecting every minute to strike upon a sunk rock which lies about a mile from the shore, but we were providentially delivered and the wind has died away since, so that I have great hopes we will have a fair wind to carry us off this barren coast. Not a house have we seen for miles. O that God may grant me the strength to carry me through, and enable me to act the part of a Christian in every trial.

By this time Bryce Allan and his passengers had restricted themselves to two meals a day and the crew had been put on short allowance. Captain Ramsay of the *Eromanga* walked across the intervening ice with one of his passengers who was a Free Church minister, a visit which nearly ended in tragedy:

We joined in prayer and were all much refreshed. I think they were very rash in attempting to come; as the ice was so bad they had great difficulty in reaching us and when they were returning the ice gave way and I was obliged to launch my lifeboat and get them safe on board, for which we were very thankful.

On 10th May crew and passengers were put on an allowance of half a pound of biscuit a day. The captain kept some beef for his sailors, for the strength of their muscles was the machinery on which all depended. On 12th May he noted:

I daresay you have never experienced what it is to feel very hungry and have nothing to satisfy the craving and I trust you never may. I can now sympathize with the poor starving Irish and Highlanders, Although we are not so badly off as many of them with half a pound of bread. I am trying to save some for fear of being obliged to reduce still further and frequently feel hungry when I have to refrain from eating.

On the following day, 10th May, the ice was again solid and found to be six feet thick. The *Albion* was as firm as if in drydock and although it was four miles to the *Belleisle* Captain Ramsay again paid a visit. The two masters talked things over and when Ramsay left Bryce remarked "He is, like the rest of us, very anxious to get out and heartily tired of the Canada trade."

On 17th May all hands were put to work at cutting round the ship with axes and saws, at best a hopeless proposition but at least a positive activity. In three days they moved the *Albion* four feet, the crew working to exhaustion in wet and cold, their hands and feet numb from constant exposure. On the 21st the *Belleisle* unexpectedly got clear and in full view from the *Albion* romped away as she set sail above sail to a strong breeze which blew up to a gale that night. Next morning, with the wind whistling in the rigging, it was snowing again and very cold. The ship remained motionless in the ice as firmly as ever. The *Eromanga* had got out on the 15th and the *Albion* was now alone in her long drift up the north-west coast of Newfoundland towards Point Rich. It was anything but a cheerful prospect as food ran out, far away from the track of other ships approaching the Strait of Belle Isle. At last came the day of deliverance:

Monday 24th May. It blew a gale yesterday from the South which broke up the ice and caused a heavy swell to come up. The ship made a fearful noise; the heavy ice beating alongside caused us to shake and quiver all over. Today I am thankful to say we have at last got into clear water. We were 46 days from the time we entered the ice until we got out again and 28 of these we never had a man at the helm; the ship was frozen so hard that it would not move.

On Friday 4th June at four in the morning the *Albion* arrived at Quebec, where she was taken in tow by the steamboat *Princess Victoria*, finally arriving at Montreal on 6th June after a passage of 72 days from Greenock. They had been unlucky, for some ships had arrived weeks before. But once rafted in the ice on the west coast of Newfoundland, ships in that predicament could only wait, and there were many such. The *Chronicle*, many of whose readers were impatiently awaiting spring merchandise, remarked that "Mercantile men scarcely know what to do, so embarassing has become the delay in the arrivals from sea." But, embarassing or no, at least they could turn the page and amuse themselves with *Dombey and Son*, the latest serial from the pen of Mr. Dickens.

When the *Albion* at last hauled alongside at Montreal it was no consolation to Captain Allan to find that the *Belleisle* and *Eromanga* were already homeward bound and that, in his own fleet, the *Caledonia, Canada* and even the *Favourite* had beaten him that year. But there was some consolation in that all on board the *Albion* arrived well, though hungry. As he passed through the boarding inspection by medical officers at the quarantine station at Grosse Isle below Quebec Captain Allan must have noticed that no less than thirty-five sail of emigrant ships had been detained at anchor there, each with 250-500 passengers, and a total estimated to number 12,000 souls. Most of the ships had dead and dying on board, all beds in the hospital were full, and the situation had plunged into a public scandal. The *Albion* was indeed lucky.

CHAPTER THREE

The Montreal Ocean Steamship Company

"Wha does the utmost that he can
will whyles do mair"

R.B.
To Dr. Blacklock

When Hugh Allan landed in Canada on 21st May, 1826, Montreal was very different from the modern port. The brig *Favourite,* small as she was, was as deep as the port could handle. Few sailing ships even attempted to get this far inland, and not for half a lifetime would there be ocean steamers. Most of the consignments awaited eagerly each spring by the Montreal merchants arrived by barge after transhipment at Quebec, or were hauled overland from New York and Vermont by horse-drawn sleighs in winter.

At this period there was only one towboat on the St. Lawrence, the sidewheeler *Hercules,* which ranged alongside the *Favourite* anchored at some point above Lake St. Peter as near Montreal as she could reasonably get under sail. One can imagine the bargaining between Sandy Allan and George Brush, skipper of the tug, for only by the utmost economy could extras be squeezed into the frugal voyage accounts of a Greenock shipowner. As the *Favourite* hove her anchor underfoot, the *Hercules* took the strain at full throttle until the current became too much for her, and a team of ten oxen, kept handy for the purpose at Hiram Gilbert's slaughterhouse, was yoked to a second line. Even this was not enough. Not until the struggle was sighted from Johnson's Shipyard at Hochelaga, where the *Favourite* had been built, did the addition of 50 men on a third hawser prove strong enough to warp the brig upstream to her mud berth below Commissioner Street. Small wonder that the Montreal trade had been slow to start; only valuable cargoes could stand the oncost.

The sight which met young Hugh that May morning was never to be forgotten. Years afterwards, when talking to a group of young men at St. Andrew's Church in Montreal about 1880, he recalled his impressions. There were no docks and wharves such as he had been used to in Greenock, the brig lying uneasily with her bilge against the river bank, held off by an anchor in the stream where St. Mary's Current swept by in the full grandeur of spring flood. Dock labourers, speaking French (a tongue which at that time he could not understand), had laid a rough gangway across spars connecting ship and shore. They discharged cargo manually or with a horse, one piece at a time. As the bulky cases and casks were broken out from the hold, they were skidded to the beach where waiting carters backed their wagons up to the axles in mud.

While the *Favourite* was in port the boy could save money by living on board with his father and brother and he recalled how he landed to find his feet on solid ground and to explore the unfamiliar streets of Old Montreal. Behind Commissioner Street with its waterfront activity, street after street ran parallel to the River. Hugh Allan would walk up Francois-Xavier to cross in succession St. Paul Street with its busy warehouses and traffic, pass by Notre Dame Cathedral which jutted into the Place d'Armes, then across St. James' and Fortification Lane until he reached Craig Street, then the northwestern limit of the City for all practical purposes. Here was a stream doing duty as a sewer which, Hugh recalled, was fronted by buildings from Champs de Mars to Dow's Brewery. He remembered crossing a bridge after which, turning right and then left, the route would take him up rising ground on St. Urbain Street as houses began to thin out where Ste. Catherine Street now stands.

It must have been a relief to a warm lad to saunter by fields of grass and grain after the confines of the ship. One can well imagine that he threw himself down to rest and admire the view. If so, he can hardly have failed to have noticed a similarity to a favourite spot in the hills of his native Ayrshire, known as the "Ravenscrag," where the map still shows a knoll of moorland sloping down to villages below. Certainly the name "Ravenscrag" was in his mind throughout his life, and he seems to have associated the view across the rooftops of Montreal with boyhood memories. Behind him, rough pastures rose steeply to become densely-wooded cliffs, thrusting upward to Mount Royal, where an enormous wooden cross marked the summit. In front, far across City and River, the plains of the South Shore with two prominent hummocks in the middle distance would fade into the blue of the Vermont Hills.

Among the half dozen passengers on the voyage out had been William Kerr, partner in a dry-goods and smallwares business on St. Paul Street, possibly one of the family of that name who were the Allans' agents at Greenock. Probably he knew Captain Allan and his sons; but when he returned after spending the winter in Scotland buying stock he got to know them better. Young Hugh made an impression on his fellow passenger, the intimate round of shipboard life encouraging confidences among passengers while Captain Allan and Bryce sailed the ship. If the son was anything like the father, and as he appeared to have no plans more definite than to seek his fortune in Canada, it was a natural consequence that within a few days of landing he should be offered a job with William Kerr & Co., nominally as a clerk but in today's terms something closer to the accountant. Someone outside the family had noticed that the lad had a head for figures.

When the *Favourite* completed loading and hauled off with her cargo of wheat and potash, the stocky figure of Hugh Allan watched from Commissioner Street as his father made sail, pleased at the prospect of learning the Canadian import business on his own, and confident in the knowledge that he could now fend for himself. He was sixteen. He remained in Kerr's employment for just over four years, living frugally with others of his kind above the warehouse and store. He continually absorbed the atmosphere of the Colony, while acquiring a useful knowledge of the commodities most likely to sell in Canada.

By the time he was twenty Hugh Allan was a trained businessman with a growing familiarity of the ins and outs of the Montreal trading fraternity, many of them fellow Scots but a surprising number French and American. Whatever their apparent differences, Allan soon learned that one trait was common to all – each was out to make money and every transaction stood on its own, sink or swim.

In a way it lacked the breadth of the shipping world, where risks were longer in term and more difficult to judge, but it sharpened the wits and perhaps gave a new perspective to the familiar Allan business, with its long-headed conservative outlook. The question was, how to advance his career? First he would take a good look at this New World of North America with its boisterous ways, then he would go back to Scotland to think things over, renew family ties and digest his ideas. So far he had hardly made a fortune, for his assets totalled barely $100. This was not much even in 1830; but it was enough, with strict economy, for a quick reconnaissance before taking passage in one of the Allan ships.

Like any tourist today Hugh wanted to see New York and Niagara Falls, a rough-and-ready journey when there were no railways and the only way to travel was by steamboat and stagecoach, the first primitive but reasonably comfortable, the second merely primitive in the appalling state of colonial roads. Crossing the St. Lawrence to Laprairie, the coach took him to St. Jean from whence the steamboat ambled down the Champlain route to Whitehall. From there another stage bumped its way across to Albany where the river steamer left for New York. Refreshed by the trip down the Hudson River, but with no money to spare, a hard day's tramping round lower Manhattan and the Battery was all the sightseeing that an inquisitive Scots lad could afford. The following morning found him afloat again on his way upstream to Albany for the canal boat to Lockport and connection by stage to Buffalo and Niagara.

With one day at Niagara, the route lay through Upper Canada by stage and corduroy roads to Hamilton, York and Kingston through scattered hamlets with wooden houses amidst endless bush and occasional clearings. Even their arrival at "muddy little York," as Allan called it, gave no hint of its impending change into the good city of Toronto. Indeed a tree stump in the road, near what is now St. Lawrence Market, hardly to be distinguished among the many obstacles of ruts, logs and potholes in the way of wheeled traffic, overturned the coach while the driver dozed. All hands had to scramble out, nursing sore knees and ruffled dignity to set things right again. Eventually, by steamboat from the pleasant limestone-fronted City of Kingston to the landing stage at Prescott and thence by coach to Montreal, a penurious young man with a taste for travel was extremely relieved to see the blue-white-and-red houseflag of the *Favourite* waving gently in the autumn air over the rooftops of Commissioner Street. In the cosy comfort of the after cabin he dined once more with his father, while an attentive steward looked after his employer in peace and privacy before passengers embarked.

With a heavy cargo of wheat the *Favourite* took her time in working downstream over the shallows of Lake St. Peter after a dry summer. Clearing customs at Quebec with the last of her cargo on 20th November she made sail for a rough and stormy eastbound crossing, arriving safely at Greenock on 18th December. With the last ship in from her fall voyage, Jean Allan and her daughters were reunited with husband, father and brothers for New Year and the comfortable months of winter, secure and happy that their men were off the seas as wind and rain swept the Greenock streets.

By March, with Canadian cargo piling up in the sheds as the vessels completed their fitting-out in the Old Harbour, Hugh Allan was again ready to move with events. This time he had made up his mind – if ever he was to make his mark it would be in Montreal, where the free and easy ways of colonial life offered intriguing prospects for a young man determined to make his way in business. But first, while the opportunity remained, he would see something of England: where centuries of trade had established the greatest commercial houses of the world, and where the docks at London and Liverpool handled riches and harboured fleets which must be seen.

He was not long in finding something new. The Liverpool and Manchester Railway had been opened only the previous year by the Duke of Wellington in a ceremony marred by the tragic death of the Tory reformer William Huskisson – who thus had the unlucky distinction to become the first person of note to be run over by a train – and had captured the imagination of promoters and visionaries alike. Hugh Allan rode on this line and was greatly impressed by his first railway journey, "A modern railroad" as he called it using the North American term, which caused him to think ahead. But in 1831 the mail coaches and turnpike roads of Britain were yet to approach their brief hour of final glory and the short line of railway at Liverpool was as yet a local wonder awaiting the bombshell of speculation, fortune and failure which would burst across the green countryside of England in the ensuing decade. Young Allan, with his active, far-seeing mind, must have sensed that railways would transform the world. Meanwhile, he rattled up to London in the time honoured way, outside passenger on the Royal Mail coach, a four-in-hand clipping cheerfully with horn and whip and relays of good horses over macadam roads. With good fare in bustling inns, the passengers swayed in unison between stops, arriving finally at the metropolis which was becoming increasingly scarred with the smoke and grime of the industrial revolution.

Hugh Allan was by no means the gilded scion of a wealthy family. On the contrary, having only the wages earned in his father's office during the winter, he was short of funds and his journeys were more in the nature of field trips with a purpose than outings for idle pleasure, a concept which would not have occurred to the grandson of James Allan brought up in the strict Ayrshire tradition of Kirk and work. Remaining in London long enough to see only what he wanted and to take in the usual tourist round by St. Paul's and Westminster Abbey, he made his way to Tower Wharf where the Leith Packets berthed. These hardy little cutters with their cramped and communal accommodation – one cabin for women and one for men – were then the cheapest way to travel between London and Scotland. Before long the "iron horse" with its train of third-class carriages would carry more in a single trip than the packets in years. But for the moment the cheapest way was the best way, and a trying beat up the North Sea in a sailing smack held no qualms for the son of Captain Allan. After a stormy passage he stepped ashore at Leith for a quick look at Edinburgh before arriving at Greenock on the last day of March.

He was just in time to catch the maiden voyage of the full-rigged ship *Canada,* pride of the Allan fleet, with his father in command. New out of Steele's yard, the *Canada* was the largest vessel in the Montreal trade, and her arrival there on 4th May after a quick passage delighted her owners. For Hugh Allan, despite having given up his first job, Montreal felt like home. Hearing of the death of one of his previous employers, he can hardly have been surprised on visiting St. Paul Street to find that William Kerr wanted to take him back and proposed to give him the vacant share in the business. It was a tempting offer, but with recent impressions of shipping in mind Hugh Allan knew that he must get out of merchandising.

A more likely chance came a few days later in a casual meeting with James Millar, an older man and previous acquaintance, who stopped young Allan in the street. Millar asked him what he was doing, and with Presbyterian bluntness warned him of the dangers of idleness. Needless to say Millar was another Montreal Scot, a man of considerable fortune who built, owned and managed ships, imported rum from Greenock and the West Indies, and rounded out an unusually versatile business by the purchase of wheat and ashes from Quebec farmers for shipment to Britain. Each took a fancy to the other and, without bothering to enquire about salary or conditions, Hugh Allan promptly reported for work. Next morning found him auctioning 150 puncheons of rum which completely blocked the laneway to Millar's office in St. Paul Street. Fortunately for Hugh Allan he had acquired an instinctive and fluent command of the French language as a dry-goods traveller for Kerr in his previous job, an accomplishment by no means usual among English-speaking Montrealers and of immense value throughout his life.

For the ensuing five years Hugh Allan worked wholeheartedly with Millar, turning his hand without question to the needs of the hour. James Millar, on his part, trained his young assistant by giving him responsibility under the shipyard manager at the building berths near the Longueuil Ferry. Here was the opportunity to learn something new and useful which might eventually profit the Allan interests, for Millar built several ships for Alexander Allan. There was a sense of pride and pleasure in occasional meetings with his father in this connection and in working on his ships under Millar free from the restraints of direct paternal supervision which, however well meant, can be a source of friction between father and son in the best of families.

51

Wheat buying had a fascination of a different kind for an Ayrshire man whose heritage, judgment and growing experience of human nature was pitted against farmers and merchants themselves canny, suspicious and wise. On top of this there was, of course, competition from other Montreal buyers. The primitive communications of the period necessitated a lengthy journey in which decisions must be made without reference to head office. The custom was to buy in September, renting barns for storage of the wheat until April when another trip would arrange for delivery by "pin-flat" – a kind of sailing lighter with flat bottom peculiar to the St. Lawrence – or by one of the growing number of side-wheeled steamboats.

James Millar was a large operator in the wheat business, taking his crops mostly from the flat country between Laprairie and St. Jean, from that long string of quaint villages winding down the South Shore to Sorel, and on the North side of the St. Lawrence from Trois Rivières towards Montreal. As he made his rounds along dusty roads in each of the years 1831 and 1832, Hugh Allan accumulated some 100,000 bushels from the Chambly area and another 50,000 from the North Shore. It was a pleasant life for a young man, his meanderings reaching into warm summer weather after being cooped up in Montreal for the winter, taking care always to return before the snow changed life for another year; but other changes were afoot.

In June 1832, returning to Montreal from the spring wheat buying, Hugh Allan was sent down river in the sailing ship *Dryope,* newly completed at the Longueuil yard. He was to see her safely through Lake St. Peter, where a spell of hot weather was rapidly drying up the channel. The *Dryope* had loaded cargo until her draft was 14½ feet, too deep to negotiate the shallows. Enquiring about the depth that morning from the master of the steamboat *Voyageur,* newly arrived at Montreal with Irish immigrants from a sailing ship at Quebec, Allan was told that the level was down to 14 feet, which meant that he would have to lighten the *Dryope* by discharging part cargo overside into lighters. Annoying as this must have been to Millar it was something of a challenge for an energetic young man, more than could be said of another piece of news painfully obvious on the *Voyageur.* She had brought cholera to Montreal.

Years later, recalling the impact of this confrontation, Hugh Allan said that "The first case was an emigrant woman; she was lying on deck when I saw her and had reached the collapse state. She was later removed to the emigrant sheds at Point St. Charles and died in a few hours."

Still wondering at this tragedy, Allan sailed as ordered that night under tow of a steamboat, sounding anxiously at intervals, sometimes pacing the poop with the master and pilot where each was engrossed with his own thoughts. At daylight, hopes rose with the sun but fell in the forenoon when the *Dryope* grounded in the mud, the tug straining ineffectually against the taut rope as her paddles churned. There was nothing for it but lightening the ship.

This was easier said than done, for news of the cholera had swept through riverside communities, and the crews of bateaux and schooners had secured their vessels and returned home. With much difficulty and delay, paying famine prices for unsuitable craft, Hugh Allan managed eventually to lighten the *Dryope*, tow her to Trois Rivières, and re-stow the cargo for sea. On completion of this job, and sighting Molson's steamboat *John Bull* at the wharf just up from Quebec, he pulled over in the *Dryope's* boat to ask for a passage back to Montreal. Captain Armstrong of the *John Bull*, an old acquaintance, had bad news and advised Hugh to wait for a later steamer as the cholera had swept his ship like a scythe. There had been several deaths among the 900 passengers and more were expected. Allan knew very little of the dangers of cholera – in the medical sense nobody did. But he finished up by sharing a cabin with an immigrant doctor who had come over as surgeon in one of the ships, comforted in the expectation of professional help if need be. Unfortunately for Hugh Allan's peace of mind and the doctor's reputation, the medical man had travelled in a cholera-free ship, had never previously seen a case, and had neither the knowledge, the medicines nor the desire to treat the disease now. Indeed, as a strictly personal palliative, he had taken the precaution of shedding any responsibilities he might otherwise have thrust upon him, by the liberal use of a private stock of brandy.

This would have been bad enough if kept quiet. But when the news leaked to the other passengers that a doctor was on board, a riot nearly broke out and Armstrong and his crew had difficulty in restoring order. As the *John Bull* steamed slowly up river against the current, boats from adjacent villages came off to hail the announcement that no dead or sick persons were to be landed, no corpse thrown into the river, by order of the Board of Health. All that night, hot and sultry as only the St. Lawrence can produce, tensions rose as showers of blinding rain followed flashes of summer lightning to reveal the overcrowded decks. It was noon next day before hopes began to rise as the steamboat was ordered to anchor in quarantine off the tip of St. Helen's Island. From here the City of Montreal looked eminently desirable under a high summer sky.

No sooner had the *John Bull* complied with this instruction than hopes were again dashed. The Medical Officer of Health came off in a shore-boat; but instead of boarding, he lay off at a safe distance despite piteous pleas to come on board. His orders were clear and to the point: nobody was to be landed until the sick, the dying and the dead had been removed, following arrangements already in hand. To Hugh Allan, never one to suffer officialdom lightly, the order was frustrating in the extreme and he argued with the medical officer that delay might be fatal for the lives of those now well. It also seemed illogical that two cabin passengers who had taken care to remain apart from infected immigrants should not be allowed to land immediately. Fortunately or otherwise, a passing boatman was later persuaded for a price to land the two cabin passengers. Hugh Allan reached St. Paul Street where anxious days were passed before realising that all was well. When the immigrants reached the cholera sheds that night 17 were found to be dead already and 42 were dangerously ill. "How many subsequently died at the sheds," he wrote, "I never knew."

Despite the epidemic life went on much as usual. Three days later, starting a journey to ship out wheat from Maskinonge on the shores of Lake St. Peter, Allan was surprised to find that guards had been posted to prevent strangers from entering the village. After a day or two, when it was seen that the visitor remained hale and hearty, precautions were relaxed due to the kindness and hospitality of the wheat seller, Mr. Boucher, who sheltered the young man when the local hotel refused to take him in. Montreal that summer went through a period of death and anxiety known as the "sickly season," and people struggled through each humid day, hoping for the best. Of this period Hugh Allan wrote:

> The population of the city was then about 36,000, and the number of deaths being about 4,000 it follows that every ninth person died in about six months. It did not appear that medicines had much effect on it. About one half of all those who were attacked died whether they had medical attendance or not, and although every kind of treatment was tried and experimented upon the result was about the same. The city was subsequently attached by cholera in four different years, 1834, 1849, 1853 and 1854, and though in proportion to the population the persons attacked were fewer in number at each successive visitation the proportion of deaths of those attacked remained nearly the same. It would seem that the disease is no better understood now than at the first visitation.

The above was written in 1880 when the horrors of the Crimean War had served only to emphasise the validity of Hugh Allan's assumption.

Meanwhile, recurring bouts of ship fever alternated with sporadic upheavals of political unrest in Montreal. These were being neglected to the point of disaster. Through it all Millar's shipyard had a brief period of activity and perhaps prosperity. Ships and lumber were in demand in England and vessels could be built on speculation, there being a ready market on the other side of the Atlantic if they failed to show immediate profit trading from Canada. Some ships, as was the case with Allan's *Favourite,* were built in Montreal to British order.

From a practical point of view Millar's shipyard was well situated as both raw material and component parts could be delivered by water. Most of the cordage, canvas and hull fittings were imported from Britain but as early as 1825 there was Canadian competition when J.A. Converse opened his ropewalk and block-making plant in Montreal using Russian hemp. On the engineering side Montreal shipyards had been turning out steamboats since 1809 when Molson started the first regular service in the world with the sidewheeler *Accommodation* which ran between there and Quebec. Iron foundries in Montreal and St. Maurice downstream were making cast-iron columns and cylinders. As for labour, a growing number of immigrants were skilled in the newer trades and when the steamship *Royal William* was built at Quebec in 1833 she was towed to Montreal for installation of machinery by the firm of Bennet and Henderson.

The main supply of timber came floating down the Ottawa River, squared from tree trunks in the forest during winter before rafting to join the St. Lawrence at Île Perrot a few miles upstream on the shoreline of Montreal Island which is formed by its drainage. Indeed this fortunate conflux, in itself a basic element of Montreal's history, was there for all to see. It was obvious in the contrast between the brown waters of the Ottawa, which swept past the shipyard frontage, and a pleasantly greenish tinge near the opposite bank which showed the origin of the St. Lawrence in the Great Lakes of Upper Canada. This distinction, somewhat obscured downstream, in the open water of Lake St. Peter, was finally lost by the approach of tides at Trois Rivières, whence brackish water gave way to salt at the Port of Quebec.

Among three shipyards more or less side by side, James Millar's yard produced a number of sailing ships for Alexander Allan and for Millar himself or their associates on both sides of the Atlantic. Mostly barques, these included the identical *Brilliant* and *Thalia* of 472 tons which were sold to Britain in 1834 for the Baltic trade, the *Glasgow* of 437 tons laid down in 1835, and two West Indiamen of 260 tons, the *Thistle* and *John Knox.* In 1838 Millar built a fine full-rigged ship for himself, the *Gypsy,* which was put into the Scottish trade to sail with the Allan packets. Among all these vessels, the barque *Glasgow* is especially notable and perhaps aptly named as marking the arrival of Hugh Allan on the threshold of corporate business.

It came about on 1st May 1835 when one of Millar's partners retired and the firm was reconstituted as "Millar, Edmonstone & Co.," Edmonstone being a senior employee admitted by name while Hugh Allan, whose share was financed from a raise in salary in lieu of ready cash, became the anonymous partner described simply as "& Co." But the real joy of the situation came with an allotment of some of the sixty-four shares in the *Glasgow*. For the first time Hugh Allan was now a shipowner in his own right. Millar, a man of few words not given to the vanity of praise, confirmed this solid mark of confidence in December, when he sent his junior to England to drum up business for the ensuing season.

For an Allan, all things started at Greenock. Sailing in the *Canada*, now under command of his elder brother James, Hugh made the rounds of his family and friends before setting out on a business trip which brought his first taste of financial responsibility. It came about in a classic situation. One of Millar's agents, entrusted with collection of a large sum due from insurance on a lost ship and cargo, broke the news to Hugh Allan that the money would not be forthcoming immediately as it had been applied to the payment of other debts and that the deficit would be made good later. The situation was made more difficult as the defaulting agent was a close personal friend of James Millar and Captain Alexander Allan. But in a stormy interview, an embarassing confrontation of youth and age, principle and compromise, the matter was conclusively settled when Hugh Allan cut short the agency agreement and sued successfully for payment of the money to Millar, Edmonstone's account. Arriving back at Montreal about May 1836, before the uncertain mail from England had reached its destination, it was in fear of burnt bridges and wrecked friendships that Hugh Allan reported to his boss. He need not have worried. True to form, James Millar was reticent and tight-lipped as befitted an Elder of the Auld Kirk, making no comment at the time but showing an increasing trust in his decisive junior partner.

This question of communication by mail overshadowed every transaction between Canada and Britain. While the British Post Office ran sailing packets from Falmouth with mails for Halifax and Boston, the overland route to Upper and Lower Canada was notoriously bad. The mail via Boston by courier was quicker in winter than by the all-British route. In summer casual deliveries by ship from Halifax to Quebec were somewhat better, but in general the Allans and their friends depended on their own vessels. This pitiful slowness in Canadian mail served to emphasise more serious difficulties in 1836 when the troubled state of Lower Canada was tardily acknowledged by appointment of a British Commission headed by the Governor-in-Chief Lord Gosford to report on what should be done. In fact, nothing was done. A threatening crisis of political impasse was followed by an equally depressing slump.

Ruminating on this unsatisfactory state of affairs, Hugh Allan set about the usual round of seasonal business. In July 1836 his sidelong fascination with railways was whetted by the opening of the Champlain and St. Lawrence Railroad, the very first in Canada. This railway connected LaPrairie with St. Jean in that fifteen miles of the route to the United States which he had found so bumpy by stage coach fifteen years ago. Railways would grow: their potential was already obvious in a country crippled by the harsh seasons of nature. Whatever might be the problems of business, constitutional government or even the continued acceptance of British rule in the face of mutual distrust between malcontents and government, fanned by a growing republican influence from the south, one conclusion was evident – communication with Britain must be improved. Steam would provide the answer, steam by sea and steam by rail with overland connection to an Atlantic port in winter, direct by ocean steamship to Montreal in Summer. But to convert the primitive inconsistencies of sailing ships, stage coach and Indian mail courier to the emerging technology of steam would require financing on an unheard-of scale. The proposition was the more difficult as the population of Montreal was then less then 40,000, although growing. With steam navigation the rate of growth would increase, with railways it would spread to the Great Lakes basin, and the port of Montreal would grow in proportion. The first group to raise the money might well reap a fortune.

Meanwhile as the uneasy year wore on, grumbling discontent grew into open rebellion with the approach of winter. On 6th November 1837 a climax was reached with the reading of the *Riot Act* in Montreal following a clash on St. James Street between the Sons of Liberty and the Doric Club. That afternoon the steady tread of British regulars was followed by the clank of ordnance and the clatter of horse artillery as they followed the magistrates. The militia was called out, new units were hastily raised, and a call for reinforcements went to Upper Canada. For Hugh Allan, raised in a settled Scots community, the issue was simple – revolt must be crushed. Enlisting in the 5th. Battalion of Montreal Militia, he exchanged his newly-won partnership in business for a place in the rank and file of foot. The militia tradition was strong, the officer corps was up to strength, and as has happened since many a young executive was content to march with knapsack and musket under the unthinking discipline of the drill sergeant.

While the political issues were complicated, the immediate and more personal attitudes of a young man called to the colours were much as they always have been. Of this period of his life Hugh Allan wrote:

The regular military force then in the country was very small and in

November when the Rebellion broke out we were called on to do garrison and guard duty. The first outbreak was at the village of St. Charles on the Chambly River and Colonel Gore was sent with a moderate force round by Sorel, while Colonel Weatherall with the first Royals was despatched by way of Chambly to attack the rebels on both sides. Colonel Gore's expedition failed but Colonel Weatherall was entirely successful. Public feeling was greatly excited by the treacherous murder by the rebels of Lieutenant Weir, and when on St. Andrew's Day Colonel Weatherall marched into town bringing a large number of prisoners from St. Charles, the enthusiasm was very great. Our anniversary dinner that day was partaken of in uniform with muskets stacked in the passages and there was no limit to the feelings of joy and congratulations. All the entrances to the City were barricaded, martial law prevailed . . . and there was a strong guard at all these places. There was a great deal of excitement all winter and but little business was transacted.

Despite this note of enthusiasm from a young militiaman, 1837 closed as a tragic year in Canadian history. *Patriotes* and British troops clashed at St. Eustache in a brief and bloody flare-up north of Montreal. Hugh Allan's detachment witnessed this attack during a period of three days in which they marched with the regular army.

In the months following the December rebellion, Montreal became virtually a military camp under martial law. More than half of the male population were by then engaged in support of regular troops brought in from New Brunswick and Nova Scotia. Understandably, business was slack: but a period of frustration for Hugh Allan ended abruptly in August 1838 with the death of James Millar. With this event the business was again reviewed and Allan's position as a coming man was confirmed for all to see. On 1st May 1839 the firm became "Edmonstone, Allan & Co., Ship Agents, Shipbuilders and General Merchants." One other interesting development, routine at the time but to have lasting significance later, occurred that year: Andrew Allan, Hugh's younger brother, then aged 17, was brought out from Greenock to start his training as a clerk in the Montreal office.

In December, 1839, with commerce slowly returning to normal. Edmonstone & Allan decided to bring themselves up to date with first-hand knowledged of the state of trans-Atlantic steam navigation. In 1833 the Quebec steamer *Royal William,* which had been built to connect the St. Lawrence with Halifax, was sent to England for sale, making the passage from Pictou to Cowes in 19 days. Despite very bad weather she had been under steam entirely, except for intervals when her boiler had to be blown down to clear it of salt. But as she consumed almost a full cargo of coal on the voyage, shipowners were not impressed with the economics of the situation: and neither in Quebec nor Montreal had anyone seen fit to repeat the experiment. It was now time to see whether others had made progress in the interim.

In fact, things were looking up. In April, 1838, the British steamer *Sirius* had made a 19-day passage from Cork to New York to be joined the same day by the much larger *Great Western* – first of Brunel's immortal trio *Great Western, Great Britain* and *Great Eastern* – which had sailed from Bristol four days later. The *Great Western*, with her Maudsley engines enabling her to average 215 miles a day, had demonstrated that ocean steam was already emerging from the experimental stage into the realm of practical shipowning. Indeed Sir John Rennie, the famous engineer, said of this first crossing by the *Great Western:* "The success of this voyage across the Atlantic having exceeded the most sanguine expectations of its promoters, and indeed of the world, there seemed no bounds to the extension of steam navigation." If the founder of the firm of J & G Rennie of Blackfriars, who had been knighted for his services to steam navigation, was of this opinion, here was something worth looking into.

With this in mind Hugh Allan got extended leave from his military duties. Changing the high stock and scarlet tunic of a soldier for the more natural cravat and coat of a private gentleman and shipowner, he booked a berth for England in the only steamer available at the time, the *Liverpool,* which then lay at New York. "I might have gone in a sailing ship," he later said, "but I wanted to have the experience of a steamship." In this he was less than fortunate, for the *Liverpool* was no *Great Western.* But to put this in perspective it must be remembered that the relative comfort and safety of steam and sail was a subject of concern to travellers long after 1839. As late as 1860 an anonymous writer in *Sketches of a Visit to Canada West* wrote:

> I know that you will not relish the passage in one of those hot crowded steamers that give one time for nothing but to be ill and complain. You will go in a nice comfortable leisurely way, in a good sailing ship. . . .

On her westward voyage before Hugh Allan joined her, the *Liverpool*'s best day's run had been 242 miles, a result which had been helped by strong fair winds and was above her average. She had demonstrated, however that 10 knots was by no means an impossible goal. Unfortunately the *Liverpool* was a great coal-eater, even by the standards of the period. There was little room for paying cargo when her bunkers were full. Hugh Allan was disappointed in the ship and said of her:

There could hardly be a vessel less adapted for Atlantic passages than the *Liverpool* was. She had been built to carry cattle between Dublin and Liverpool and had a high poop and forecastle with solid bulwarks five feet high extending from one to the other.

There were twelve cabin passengers of whom Allan remarked that four besides himself were "Canadians," among them G.B. Symes, the Quebec timber merchant, with whom he struck up a friendship. Sailing from New York on 14th December 1839, the *Liverpool* ran slap into a heavy gale. The waist was continually flooded with large quantities of free water, which sloshed from side to side because the scuppers and washports were quite inadequate. This highly dangerous situation made a great impression on Hugh Allan and remained to influence the design of his steamships later.

They had a wretched voyage towards England as continuous bad weather forced the master to bear up for Fayal in the Azores as the last few shovels of coal gave out, arriving eventually at Liverpool 31 days from New York and given up for lost. Well might Hugh Allan recall that most of his friends were distrustful of steamships; he now saw for himself the embryo state of steam navigation on the Atlantic service. Steamships would improve, without doubt; but in the meantime it was clearly hard enough to make them pay in year-round operation on the much-travelled New York route, never mind the difficulties inherent in seasonal sailings to Montreal and the added question of a railway to the coast. Yet despite these difficulties, and despite its small population, Montreal had been among the first cities to benefit from river steamboats and it was clear that future development would depend on ocean steam navigation.

Perhaps the best memory of that miserable month in the *Liverpool* was a superb view of Fayal from 7,000 feet up Mount Caldura as Symes and Allan looked down on their tiny ship far below. Those on board hung on grimly as she rolled to the gunwales in the heavy swell of an open roadstead.

Meanwhile, political affairs in Canada reached a climax with Lord Durham's famous Report. The resultant decision to combine the Upper and Lower Canadas into a United Province brought an unexpected benefit to Edmonstone & Allan through the efforts of the Governor General, Charles Edward Poulet Thomson. Thomson, later to become Lord Sydenham, made valiant efforts to promote St. Lawrence shipbuilding by persuading the British Admiralty to place naval orders. The Governor sent for Hugh Allan to discuss ways in which the industry might respond. Shortly afterwards Edmonstone & Allan were the successful tenderers for the *Lord Sydenham,* a wooden dispatch vessel with engines by Ward, Brush & Co. of Montreal, which was completed in

1841. This job was followed by the launching of a pleasure yacht to His Excellency's personal account and a steam tug called the *Alliance.* But despite vice-regal encouragement during Sydenham's period in office, the outlook for Montreal shipbuilding was beginning to be obscured by the coming of iron.

By this time Hugh Allan was convinced that technical limitations in steam navigation would be overcome and that financial capability would be the decisive factor in Montreal which was too far inland to be served much longer by sail. When the change did come, wooden hulls would go the way of sailing ships and, in the meantime, it would be a mistake for Edmonstone & Allan to over-extend in the wrong direction by building obsolete types when capital would be required for steamships. They had one final fling at building for themselves in the barques *Blonde* and *Brunette* of 676 tons which were launched in 1840 with ownership equally divided between the two principals. Shortly afterwards Edmonstone & Allan closed their shipyard to concentrate on ship management and agency work. This was more profitable and more likely to open up prospects for steam.

One wonders about the inspiration behind the names *Blonde* and *Brunette,* a pleasing flight of fancy after the heavy Presbyterian flavour of *John Knox* and *Glasgow*. It might well have been that memories of the successful *Jean,* named by Sandy Allan in devoted admiration for Jean Crawford, had been recalled in connection with a double romance as yet undeclared. Certain it is that about this time Hugh and Andrew began their courtship of the sisters Matilda and Isabella Smith, daughters of yet another among the elite of the Montreal-Scottish business world. In the strict propriety of early Victorian society it would have been a pleasing and ingenious compliment from young men with an unsuspected sense of fun.

The *Blonde,* as mentioned earlier, was advertised to intending travellers in April 1843 as a particularly comfortable ship on which high "econiums" had been passed by appreciative passengers. But it is a measure of the decline of the Montreal shipbuilding market that she was running for her builders' management account only because they had been unable to sell her when new. An advertisement in the *Glasgow Herald* of 24th February 1841 reads:

> For Sale – Fine new barque *Blonde* 603 tons O.M. 676 tons N.M. built at Montreal last year under particular inspection, framed with tamarack, planked with best white oak and completely copper fastened. Rigging and materials of best Greenock manufacture. James Allan, 87 Union Street.

From subsequent sailing announcements it is clear that no sale resulted.

The *Blonde* was lost at sea in 1849 while the *Brunette* lasted only till 1843 in which year she was wrecked on St. Paul's Island. From tables of casualties in annual reports of the Commissioner of Works of Canada 1843 was not regarded as a particularly bad season: losses in the Gulf amounted only to twelve ships.

The young ladies fared better than the ships. On 16th September 1844 the *Montreal Gazette* announced Matilda's wedding:

> On 13th. inst. at Athelstane Hall, by the Rev. Dr. Anderson, Hugh Allan Esq. to Matilda Caroline, second daughter of John Smith Esq. . . .

When the ship *Caledonia,* Bryce Allan commander, arrived at Glasgow on 6th October that year after logging "A fine passage of 21 days," the young couple stepped proudly ashore as Mrs. Hugh Allan was introduced to Jean and Sandy and the family. It was a happy moment for all, a delightful climax in which their sons and daughter-in-law had demonstrated that a beautiful Allan sailing packet could make a much better passage than that dreadful tin kettle of a steamer which had brought Mr. Hugh in 1839. Captain Allan rubbed his hands in delight: well might passengers sixteen years afterwards remark on the pleasures of a "nice comfortable, leisurely sailing ship." Apart from the description "leisurely," he would have been the first to agree with them.

After a tour of Europe, Mr. and Mrs. Hugh Allan returned to Montreal in the spring of 1845 and took up residence in a fine new house on St. Catherine Street which had been building for them over the winter. It was a good address on high ground, not quite on the slopes of the Mountain which had fascinated young Hugh on first scrambling ashore from the *Jean* in 1826 but within easy reach of the docks. Here they lived for eighteen years and here most of their twelve children were born. The second marriage between the Smiths and the Allans came in 1846, the year when Edmonstone & Allan admitted Andrew as a partner and in which Andrew and Isabella were married in Montreal.

By this time the military emergency of 1837 had died down but the place of the Militia had been firmly established in the social life of Montreal. Many an employer regarded it as a seal of approval that his young office staff should join the ranks and a commission was decidedly a business and social asset. With his previous experience of active service when the need was urgent, Hugh Allan's name had slowly worked up the eligible list for vacancies until, on 14th July 1847, he was gazetted Lieutenant in the Third Battalion of Montreal Militia under the seal of "Elgin and Kincardine," Governor General of British North America.

Despite the attractions of a widening family and social life, there were many real dangers and difficulties in the forties. With famine in Ireland mortality among newly arrived settlers was high. The worst type of emigrant ships, many of them grossly overcrowded and operated by unscrupulous owners, brought typhus fever, and this cast a loathsome cloud over the entire Canadian passenger trade. The Allan packets, which sailed mainly from Scottish ports with "respectable" passengers of self-sufficient artisan or farming types, were notably free from this scourge. But the fact remained that even from a practical point of view, to say nothing of the vicious inhumanity which was everywhere apparent, people would not put up with it much longer. Improvement would depend on steamships which, for successful commercial operation, would need to sail continuously throughout the year and would be dependent on railways. Never far from Hugh Allan's mind in this connection, his interest in railways had been consistent since their very beginning. On the financial side his willingness to invest in railway development appears as early as 1842 when a letter dated "Greenock, 1st April," informed James that:

> I am desirous of investing in some way that will return me a greater dividend than I would get from a bank – and as I understand that the Glasgow and Edinburgh Railway Company are borrowing money on the security of the Railway at five per cent interest – I hereby authorise and request of you to give them my money above mentioned taking a bond for same with interest payable half-yearly. . . .

In laying out this modest private investment of 2,500 pounds sterling, Hugh concluded with the assurance that "I am, my Dear James, your affectionate Brother."

Although he was comfortably off by the time he was married and settled in Montreal, Hugh Allan was by no means wealthy as a capitalist; and if he had not so far invested in Canadian railways, it was simply because he could see no reasonable prospect of "A greater amount of interest than I could get from a bank." In fact, some investors in railway stock had lost their all, and where would that leave steam navigation?

Undoubtedly he had followed the slow progress of one railway, the St. Lawrence and Atlantic, which was planned to join Montreal over 300 miles of rough country to the fine natural harbour of Portland in Maine an inlet which was completely ice-free. This scheme was directed by another Ayrshire man, John Galt, who was that unusual type, an entrepreneur with talents in poetry and writing. It was backed by the British American Land Company which optimistically hoped to make money from lands acquired for colonisation in the early thirties. Opened in 1853, the St. Lawrence and Atlantic Railway was originally financed from Montreal but later merged with a group of Toronto financiers, including the son of John Galt the novelist, a notable engineer called

Casimir Gzowski, and David Lewis MacPherson. These men, and many favoured contractors, made fortunes out of the Grand Trunk Railway which rose from the merger. But despite riches for promoters and others, the Grand Trunk lost enormous sums of public money. It was a mis-marriage of government, railway promoters and politicians which cost Canada dearly and set an unfortunate precedent. The Grand Trunk, bankrupt in every way, was eventually wound up in 1922 when it was absorbed by Canadian National Railways as a government line.

Unknown to Hugh Allan at the time, this group of Toronto capitalists, particularly D.L. MacPherson, would become his bitterest enemies, when he too would become mesmerized by railway dreams and play for the greatest stake of all, the Pacific Railway contract.

Meanwhile the government's position on ocean steamers, quite apart from the opportunity arising from completion of the St. Lawrence and Atlantic line, had been maturing since 1839. In that year the Admiralty had signed a contract with the British and North American Royal Mail Steam Packet Company to provide a mail service to Halifax and on to Boston. Everyone, including the Allans, had been fired with ambition. The already famous quartette of Royal Mail paddle steamers *Britannia, Columbia, Acadia* and *Caledonia* had been financed mainly by that remarkable Canadian, Samuel Cunard, with Burns and McIver as the other principal shareholders. These ships, which provided a regular and efficient service, brilliantly confirmed the views of their designer, Robert Napier of Glasgow, who for many years had been urging shipowners to exploit the advantages of steam in the Atlantic passenger trade. From the first sailing of the *Britannia* in July 1840 the Cunard Company were bound to provide a connection to Quebec, by mail steamer from Pictou, whenever ice permitted. This service was provided by the *Unicorn,* which was sent out from Britain for the purpose. It came to Montreal for one trip in 1839, being probably the first steamship to arrive in the port from an Atlantic crossing.

But in 1845 the Cunard branch sailing to the St. Lawrence was dropped. Public opinion in Canada came out against the imperial government and the British and North American Royal Mail Company. The imperial mail subsidy, originally intended to help the British North American Colonies before the Atlantic Railway had been built, was of more use to the United States than it was to loyal British colonists. The latter then had to revert to the uncertainties of overland mail from Boston or New York despite the completion of the railway to Portland. With this in mind, and with a lack of shipping progress holding back the Canadian economy, the Province of Canada, by a contract dated 13th August 1853, arranged for a line of steamships to open regular sailings from Liverpool to Montreal. The sailings were to be fortnightly in summer, and from Liverpool to Portland monthly in winter.

To Hugh Allan's disgust and mortification, this contract went to Liverpool shipowners McKean, McLarty and Lamont, who had a motley fleet of highly unsuitable steamers. Although not a man to allow personal feelings to sway his business judgement, Allan's disappointment was understandable. The reputation of the Allan sailing packets was second to none. It was known that they intended to go in for steam, and that Hugh Allan was firmly of the opinion that regular sailings could be maintained only by a group of ships designed and built for the purpose, all having the same speed and power and general characteristics. Surely this was the outstanding lesson of Cunard's success. Contrary to these logical ideas, the Canadian government had in fact been influenced in favour of a Liverpool company with steamships in being, however unsuitable. They were opposed to a Montreal company with an established reputation who were prepared to back their views by building iron steamships of the latest type especially designed for the St. Lawrence trade.

The firmness of Allan's intentions is evidenced by the fact that he had persuaded his family – with the exception of Captain Alexander Allan who was now seventy-three – to invest in new steam tonnage. This firm intention, hindered only by an insufficiency of capital within the family, is clear from the following letter to Isaac Buchanan, a Scots capitalist and politician in Canada West. It is also clear that Hugh Allan foresaw that the Liverpool ships would be quite unable to fulfill the obligations of the contract.

Montreal, Sept 10 1853

Isaac Buchanan Esq.,
Hamilton C.W.

Dear Sir,

Overtures having been made to us by influential parties here to this effect that as there is apparently no prospect of the present contractors for screw steamers between this city and Liverpool carrying out their contract, and about as little of the proposed joint Stock Company going into operation, we should take up the matter and undertake to carry it out. I have so far gone into it as to have got 75,000 Stg. subscribed, I think, by the time contracts will have been closed in Glasgow for the construction of two iron steamers of 1800 tons each and 300 to 350 Horsepower – the cost of which will be about £ 40,000 Stg. each. One of these vessels may I hope be ready in June and the other in August next – but in going into them at all my views are not limited to two vessels. To carry it out effectually there should

65

be four steamers from Liverpool, one from Glasgow, and at least one from London, and my object in now addressing you is to ask whether you would be disposed to take any stock in such an enterprise. There is little doubt that it would be highly remunerative if properly managed and I am persuaded that the state of trade now requires it. In order to put you in full posession of all the facts connected with the matter I annex a list of those who have already taken stock, and as it is desirable to have it in as few hands as possible, I am anxious that those who subscribe should do so largely. If in accordance with your views I would be much pleased to have you as an owner in the vessels and to have your countenance and support in the enterprise.

Will you therefore be pleased to let me hear from you as early as convenient, & believe me,

> Yours faithfully,
> Hugh Allan

The vessels will make the passage in 12 days

On the back of this letter, all of which is in Hugh Allan's handwriting, appears the subscription list, including the five Allan brothers whose names are listed in order of age where shares are equal, and otherwise by the amount invested.

Subscribers names	Number of Sixty-fourth shares in each steamer	Amount subscribed to each steamer	Total amount subscribed
James Allan Glasgow	8	£ 5000 Stg	£ 10,000 Stg
Hugh Allan Montreal	8	5000	10,000
Bryce Allan Liverpool	8	5000	10,000
Jno. G. MacKenzie Montreal	8	5000	10,000
George B. Symes Quebec	8	5000	10,000
William Edmonstone Montreal	4	2500	5,000
Sir George Simpson do	4	2500	5,000
Robert Anderson do	4	2500	5,000
Alexr. Allan Jn. Glasgow	4	2500	5,000
Andrew Allan Montreal	2	1250	2,500

It should be noted that the above lists shareholders in vessels rather than holdings in a stock company. As the Allans and their close associates had subscribed for 58 out of the 64 shares into which the law divided their ships, it is clear that Isaac Buchanan was regarded as a prospect for the remaining six, a holding which would have placed him immediately behind the senior Allans. He may have regretted his decision not to join for in later years, in a number of involved transactions, he was heavily indebted to Hugh Allan as a bank director.

Hamilton, 16th. Sept 1853

My Dear Sir,

   I was truly glad to learn from your letter of the 10th inst that you & your friends are at length going into steamers – there is no doubt in my mind that they are called for by the state of trade and that they will be a highly remunerative property if properly managed. At the moment however I am not prepared with money for this enterprise & must content myself with supporting you (as I feel sure you will make it our interest to do) as far as I can in the way of freight which is I suppose your vital consideration. With my best wishes for the success of your enterprise,

    I am,
    Dear Sir,
    Yours faithfully,
(Signed) Isaac Buchanan

Give my regards to Mr. Edmonstone
Hugh Allan Esq
Montreal

Hugh Allan's reaction to this refusal is not recorded but clearly he had not counted on Buchanan's acceptance as on 5th. October, before news of the refusal could have reached Scotland, a previous decision was put into effect when the Glasgow office ordered the first Allan steamship from Denny of Dumbarton. This was a very bold decision, for as yet the Allans had neither the government mail contract nor subsidy for freight and passenger services. Indeed, they had no guarantee that they would be supported officially if, as appeared inevitable, the existing contractor failed to meet his commitments.

  Meanwhile, true to Hugh Allan's expectations, the firm of McKean, McLarty & Lamont had run into serious trouble. The Liverpool firm had a seven-year contract, commencing with the navigational season of 1853, by which they had to run a monthly service in the first year of operation, increasing the frequency to two-week intervals by 1854. The Province of Canada, the City of Portland, and the St. Lawrence & Atlantic Railway were each to pay agreed amounts to the contractor, depending on the number of trips. It was also agreed that the steamships should be of not less than 1200 tons and 300 horsepower, and that they should make westbound passages of not more than 14 days, and 13 when returning to Liverpool. Even in mid-nineteenth century this was by no means a difficult schedule to maintain, provided they had a fleet capable of reliable and sustained operation.

In their attempt to meet this contract the Liverpool firm put on three ships, the *Genova, Lady Eglinton* and *Sarah Sands.* Of this fleet the *Genova* and *Lady Eglinton* were smaller than the stipulated tonnage and power. But on 13th May 1853, the *Genova* was acclaimed with great enthusiasm when she arrived at Montreal, becoming the first regular trans-Atlantic steamship to use that port.

In some ways it was the biggest of the trio, the memorable *Sarah Sands,* which was least adapted to the St. Lawrence trade. Launched at Liverpool in 1846 and named after the wife of her first owner, the *Sarah Sands* was among the first ocean-going iron screw steamers and had been intended to demonstrate that steam and sail would make an economical combination on the long run from England to Australia. This concept was completely at variance with requirements on the Atlantic where Cunard had demonstrated, and Hugh Allan was equally convinced, that regular passage-making depended on having sufficient power in reserve to keep up a sustained average speed in all weathers.

For some reason the *Sarah Sands* was put into the New York trade on completion. She was very slow, averaging about 18 days per voyage. Many voyages were considerably longer. When McKean, McLarty and Lamont chartered her in 1853 for their Canadian Steam Navigation Company, she averaged 22 days from Liverpool to Montreal, with an average return passage of 18 days. This was well below contract performance.

On 5th June 1853 the *Sarah Sands* stranded in the Belle Isle Strait in a night of thick fog and was extremely lucky to get off. On return to Liverpool for repairs the unfortunate ship capsized on leaving drydock, owing to an error in ballasting. Her strong iron hull enabled her to survive without significant damage and she was refitted. But her most dramatic moments, recalled by generations of English children brought up on the epic sea stories of Victoria's reign, came in November 1857 while on a trooping voyage to India. On this occasion a disastrous fire reduced the *Sarah Sands* to a charred and blackened shell. This contained the fire, while the courage and discipline of officers and men of the 54th Regiment of Foot brought her eventually to safe anchorage at Mauritius without loss of life.

In 1854, their second season of operation under the Canadian Government contract, McKean, McLarty & Lamont made equally futile attempts to recover the situation by chartering in addition the steamships *Cleopatra, Ottawa* and *Charity,* names which can hardly have attracted the travelling public. Not only did the Canadian Steam Navigation Company fail to meet the stipulated requirements of power and size in their oddly assorted chartered vessels, they rarely achieved a passage in anything approaching contract time. In 1854 a report of the Commissioners of Public Works of the Province of Canada – who administered the ocean steamer contract – complained that fifty sailing ships arrived at Quebec to open the season ahead of the unfortunate *Cleopatra.* There is no doubt that the government would have been justified in cancelling the contract there and then, or even in the first year. But there was no alternative: they had backed the wrong firm and the man who could have saved the situation had been struggling to raise the money.

Now after years of careful thought, after years of waiting for the railway, after years of beating the bounds of Canada among financiers and politicians alike, Hugh Allan was ready to go ahead. He would not do so alone, but with ships owned also by his brothers and trusted associates. In contrast to incompetent contractors with chartered ships, there was to be a company owning vessels of thoroughly up-to-date type, the entire organization directed from Montreal by men who knew the Canadian trade.

After eighteen months of failure and frustration in their first attempt to encourage ocean steamships, the Canadian Government approached Hugh Allan. Negotiations were formally concluded on 18th December, 1854, when royal assent was given to a parliamentary bill in Chapter XLV of the *Statutes of Canada* for that year, *An Act to incorporate the Montreal Ocean Steamship Company.* Besides Hugh Allan and William Edmonstone, partners in a firm known to Montreal shipping men for upwards of half a century, the stockholders were: his brother Andrew Allan; his old cabin-mate George B. Symes of Quebec, with whom he had climbed Mount Caldura at Fayal on that memorable trip in the old *Liverpool;* Sir George Simpson, the Governor in North America of the Hudson's Bay Company; William Dow, the brewer; and Robert Anderson, both of Montreal; and John Watkins, a Kingston merchant.

CHAPTER FOUR

Denny of Dumbarton

"Few heads with knowledge so informed"

R.B.
Epitaph on Wm. Muir

James Allan's office at 40 Union Street, Glasgow, was in a row of stone-fronted tenement buildings, many of them still standing, with occasional shops at ground level. This was the newer business area of the City, which had moved westwards from the Trongate since the days of the West Indian tobacco trade. But the rumble of heavy carts drawn by teams of Clydesdale horses would be a sign that Scottish trade with North America was greater than ever before, and that cargo could be delivered alongside ocean ships now berthed at the Broomielaw not far away. A growing traffic in carriages and cabs betokened an increasing affluence among the business community.

The partnership of "James & Alexander Allan, Shipowners," which had been founded in 1846, marked the end of the Greenock agency and the virtual retirement of Sandy Allan. The junior partner was the youngest son, also named Alexander. He had gone into business with Captain James after a brief apprenticeship in Ireland with their freight and passenger agents. This was a good arrangement: the brothers pooled their talents and experience in ship management and commerce. Their father, founder of the firm, now lived in a Georgian town house in Newton Place. He and Mrs. Allan had been among leading families who had all but moved *en bloc* to the new and fashionable West End. Now seventy-four, his life had been spent under square sail, sails which in the end had brought him from Hamilton Street in Saltcoats by way of Greenock to this quiet terrace, with its carriage steps and ornamental railings. Steam navigation had come too late for Sandy Allan.

Following the Montreal Ocean Steamship Company's decision to build iron steamers, J & A Allan negotiated with William Denny & Brothers of Dumbarton to build the first vessel, an exchange which resulted in the following offer:

Iron Shipyards,
Dumbarton, 5th Octr 1853

Messrs J & A Allan,
Glasgow.

Dear Sirs,

We offer to build you an iron screw steamship, according to specification of yesterday's date signed by us and now referred to, for the sum of Forty-four thousand pounds (£44,000) or with second class berths in lieu of third with companions, cupolas etc requisite for same, including cabinet and upholstery work but no beds, bedding or other stewards furnishings, referring in this also to the *Andes* and *Alps,* for the sum of Forty-five thousand pounds (£45,000). If wood stanchions and bulwarks are preferred you can have your option.

Contract payable in three equal instalments, first keel laid and cylinders bored, second ship decked, and third when contract is finished and approved of. First two cash, last pyble @ 6 mths.

The vessel to be finished ready for sea by 1 June 1854 under penalty of one thousand pounds.

We are etc.
(signed) W.D. & B.

Allan's acceptance has also survived in a letter signed anonymously in the name of the firm, most probably by Nathaniel Dunlop, a hardworking young man of ambition who had risen from office boy and would one day reach the top.

40 Union Street,
Glasgow, 5th October 1853

Messrs. W. Denny & Brothers,
Dumbarton

Dear Sirs,

We accept your offer to build us an iron screw steamer according to specification signed by you and dated 4th instant and in terms of your letter of this date.

The price complete with first and second class accommodation to be Forty-four thousand pounds, or forty-three thousand pounds if not finished ready for sea by 1st June 1854.

If fitted with second class accommodation instead of third in terms of said letter the price to be one thousand pounds additional.

Although you only to provide furnishings for fifty 1st class cabin passengers we understand that there is to be accommodation made for seventy.

We also understand that the vessel with her equipments and machinery is to be in every respect equal to the *Andes* and *Alps* and the boilers to be at least equal in size and strength to those on board said steamers – the sails to be of best Gourock extra canvas, and the cordage to be equal in quality to that supplied by the Gourock Ropework Co. One at least of the bower anchors to be of Trotman's patent, and one of Fox & Henderson's 'Rodgers' patent. A suitable mooring chain to be supplied in addition to the chain required by Lloyd's Rules. The principal blocks to have patent bushes, and brass sheaves to be put in the catheads. The vessel to get four coats of paint.* Two at least of which to be of Peacock's Patent or any other composition that may be found more useful for the prevention of fouling.** To be supplied with at least two guns and carriages and one of Massey's patent sounding machines. The compasses to be adjusted and a trial trip made with vessel after the steam is up at your own expense and risk.

The machinery is to be guaranteed for six months free from defective material and workmanship, and notwithstanding any omission in the specification we understand that all materials and fittings connected with the ship and machinery usually supplied to Burns' screw steamers are to be furnished and fitted to our vessel to our satisfaction or to that of any inspector we may chose to appoint.

If the particulars we have mentioned are in accordance with your views we shall be glad to confirm them by letter and you can then proceed at once with the building of the vessel.

Any dispute that may arise between us to be referred to arbitration by Captain Walter Douglas.

* 2 only inside the iron hull
** On ships bottom

We are,
Dear Sirs,
Your able servants,
Jas. and Alex. Allan

The following alterations made in specification by and with consent of your Mr. Denny:

Beam tyes – to have a tye plate of iron 15 inches (instead of 10) by ¾ inch.

Machinery etc – "With a boiler" altered to "With boilers"

The vessel referred to in this correspondence between J & A Allan and William Denny and Brothers, appropriately named the *Canadian* at her launching in the Summer of 1854, marked a great step in the history of the St. lawrence trade. In one fell swoop the Allans had moved from sail to steam, from wood to iron, directly to screw propulsion. Putting aside, of necessity, the intermediate stage exemplified by Cunard's *Britannia* class of paddlers and their successors, Hugh Allan was motivated by the inescapable logic of the St. Lawrence route. Sidewheel steamships might or might not survive for a while on the open sea crossings but the ice which had imprisoned Captain Bryce Allan in the sailing ship *Albion* would have sunk a paddler. This decision emphasised that ocean paddlers were now hopelessly outdated and that iron had come to stay, a policy which placed the Allan Line in the front line of marine technology at a time of rapid change. In this connection it might be mentioned that the first iron Cunarder was the paddler *Persia* of 1856 and their last paddle-wheel steamship the *Scotia* as late as 1862.

Although the liners *Andes* and *Alps* are mentioned in the Denny letter as convenient standards of comparison for equipment for the new Allan steamship, and there is a reference to the specification of Burn's screw steamers, it is probable that the design of the *Canadian* was influenced by the Inman Liner *City of Glasgow,* a beautiful and successful Clyde-built ship which since 1850 had demonstrated the superiority of the iron screw steamer in regular trans-Atlantic service. The tragedy of her loss without trace only eight months before completion of the *Canadian* was accepted as but another in the long catalogue of missing vessels: a catalogue which, steam or no steam, gave little sign of decreasing.

The Allans and the Dennys had much in common. Each family had formed successful business partnerships in a changing and highly competitive world, and the hard-headed commercial outlook of the shipowners was matched by an equally hard-headed and impressive technical capability on the part of their chosen shipbuilders and engineers. The original William Denny, who had died in 1833 after founding the business, left a large family, of whom five sons became well known in the shipbuilding world. Like the five Allan brothers, they moved around to gain experience. By the time that the contract for the *Canadian* was placed, the firm of William Denny & Brothers comprised William, Peter and James in their shipyard on the River Leven where it drains from

Loch Lomond to join the Clyde under the shadow of Dumbarton Rock and Castle. With William Denny & Brothers was associated the business of Tulloch & Denny, which made propelling machinery.

The *Canadian* took form on the building berth of the old Iron Shipyard in the winter of 1854, growing from a skeleton of frames and plates surrounded by a thick forest of wooden poles and scaffolding. The rattle of riveter's hammers and the sharp tang of smoke from their portable forges foretold the end of the ancient craft of the shipwright in wood but as yet gave no sign that in time both would disappear before the splutter and flash of the automatic welding machine. A half-circle of glowing rivets would be laid neatly around each fire to the riveter's shouted instructions for the work in hand. "Hey boy, efter three mair gie's a half-dozen five-eighths snap-heid . . . ." The "boy," who might in fact be any age, tossed the first rivet from his tongs to the "holder-on" somehere in the adjacent staging, who caught it expertly by the same method, popping it in one swift movement into the waiting hole where he held it while the riveter and his mate fell like demons on the unsuspecting point. As it changed through the colour spectrum from red-hot to shining metal by sheer manual dexterity, the rivet would be finished off by a resounding tap from the outside of the plate while the holder-on inside gave a final lick of his flat hammer to the head. Rivet by rivet, plate by plate, strake upon strake of fair plating testified to the skill of the naval architect William Denny and to the sweat of countless trades from mine to mould-loft. This was the new Scotland, unheralded when Saw'ny Allan was apprenticed to the Kilmarnock shoemaker.

Sandy Allan, the patriarch of the Allan Line, never saw the results of his sons' new and courageous policies. As William Denny scanned the *Glasgow Herald* of 20th March 1854 the name of an old friend and that of a new client would be sure to catch his eye:

Deaths:
At 16 Newton Place, Glasgow, on the 18th inst Alexander Allan, aged 75 years.

Farther down the paper, the weather report for the past few days noted a period of windy showers, days of typical light and shade in which a fair tops'l breeze brought tall ships with square sail safely in from sea, past Saltcoats through the Gate of the Clyde, to good holding ground on the Tail of the Bank off Greenock.

The iron screw steamship *Canadian,* although small by modern standards at 278 feet in length and 1,764 tons, was described by the *Dumbarton Herald* as being of " . . . immense size." Few would dispute the same reporter's opinion that she was a beautiful ship, a model which at that time and for years to come was based on the best practice of sailing ship design. With her graceful clipper entrance sweeping aft in a continuous sheer except where the forecastle was decked to the rail, a few modest deckhouses amidships and right aft served only to emphasize the symmetry of the design which was crowned by three nicely raking masts rigged as a barque, with stu'n'sails on fore and main. She had two funnels, red with a white band beneath their black top, which complemented the blue-white-and-red of the Allan houseflag at the main truck. The houseflag was surmounted by a long red pendant to differentiate the steamship from her sailing sisters with Alexander Allan's *tricoleur*. This custom was adopted by many shipowners of the sail and steam age when more obvious evidence of mechanical propulsion was liable to be concealed by masts and yards.

The *Dumbarton Herald* of 7th September 1854 carried an excellent description of the ship as seen by their reporter:

The *Canadian* is constructed to carry sixty-eight cabin passengers. The staterooms are perfect models of elegance and comfort. They contain every convenience of life on board ship, from luxurious velvet-cushioned sofas and snug berths tastefully curtained, to mirrors, patent lamps and wash-hand basins. They are each seven feet three inches in length and eight feet six inches in breadth, fitted up with two berths two feet wide. The saloon is an apartment of surpassing beauty fifty-eight feet in length. The style of carving is the old cathedral, and nothing could have been more finely adapted to give the great length of the saloon its full effect than the plainly arched roof and unobtrusive panelling which belongs to this style. From the large gilt mirror between the two entrance doors to the farther end of the saloon there is quite a vista of refulgent things – gilding on the walls and crystal on swinging trays above the centre tables. These swinging trays more closely examined are wonderfully contrived. In foul weather they can let down with all their brittle load of tumblers and glasses to almost a level with the table which being fixed to the floor of the ship is liable to all varieties of motion. In the way of furniture we noticed that the saloon is adorned with handsome telescope chairs, as many as will seat comfortably at dinner no fewer than 70. The light in this magnificient room is excellent, being admitted from the end of the cupola by four panel panes of stained glass, the work of Messrs. Ballantyne and Allan of Edinburgh. The cupola is constructed so as to ventilate the saloon freely. And when we have added that that apartment is heated by steam, endowed with appliances for a little friendly gambling, and so handsomely finished and decorated that it is quite a pleasure to look upon, we have said all that we intend to say of its unrivalled beauty and comfort.

The ladies cabin, which is to the right of the saloon on going out, contains fourteen berths and is everything that could be desired for privacy and comfort. This cabin is also heated by steam. Before ascending to the deck again we are conducted to the steward's pantry, a splendid room eighteen feet by eight superbly garnished with silver plate of all dimensions and crystal of every imaginable cut. A happy man the steward must be with quiet surroundings and so much silver plate about him.

On deck are the master's and mates' rooms, snug little apartments compactly furnished with the requisites of the nautical profession, as well as all personal conveniences that seamen might be expected to care anything for. The wheelhouse astern is a handsome room with a glass front, more comfortable in the cold season we should think, by a long way, than an upright exposure to the heavenly breathings. There is also another wheel at the bow which will be of great use it is said in navigating a narrow channel. The cooking range has been fitted up in a most complete style and on the most improved principles. On deck also there are two large ice-houses, 12 feet long each by 7 deep and 6 in breadth and as was to be desired, a most respectable cow-house. The rooms of the third mate and petty officers at the bow are fitted up much in the same style as the other staterooms, with the exception of two messrooms which are of course long apartments with seats and a table. Many a jolly laugh, we have no doubt, will resound through the length of these rooms when they and the brave fellows they shelter are dancing on the wide Atlantic.

The fore cabin is as admirably fitted up in its own way as the rooms we have been describing. There are 280 berths in all, disposed in two single ranges along the sides, and one double range in the centre of the ship. Air and light are abundant and there is no lack of space to promenade when the deck would be a doubtful scene for bodily exercise. About a ninth of the whole number of berths are boxed off from the rest for the use of unmarried females. There are also two hospitals for the use of steerage passengers, one for males and the other for females.

The store-rooms are of great size and rather resemble honey-combs in the minute care with which every particle of space is husbanded.

The carving of the *Canadian* has been executed with consumate ability by Messrs. Kay & Shanks of Glasgow, and the painting has been beautifully done by Mr. Ballardie of this town. The rigging we believe was supplied by Mr. Cullen.

The machinery of the *Canadian* is on a scale commensurate with her size. She is fitted with a pair of direct action engines, cylinders 62½ inches diameter, 3½ feet stroke; they are immensely strong and are expected to make upwards of fifty revolutions per minute. The boilers are two in number, fire at both ends, have brass tubes, and are constructed to give an ample supply of steam. The propeller is sixteen feet in diameter.

In concluding this description of the first Allan Line steamship the *Dumbarton Herald* informed its readers that the *Canadian* had sailed for the Gareloch for adjustment of compasses and that " . . . a more substantial or elegant specimen of naval architecture had never been built on the Clyde."

As it was not until September that the *Canadian* was handed over to her owners, the builders would normally have forfeited the penalty of £1,000 applicable to late delivery. This was waived as the delay was due to strikes. Even so, it was a creditable effort to complete such a vessel in eleven months from date of order for the *Canadian* was by no means an ordinary ship and had more in common with those which followed than with earlier vessels.

However improbable it may seem to modern engineers, the use of brass tubes in the boiler was quite common at the time in warships and high-class merchant vessels. With salt-water feed and jet condensation corrosion was not nearly such a serious problem as it became later with the general use of surface condensers, and boilers had a surprisingly long life. Steam pressure was about 25 lbs per square inch and the boiler shell, which was rectangular, was made of wrought iron stiffened by inumerable stays which held together the top, sides and bottom.

The Tulloch & Denny engine marked a recent and distinct change from the first generation of ocean steamers, in which machinery of various quaint and cumbersome designs had been tried and discarded, to the emergent type of upright reciprocating engine with cylinders on top and direct-coupled crankshaft below. As yet, the steam was put to work in simple expansion with twin cylinders, virtually two single-cylinder engines bolted together. But in essence marine machinery of this type belonged to the classic school which dominated the oceans of the world until the advent of the turbine and the diesel, and brought with it a way of life which Kipling immortalised in *McAndrew's Hymn*.

The *Dumbarton Herald* mentions the comfortable glass-fronted wheel-house aft, from which it is probable that age-old custom and a certain practical advantage pointed to its use when carrying sail in open waters. The " . . . other wheel at the bow . . . " referred to the navigating bridge forward of the funnels, an innovation which had come to stay. Although hand steering gear with rods and chains must have made the forward steering wheel heavy to handle, the coming of the steam steering gear in the ensuing decade overcame this difficulty.

But the greatest change benefited the passengers to whom the Company owed its existence and to whom, throughout its long life, successive directors bent their energies in times of progress or neglected at their peril. Compared to previous ships in the St. Lawrence trade, the *Canadian* was a great improvement. She opened up a new era in which sustained speed and reliable passages were complemented by superior standards of accommodation. With choices ranging from luxurious cabins in terms of the day, for those who could afford them, to relatively spacious communal messdecks for travellers of more modest means, all passengers had steward service of some kind and cooked meals. In general the coming of the *Canadian* marked an efficient and humane approach to emigration at a time when many sailing ships under less progressive owners were still carrying unfortunate people as they had done for the previous century. These were lodged in rough wooden shelves almost on top of the ballast, with a bare subsistence of food – of which very little was supplied by the ship.

Sailing from Liverpool on 16th September 1854, the *Canadian* arrived at Quebec on 28th September after her maiden voyage. But the Allans knew that they could not hope to provide a regular service with one ship or even with two, for a sistership called the *Indian* had been ordered from Denny within a few weeks of the *Canadian*. The Montreal Ocean Steamship Company were now faced with the problem of finding profitable employment for individual ships while financing a comprehensive building program as disbursements mounted. Meanwhile the Canadian Steam Navigation Company under McKean, McLarty and Lamont had by no means given up despite their poor showing with the Canadian government contract, and the Allans allowed them to charter the *Canadian* to augment their motley fleet. Under this stop-gap arrangement, the *Canadian* made one interim round voyage from Liverpool to Portland in November.

By this time the shipping market was looking up elswhere. In March 1854 Britain and France had declared war on Russia. When the Allies landed in the Crimea in September to besiege Sevastopol the appalling casualties of the battles of Balaclava and Inkerman (which were brought to public attention dramatically by the Charge of the Light Brigade) necessitated immediate large-scale reinforcement of the British Army. Tenders were called in Liverpool for fast troopships. As always in wartime, the charter market was high, few modern ships were available and the British government had difficulty in finding sufficient vessels of the right kind. Here was a situation made to order for the fledgling Allan Line. With two powerful ocean steamships of the highest class ready for sea, it is not surprising that the Allans had no difficulty in arranging time-charters for the *Canadian* and *Indian* as troopships, the *Canadian* after her two trial runs on the Atlantic, the *Indian* direct from Denny of Dumbarton. On 26th February the *Glasgow Herald* reported the arrival of the *Canadian,* Captain William Grange, at Constantinople, to be followed on 13 April by news of the *Indian* under Captain Andrew McMaster at the same port.

Both ships did well as transports, providing an outstandingly efficient use of well-manned merchant ships in a campaign which was otherwise notorious for military and administrative chaos. While many of the Crimean soldiers went to war battened down in the holds of sailing ships, differing only in size from Sandy Allan's little brigantine which took their fathers to fight in Spain under Wellington, troops bound for the Bosphorus in the new Allan Liners had their eyes opened to a new world. Leaving Plymouth on 25th August 1855 with troops and horses McMaster brought the *Indian* into Gibraltar after a near record passage of 4 days and 15 hours. Stopping at the Rock only long enough to take coal and water, he was at Malta by 3rd September. Among other successful operations the *Indian* laid heavy mooring buoys at Kinburn for use of ironclads bombarding enemy forts. As the Crimean War did not spread to the high seas, there was no question of troopships having to sail in convoy to the scene of action. The hired transports *Canadian* and *Indian* showed what steamships could do, making passages which were impossible of attainment in later conflicts involving submarines and aircraft.

Thus assured of a steady return on their hard-won investment in the *Canadian* and the *Indian,* the Allans made the best possible use of a welcome breathing space by ordering two more ships from Denny. These were the *North American* and *Anglo-Saxon,* vessels of much the same type as the first two.

As the War ground on remorselessly the Allans and their affiliates on both sides of the Atlantic prepared for the familiar struggle of the St. Lawrence trade which must soon be renewed under new and untried circumstances. They had a joint stock company, they had ships on British government charter and others on the building berth, but as yet there was no guarantee of support from the Canadian Government – small prospect of success without it. McKean, McLarty and Lamont had shown how the wind was blowing when they chartered the *Canadian* for her second voyage: it was always possible they might make a comeback. There was no time to lose.

With an eye to the future, the Montreal Ocean Steamship Company, by now more widely known as the Allan Line, opened a chain of passenger and freight agencies which laid the administrative foundation of the new service. The financial control of the entire group was in Montreal: a brass plate at the doorway to 16 Common Street adorned the office of their Canadian agents, Edmonstone, Allan & Company. This building overlooked the wharf which had been built to replace the muddy riverside berths of Sandy Allan's time. At Quebec the local agent was George Burns Symes who had sailed to England with Hugh Allan in the steamship *Liverpool* in 1839. In Glasgow the firm of J & A Allan moved to larger offices at 54 St. Enoch Square while in Liverpool Captain Bryce Allan founded the firm of Allan & Gillespie in the Derby Building on Fenwick Street. To complete this network, the London business was handled from the office of Montgomery & Greathorne at 17 Gracechurch Street, at the very heart of the shipping world.

In July 1855 the shipping papers carried rumours of trouble for the Montreal Ocean Steamship Company. The *Glasgow Herald* reported that Mr. Lamont of Liverpool was in Quebec on behalf of English capitalists and shipowners to negotiate a renewed contract with the Canadian Government. It was stated that Lamont was supported also by Canadian investors who had taken to heart the lessons of previous failure and were spurred on by the realization that Hugh Allan's steamship company was poised in the wings. Negotiations centred on Lamont's proposal to enter two steamships of great power and size, the *European* and *Columbus*. The fact was that the Crimean War had interupted the activities of Lamont's group, as it had with the Allan Line; but a welcome respite had also occurred when the *Sarah Sands* with her large cubic capacity had been the first to be snapped up by the British Government for trooping. Exchanging the difficult North Atlantic run for the certainties of profit from the Bosphorus, Lamont had shown a quick appreciation of the possibilities when he chartered the *Canadian.* Now that she in turn had been taken up for trooping, steamships virtually disappeared from the St. Lawrence trade while unexpected profits from the War boded new alignments for its eventual resumption.

Meanwhile Hugh Allan, determined that no consortium was to wrest the contract from his newly-formed and efficient Montreal Ocean Steamship Company, had not been idle. He had to secure at once the backing of the Canadian Government, in order to demonstrate to his stockholders that their investment would be successful and that the present period of capital outlay with mounting costs would be justified. Both groups came into close discussions with the Government of the Province of Canada. The *Glasgow Herald* reported that Lamont's proposal was for four new ships of 2,000 tons and 500 horsepower to operate under a subsidy of £37,800, or for two such ships and a second pair of lesser tonnage for £36,000. Discussion then centred on a proposal by Lamont that his group would provide eighteen round voyages a year, twelve to the St. Lawrence and six to Portland, for a subsidy of £32,400.

Hugh Allan countered Lamont's offer by guaranteeing nineteen annual sailings of which fourteen would be to Canada and only five to Portland, all for £24,000 "annual bonus" from the Government. This, coupled with posession of their fine new steamships, was the final argument in favour of the Allans. Under the heading "Latest Liverpool News" the *Glasgow Herald* of 25 July 1855 summed up the situation thus:

> Last week we alluded to the endeavours to form steam communication between this port and Canada. We are now given to understand that the tender made by the English Company represented by Mr. Lamont has been declined, and that the Canadian Government has decided to accede to the terms proposed by Mr. Allan of Montreal.

The *Canadian* was the first to be released from trooping but as the St. Lawrence commitment could not be honoured until the fleet of four was ready, the Allans sailed the *Canadian* from Glasgow to New York and Boston for a preliminary voyage in January 1856. As they were already under contract to call at Portland, no special significance attaches to this American sailing other than the necessity to earn money as soon as possible.

By March, the first advertisements for regular sailings began to appear in newspapers on both sides of the Atlantic, the heading *Montreal Ocean Steamship Company* striking a new note in the shipping columns. Sailings were from Liverpool to Quebec and Montreal, starting with the *North American* on her maiden voyage on Wednesday 23rd April. Thereafter, every second Wednesday would see an Allan Liner leaving Liverpool – the *Canadian* on 7th May, the *Indian* on the 21st, and the *Anglo-Saxon* making her debut on 4th June. Every second Saturday an Allan Liner would sail from the wharf below the ramparts of the City of Quebec, starting with the *North American* on 12 May.

Passages were advertised at eighteen guineas in the cabin class or eight guineas steerage, it being emphasised that emigrants would be supplied with a plentiful service of cooked provisions. Freight was accepted at the rate of four pounds sterling per ton for box and bale goods. It was thirty-seven years since the brigantine *Jean,* Alexander Allan master, had been advertised to clear from Greenock with passengers and cargo for Canada. Sandy Allan was now dead; but the tradition which he founded had been brought up to date by his sons, who had planted it firmly in Canada. By coincidence, one aspect of that tradition had been unexpectedly repeated. Profits from the Peninsula War had given Captain Allan his start in the Quebec trade, and now the Crimean War had come at an opportune time for his sons. Fortunate as this coincidence undoubtedly was for two generations of pioneer shipowners, in each case the profits were applied with judgement, ability and courage when the real test came. Time-charter to the British War Transport Service was one thing, but competitive steamship operation to Canada was quite another.

Times were changing. The Victorian world moved forward in a spirit of hope in which it was firmly believed that the advance of science would benefit humanity and that steam communication would bring nations closer in spirit as it did in time. A new era was foreseen when the Crimean War was brought to its formal conclusion on 29th April 1856. In London Her Majesty's Heralds and Trumpeters, flanked by a jungling detachment of Household Cavalry, rode at a brisk trot to proclaim the Peace from Charing Cross, Temple Bar and the Royal Exchange. The commercial world was less impressed by a sense of occasion, the *Glasgow Herald* commenting only that the weather in London was dull and the Procession was not of an imposing character.

CHAPTER FIVE

The Dangers of the Sea

"Listening to the doubling roar,
Surging on the rocky shore,
All I can I weep and pray
For his weal that's far away"

R.B.
On the Seas and Far Away

In 1856, the first year of regular operation, the Montreal Ocean Steamship Company made good passages despite the hazards of the St. Lawrence route. Government and public alike knew that a very satisfactory service had been provided, and that the Allans had spared nothing in providing first-class vessels equipped to the highest standards. The Report of the Commissioners of Public Works stated that the ocean steamers had made the westbound run that year in an average time of 12 days and 13 hours from Liverpool to Quebec. Passengers could travel to North America at fares slightly less than by New York. Westbound freight brought fifty shillings per measurement ton on fine goods and thirty shillings a deadweight ton for metals. Eastbound the main traffic was in grain, which fetched from twenty to thirty cents a bushel, with flour and timber to fill up the tweendecks. This latter trade was greatly influenced by G.B. Symes at the Quebec agency, who was also a timber merchant.

Nevertheless, business was slow in the opening years. With a general

83

economic depression and a poor harvest in 1857, the Company failed to do as well as had been expected. Together with the risks of business Hugh Allan was greatly concerned with the risks of navigation in the Gulf. To save time, the Allan Line used the Northern route through the Straits of Belle Isle from about the beginning of June to the close of navigation. Although convinced of the merits of this course, which cut some 250 miles from the run to Liverpool, there was great concern about aids to navigation in the Gulf of St. Lawrence. At that time there were no lights at all in the Straits of Belle Isle and only Cape Pine and a new lighthouse at Cape Race to mark the southern route by way of the Cabot Strait.

In the Gulf itself two lights on St. Paul Island, two on the Island of Anticosti and one on the North Shore of the St. Lawrence at Pointe des Monts where the River begins to narrow, were all that were then established. A number of others, including Pointe Amour on the Labrador shore, the West Point on Anticosti and Cap des Rosiers on the Gaspé Peninsula were under construction, but even so the situation was hazardous in the extreme. After discussing the possibilities with his captains Hugh Allan made a strong recommendation to the Canadian Government that a three-year program of lighthouse construction should be started immediately. This was based on a study of the best sites from Labrador to the Quebec approaches and included a plea for fog guns at the principal stations. It was put in hand soon afterwards. Meantime, however, the first steamship casualty in the Allan Line emphasised that deficiencies in pilotage must also receive attention.

On 1st June 1857 a brief note in the shipping columns of the *Montreal Gazette* forecast the arrival of the *Canadian* which had sailed from Liverpool on 20th May. Noted as having passed Rivière du Loup at 2.10 pm on Sunday the 31st, the vessel was confidently advertised for her return passage to Liverpool. Passengers could reserve a private cabin for twenty pounds sterling or a stateroom before the gangway for sixteen pounds ten shillings. Third class passengers could travel for seven pounds ten shillings which, as with the fares of all passengers, included the services of an experienced medical officer. In Montreal and Quebec consignees waited eagerly to clear their spring goods through customs and get them safely to market.

After picking up her pilot at Rivière du Loup, the *Canadian* steamed towards Quebec, her course taking her to the North shore in the usual way until again turning towards the south by the St. Roch Traverse which was crossed in safety despite the danger of heading diagonally into the current. Passing St. Jean-Port-Joli, Captain Ballantyne was not on the bridge – he had gone below briefly after a long spell on deck because of fog – and the pilot was in charge. He squared up for the

Beaujeu Channel about forty miles below Quebec and swept past the Stone Pillar Island at full speed, an island which had been marked with a lighthouse since 1843. Despite this aid to navigation, the pilot missed the channel and the *Canadian* struck hard aground on a rock some two or three cables south of the Pillar. It was one o'clock of a dark night. The tide was at full and change, the worst possible time for a stranding. As the vessel heeled over alarmingly in the first of the ebb, Captain Ballantyne mustered his three hundred and fifty passengers in good order while the crew got mails and baggage on deck. Later that day everyone was transferred in safety to Quebec on board the Government Steamer *Queen Victoria.*

The *Canadian* was in a bad way; lying dangerously athwart the tideway in an awkward position the flooded ship eventually settled upright with only her bows showing, everything aft of the mainmast being under water. At first it was hoped to get her off and a formal notice appeared in the *Montreal Gazette:*

> Notice to consignees per steamship *Canadian.* The above named vessel's average bond is now lying at the office of Messrs Gibb & Hunter, Notaries Public, of No 47 Little St. James Street. Consignees will please call and sign it.
>
> Edmonstone, Allan & Co.

In the language of marine insurance, this terse announcement meant that claims by consignees for "particular average" or partial loss of cargo would be adjusted to the value of goods recovered, less duty. Some cargo was recovered and delivered to its rightful owners in this way but before long the wreck settled more deeply in the ebb and flow of strong tides. The *Canadian* became a total loss. Despite the salvage of additional cargo which was sold at auction, and a promise from the salvors to pay the Company half the value of goods subsequently recovered, the Allan Line suffered a heavy financial loss.

The *Montreal Gazette* was outspokenly critical of pilotage on the St. Lawrence, blaming the wreck on the pilot. It concluded an account of the incident with the hope that the *Canadian* might yet be saved, with as little damage as had happened the previous November when she had stranded on White Island Reef by "criminal negligence" of another pilot. Whether or not this pungent criticism was justified, accidents of the kind were all too frequent. With the coming of the mail steamers they were to become more marked.

Meantime the loss of the ship posed a problem in the sailing list. Passengers booked eastbound in the *Canadian* had to be crammed into the next ship, which was the *North American.* To add to the Company's embarassment, an already heavy passenger list began with the Gover-

nor-in-Chief of Canada: Sir Edmund Head, with Lady Head was returning to England on completion of his term of office. But shipwreck was
regarded as an "Act of God," worthy only of that unspoken cognizance
reserved today for mishaps in air travel. Sombre thoughts were put to
one side in the ceremony of departure of Queen Victoria's representa-
tive, on board the finest steamer yet to sail from Canada. It was the first
of many vice-regal voyages to be accomplished safely under the Allan
colours.

As Hugh Allan went ashore after saying farewell to his distinguished
passengers the *North American* hauled out into the stream and canted
close under the heights surmounted by Durham Terrace. The sun broke
through the morning mist, glinting on scarlet and gold as troops returning to England lined her decks. On shore the people of Quebec crowded
to every vantage point from the waterfront to the boardwalk. A gun
salute cracked across the intervening water as the Royal Mail Steamer
North American gathered speed. From the ancient heights the band of the
39th Regiment broke into "Will ye no come back again . . . " A reporter
from the *Gazette,* impressed by the size of the *North American,* wrote that
"The great steamer, bent on her voyage across the broad Atlantic,
steamed out of harbour towards that fairy land the Isle of Orleans, past
the beautiful and diversified shores of the St. Lawrence." If, on his way
down channel shortly afterwards, His Excellency caught sight of three
mastheads rising at an angle from the spring flood of the St. Lawrence
by the Pillar Rock, he was too much of a diplomat to be the first to have
mentioned it to Captain William Grange of the *North American.*

Despite the loss of the *Canadian* the season of 1857 was remarkable
for good passages. The average westward time from Liverpool to Quebec was reduced to 11 days 1 hour, while the eastward voyage was cut
to 10 days 15 hours. Honours went to the *Indian* for the quickest eastward passage of 9 days 11 hours, and to the *Anglo-Saxon* for the westward
record of 9 days and 13 hours. By the close of the season the *Indian* had
made five round voyages between April and November, a performance
never previously achieved by any ship up till that time.

Results so far confirmed that policies were on the right lines, but to
many people the fortnightly service was not enough. Hugh Allan was
convinced that Canada must have a weekly service to England or remain
dependent to a large extent on the New York trade where steamships
were now sailing almost daily. The question was would there be enough
cargo to support the weekly sailings; and, if otherwise, would the
Canadian Government be prepared to subsidize the increased service in
proportion? The directors of the Montreal Ocean Steamship Company
were divided on this issue, because some felt that even with an increased subsidy the risk of financing more tonnage to handle the same

volume of cargo was too great. In addition, they had already lost one ship by stranding and the weekly service would double the navigational risk. Hugh Allan was determined and resolute. By splitting the business into a number of agencies in addition to the owning Company he had already provided an effective limitation of risk should disaster strike any part, and he was convinced that a regular and efficient mail service was essential from all points of view. Despite objections his influence finally won the day. The subsidy was increased to $4,000 per round voyage or $208,000 per year of operation.

Hugh Allan was well aware that dissenting directors would probably withdraw. It is possible that this was what he really wanted. Be this at it may, this split in policy caused the immediate resignation of G.B. Symes of Quebec, William Dow the brewer of Montreal, Robert Anderson and John Watkins, all of whom were bought out by the Allan brothers. William Rae, also a Scot, filled the vacant agency at Quebec which then became "Allans, Rae & Company." Closing ranks the Allan family were now for the first time in sole control of the firm which bore their name.

The immediate task was to provide more ships. As soon as the financial arrangements were completed Hugh Allan went to Scotland to consult his brothers and William Denny. Denny laid down a quartette of sister-ships to open the weekly sailings. There were *Nova Scotian, North Briton, Hungarian* and *Bohemian,* handsome barque-rigged vessels with a single funnel. They were twenty feet longer than the first ships and had increased cargo and passenger space, although they were slightly slower. This type of ship was expected to prove more economical in service, but any savings were more than offset by a continuance of the slump. The Allan Line informed the Canadian Government that they would be unable to carry on under their existing contract. By this time it was generally accepted that the weekly service was a necessity and the mail subsidy was doubled.

Meantime disaster struck again, this time with the loss of the *Indian* on the coast of Nova Scotia. Leaving Liverpool in November 1859 bound for Portland with the Canadian mail, under Captain William Smith, she made her landfall at Cape Race on the 19th of that month and carried on with the intention of passing midway between Sable Island and the coast of Nova Scotia. Captain Smith stopped every now and again to take soundings. Although the weather was hazy he came to the conclusion that he was on the Sable Island side of the mid-channel line. At 5 am on Monday 20th November the Chief Officer, who as usual was in charge of the morning watch, sighted land on the starboard side. He at once called the Captain, who ordered him to alter course away from the shore.

At that moment the *Indian,* under full steam and a press of sail, struck the rocks at a point of land near the village of Mary-Joseph which is marked on the chart today as "Smith Point." In the darkness and cold of early morning the boats were got ready for launching; but, as the ship worked in a heavy sea, the forward part began to break away. Some passengers rushed the lifeboats in confusion. One boat was upset, another had its falls cut, and yet others were dashed against the side of the ship. When daylight came it was found that twenty-seven people had been drowned.

Some passengers were rescued by fishing schooners which lay off the wreck during the day. As accusations of looting were made, however, Captain Smith decided to go ashore himself and make special arrangements for other boats to take off the remaining people. By this time the Chief Officer and his men were exhausted by their constant work in the remaining lifeboats and were unable to get back to the ship. By one means or another some hundred and thirty people were eventually rescued and the mail was brought ashore. Returning to the wreck of the *Indian* before daylight the next morning, Captain Smith found that the ship had been plundered from stem to stern. Besides the tragedy inherent in shipwreck, there were the suspicions and accusations by people who gave widely differing versions of a period of suffering and confusion. These included complaints by some passengers that their baggage had been plundered after reaching shore.

From the point of view of the Allan Line this was a much more serious affair than the loss of the *Canadian.* There had been heavy loss of life. While undoubted gallantry had been shown by some members of the crew and by some local fishermen, others were inevitably under suspicion – particularly Captain Smith, who was accused of leaving his ship prematurely. In addition to all this the Company suffered a heavy financial loss as the vessel was uninsured and nothing was saved from the cargo. Amidst a welter of criticism, Hugh Allan was not long in publishing an account of the story. The following letter appeared in the *Montreal Gazette* of 24th December 1859:

> . . . from the pecuniary point of view we are by far the heaviest sufferers in this calamity; hence it might be expected that we should be more dissatisfied with the captain than with any other party but a sense of justice compels us to say that while we view his getting the steamer on shore at all, where he did, as a serious mistake, we do not think his conduct afterwards in any degree deserving of the blame which has been heaped upon him. The heaviest charges brought against him were leaving the ship in the first shore boat. . . .
>
> Every officer was at his post, and each one with their crews, as

detailed in the printed instructions, manned their own boats. If it had not been for the panic in which the breaking across of the ship threw the steerage passengers, who then disregarded all orders, the captain assures us that no lives would have been lost.

Other letters supported or attacked Captain Smith and his officers, and the matter became something of a *cause célèbre* in Halifax. Israel Nickerson, a Justice of the Peace in Mary-Joseph, certified that he and Captain Smith had tried to recruit fishermen to board the wreck and save property, but that " . . . owing to the ship working on the rocks they had declared that it was unsafe." Safe or not, the fact was that few coastal communities in remote areas a century ago regarded wreck as anything but a fortuitous opportunity for individual enterprise.

Some passengers attacked the shipowners for not paying all the expenses of onward journeys to their destinations. Mr. R.S. Paterson of Peterborough complained that his hotel bills had not been honoured. After a bitter dispute in the press it appeared that the Company had paid legitimate costs but had refused to refund claims for beer and cigars. On the whole, the newspapers supported the Allan Line. In a kind of flanking action the *Montreal Gazette* took the opportunity to fire a few editorial salvoes against its rival, the *Montreal Herald*, opening with this broadside:

> The *Gazette* is at pains this morning to defend itself against an attack by the *Herald* in reference to its explanations of the loss of the *Indian*. It might have spared itself the trouble. Everyone understands how cowardly and malicious the *Herald* is when it thinks it can be so with impunity and it does not conflict with its pecuniary interest to kick a fallen man.

In the end it is hard not to agree with the statement that " . . . it does not require great effort of the imagination to believe that Captain Smith may have been misunderstood by suffering passengers at the time of the excitement and after he had been guilty of the great error of running the vessel on the ledge." The Bay where these events took place is named "Smith Cove," in memory of that cold morning more than a century ago. Whatever might be the judgment of the court of enquiry which would inevitably follow, few expected the *Indian*'s captain to escape without censure.

With the loss of their first two steamships in 1857 and 1859 the Allans no doubt thought that they would outrun this unfortunate start. In fact, they were about to receive a series of tragic blows which would all but knock them out.

After the wreck of the *Indian* the immediate problem was to get the survivors to Halifax or Portland. As there was then no convenient land transport in Nova Scotia, the inhabitants of Mary-Joseph can hardly have been surprised to find another Allan Liner at anchor in their little bay. This was the *Hungarian*, Captain Thomas Jones, which had been diverted for the purpose. Like most of the Allan commanders, Jones was highly regarded by those who travelled in his care: one passenger had taken the trouble to publish a testimonial in the *Liverpool Mercury* of 4th February 1860 on completion of the next round voyage. The North Atlantic had been as nasty as usual, the *Hungarian* had been washed out fore and aft, but she had been well handled. A grateful American was able to write:

> I left New York on the advice of friends to give the (Portland) route a trial and to report to New York papers. The moment my friend and self set foot on board we found ourselves at home. The spacious saloons and the politeness of the captain and officers made us feel all is right here. . . .

But the American spoke too soon. Three months after the loss of the *Indian*, Jones was making his landfall at Cape Sable Island off the Southern tip of Nova Scotia (not to be confused with Sable Island lying 200 miles out in the Atlantic). He was keeping a sharp lookout for the reassuring flash of a new lighthouse which had been established there. At 3 am on 20th February 1860, the lightkeeper noted in his log that the lights of a steamer had been sighted. At daylight all he could see were three masts and a funnel, surrounded by the wash of breakers on the rocks. By 10 am there was nothing in sight except a tragic trail of flotsam, mailbags, personal baggage and a splintered lifeboat which drifted ashore. Litter appeared on the coast for miles. When the alarm was raised, watchers on the shore spotted the first bodies. Two hundred and five men, women and children, the entire crew and passenger list, lost their lives. There was not a single survivor.

With the heavy loss of life involved in three shipwrecks over four years, speculation and comment filled the newspapers. Many armchair seamen vented their views, some of them blaming the disaster on the inadequacy of "Government" charts. A letter signed "John Orlebar" in the *Montreal Gazette* of 12th March 1860 put that idea to rest. Who should know better than Commander John Orlebar of the Royal Navy, Admiralty hydrographer in charge of the Newfoundland and Nova Scotia survey? Pointing out that the *Indian* had, in fact, carried privately-published "blue-back" charts without any claim to "government" authority – Commander Orlebar must have winced at the word "Government" – he went on to prove that the *Indian*'s course as subsequently plotted by naval surveyors on Admiralty charts proved only one thing.

She could only have finished up where she did, on the rocks at Mary Joseph. He came to the conclusion that unknown deviation of the compass had been Captain Smith's downfall, a possiblity which the Board of Trade enquiry into the loss of the *Indian* apparently considered to mitigate Captain Smith's error. He was absolved of full responsibility.

Another critic of the Allan Line, under the anonymity of "Nauticus," had already penned his view in the same paper on the 1st of March. Accidents such as the *Indian* and the *Hungarian* had experienced, he stated with firmness, were due entirely to the temptation to set record passages. In vain it was for Hugh Allan to reply that all the Allan Line masters were issued with written instructions to put safety first at all times: "Nauticus" was adamant. Twelve days, he opined, should be considered a short passage and then " . . . if they arrive off the coast during dark nights they will feel at liberty to stand offshore at half steam until daylight." But how was a master to know for certain that he was near land?

The *Portland Argus* was more philosophical, as were the press in general. After commenting favourably on the high standards of the Allan ships and the competence of their masters, an editorial gave the opinion generally held in shipping circles:

> The proprietors of this line of steamships have therefore the consolation of knowing that nothing was left undone on their part to invert such a calamity. They neglected nothing to make life and property secure. The calamity came however, as calamities will often come, in spite of human care and forethought. It is a stunning blow and the sympathies of our whole community go forth to all those who are suffering.

In fact, the critics were all wrong. As it turned out years later, the light on Cape Sable Island may have been out on that terrible night when the *Hungarian* was lost with all on board. James Croil, in his book *Steam Navigation* published in 1898, wrote that the lightkeeper was said to have confessed on his deathbed that he had been sick and had failed in his duty.

Meanwhile the Allans went back to Denny of Dumbarton for replacement tonnage. The first *Canadian*, whose iron frames lay rusting below Quebec, was followed by another. It was felt that there could be nothing unlucky in repetition of the name, for the Company had not been at fault when mischance of pilot stranded the first *Canadian* on that inconvenient patch by the Pillar Rock.

The second *Canadian* was commanded by Captain John Graham, a fellow Scot whose judgement and ability had been weighed carefully by James and Bryce before appointment. He was something of a character,

first-rate as a seaman, popular with passengers and a man whose imagination had not suffered from the loneliness of his position. Indeed, it
had flourished in long years of trading to the St. Lawrence and Captain
Graham was firmly of the opinion that a dam built across the Belle Isle
Strait would greatly improve the climate of Canada and the prospects
for shipping, a pet scheme which placed him among the visionaries of
his time. There came a day when he must have wished with all his heart
that it had been carried to fruition.

On 1st June 1861 Graham left Quebec in the *Canadian* bound for
Liverpool. It was a hazy summer day in the river but spring comes late
in the Gulf and he well knew that ice must be expected in the northern
route. By daylight on the 4th he was nudging his ship ahead under easy
steam while pans of ice slid by in a rising wind. Soon his worries would
be over and he could ring the telegraph for full speed and settle down
to the Atlantic crossing. Ten miles away on the starboard beam the high
stark cliffs of Cape Bauld marked the north-eastern tip of Newfoundland where a group of French fishing vessels were dodging about under
easy sail clear of the ice. At 10 a.m. the *Canadian* ran into thicker ice and
Graham stopped his engine until the pressure eased. By 11.35 he was
moving carefully ahead, turning through a narrow lead with the main
flows to starboard and lighter ones to port. There was no feeling of
icebreaking, no shock or shudder, as loose pieces parted silently underfoot to slide past the iron sides of the ship; a submerged lump was seen
from the bridge to roll under the port bows, disappear for a moment,
and then float up with a gentle splash abreast the fore rigging as it
slipped aft into the closing wake.

Suddenly an excited Irish-Liverpool voice from the bridge ladder
announced the unexpected arrival of an off-watch stoker with the
alarming news that he had scrambled out of his bunk as a deluge flooded
the firemen's mess. Hasty inspection showed that the lower hold was
filling. Despite immediate closing of watertight doors, several compartments were open to the sea: water was already up to the furnaces. It was
almost a preview of the *Titanic* disaster of half a century later: the untold
inertia of that seemingly inocuous icefloe had pressed a cutting edge
longitudinally against the flanks of the *Canadian*, to rip a gash with
surgical precision.

The ship had been almost in clear water and Graham made desperate
effort to increase speed slowly while altering course for Cape Bauld. But
already it was too late. The ship was becoming sluggish as she dipped
by the head, and as she edged clear from the sheltering smother of that
terrible ice, passengers mustered frantically on deck as boats were lowered in a rising sea. One lifeboat capsized and the mailmaster and some
of the crew were drowned in attempting to save the mail. When the

boats got clear, thrity-five lives had been lost. Captain Graham directed the abandonment until his stricken vessel lolled in the pitiless waves: sliding off the bridge, he was the last person to be picked up.

The *Canadian* then dipped steeply by the bows and went down with a lurch to starboard. As she hit the bottom, the fore and main topmasts whipped in reaction and broke off short at the caps. Survivors in the boats gazed in speechless awe as the stern slowly withdrew into the ocean. Suddenly the poop burst with entrapped air, the boilers opened their seams, and, in a shower of wreckage, ashes and steam, the *Canadian* had gone for ever.

Pulling and sailing in a heavy sea the lifeboats made Quirpon Harbour on the Newfoundland coast. A week later, with the resources of that remote settlement drained to the utmost, Graham arranged with Captain Mace of the French barque *Jules* to convey remaining passengers and crew to St. John's in return for four hundred pounds sterling. In a small cod carrier months away from her home port in Brittany, and with little room for anything except fish, there was privation and suffering in the seven days which elapsed beating down the coast to St . John's. On 14th June, under the scrutiny of curious watchers from Signal Hill, the *Jules* sailed through the narrow gut of the finest harbour in North America.

It is the custom of merchant shipmasters in port, and before discharging cargo, to lodge a "protest" with a notary public. The purpose of this document is to forestall possible insurance claims on damaged cargo by swearing an affidavit that, despite all seamanlike precautions, goods had been exposed to risk of damage because of heavy weather. In the extreme case of total loss of his ship and cargo the master or senior survivor makes as his protest a statement of the events leading to disaster. The captain of the second *Canadian* walked up Water Street with a heavy heart to enter his protest in the language of the law:

I, John Graham, commander of the said steamship, do declare and protest . . . that the loss of said steamship with its fatal consequencies is solely attributable to the dangers and accidents of the sea as hereinbefore set forth, and not by or through the inefficiency of said steamship or said commander or of any of his officers and crew. . . .

At the subsequent enquiry Captain Graham was cleared of blame for the loss of his ship. A deeply religious man, evidence of the dangers of the sea failed to disturb his equanimity in court as the reality failed to shake his resolution in that last moment of agony in the icy waters of the Belle Isle Strait. His master's certificate was handed back to him with the tribute "Sir, you did your duty like a noble British seaman."

This fourth loss in as many years was a terrible blow to the Allans, particularly to Hugh, who had been the moving spirit of the change from sail to steam. For the past half century his family had made their way doggedly to and from Quebec, first his father Captain Alexander and then James and Bryce, without either of those redoubtable seamen having had a serious accident. Now under steam the Company had suffered heavily. There were those who felt that they should give up steamships, forget the mail contract, and go back to the leisurely ways of sailing ships. But, as critical letters again appeared in the newspapers, Hugh Allan's driving and indomitable will was supported by his convincing logic. "Providence has not a special grudge against any honest enterprise, nor does it show it by bringing destruction upon innocent people. The fault is in ourselves in some disregard of nature's laws. It is we who must find out what is wrong and put it right."

The burden of putting it right fell, for the most part, on the masters of the mail steamers. For the original quartet of Andrew McMaster, Thomas Jones, William Ballantyne and William Grange the strain of bringing steam navigation to the St. Lawrence had been heavy. Jones had lost his life in the *Hungarian* in circumstances difficult to understand, Ballantyne had suffered the loss of his ship while under pilotage, and the other two must have wondered when their turn would come. They were a stoical breed, prepared to face disaster if it came, wearing their responsibilities with the fatalistic attitude of seamen. McMaster was even moved to a dry humour at times: in replying to a passenger's letter of thanks for safe arrival, he confessed that he had never seen the ice as bad as it had been that season, but suggested that " . . . it would be a capital year to explore the North Pole as the whole Arctic must be emptied of ice."

Five months later it was William Grange's turn to have his prudence and seamanship flung in his teeth. Ships leaving the St. Lawrence by the Belle Isle Strait usually go north of the Island of Anticosti which lies some fifteen miles off the North Shore of Quebec. In reasonable weather the route is simple enough; but in fog, snow or rain (particularly a century ago when there were few lighthouses and the magnetic compass was liable to deviations from mineral deposits under the sea), the coast of Anticosti was a nightmare.

In November 1861 the RMS *North Briton* left Quebec, under the command of Captain Grange, for her last run of the season. Passing Pointe des Monts in daylight, course was set for the West Point of Anticosti, where Hugh Allan's representations had been instrumental in the establishment of a lighthouse in 1858. At four on the afternoon of Monday 4th November, the *North Briton* was ploughing along in a gale with reduced visibility in snow squalls when land was sighted on the Quebec side, distant about five miles. Realising that he had been set northwards by tide or currents, Grange hauled off the land and steered for a mid-channel course between Anticosti and the Quebec Island of Mingan, taking soundings at intervals as he went. Visibility became poor, the West Point light was not sighted, and when a line of soundings indicated the configuration of the mid-channel line, course was altered to conform. At one-thirty on the morning of Monday the 5th November the *North Briton* struck a reef in a squall of driving snow while steaming at four knots with no land in sight.

Lashed by a confused and breaking sea, the vessel pounded and thumped on the rocks and, as there was danger from falling spars, the passengers were put into lifeboats with orders to make fast alongside on a long painter. When the tide changed and the boats started to bump, some of them cast off and disappeared into the darkness. Daylight of a bitterly cold morning revealed the Island of Mingan about a mile away. As the day wore on, passengers and crew were landed with a supply of food and blankets, the missing boats turned up, and eventually everyone was put ashore without loss of life.

But it was a terrifying experience. Families had become separated, and as one father stumbled about crazy with anxiety for his wife and little Emma, a childish cry rings out from the pages of a century-old letter " . . . There's Papa, there's Papa." With true Victorian spirit, people made the best of things, an accomplishment which was by no means easy when some of them thought that perhaps they would have to spend the winter there. Felix Morgan of Montreal wrote in his journal " . . . snow fell last night, it is about an inch thick, the temperature is delightful and the morning charming after the snowstorm." It was just above freezing as men, women and children huddled together under tents, formed from spars and sails, spread over rocks. There was a Robinson Crusoe ring about Morgan's words when he described this pitiful shelter as " . . . a palace compared to nothing."

About a week later, when the third mate had been sent to Father Point in a local schooner to send the news to Quebec, the Chief Officer cruised the Gulf of St. Lawrence in another fishing boat and was able to intercept Captain McMaster westbound in the *Anglo-Saxon*. Feeling his way very carefully to Mingan Harbour McMaster embarked the stranded North Britons together with most of their baggage and the mail, and landed them in good health and spirits at Quebec. At the conclusion of his report to Edmonstone and Allan, Captain Grange noted that his wrecked ship was lying on an even bottom with a slight list to port. The berth decks were awash two feet at high tide but the saloon was dry. The second mate had been ordered to remain on board for the winter to look after things. Whether or not Mr. Lang was able to fulfill this difficult assignment is not recorded. Mingan in winter is hardly conducive to existence on a wreck a mile offshore, but seamen were tough and hardships were accepted as part of a responsible officer's career.

With this fifth wreck, averaging one a year since commencement of the service in 1856, there was another outcry in the press. Public, government and owners alike were appalled at the situation. In a welter of critical letters some correspondents pointed out also that losses had occurred on the New York route. It was noted that the Allan mailboats were numerically a small percentage of total losses in the Gulf. Figures from the Commissioners of Public Works of Canada showed that accidents including total loss, stranding and serious damage had occurred to 38 vessels in 1859, rising steadily to 102 in that awful year of 1861. Practically all of these, except the Allan liners, were sailing ships. It was seen that the increasing potential of the St. Lawrence trade was overshadowed by exceptionally high risks.

There was also ominous talk of cancelling the contract with the Montreal Ocean Steamship Company and transferring it to some other concern. But as winter closed the river for another year, public interest faded. The *Montreal Gazette* of 21st November 1861 reflected a general consensus with the comment that the government had not the power, even if it had so decided, to annul the mail contract; its terms were being honoured in their " . . . true and honest" meaning. In the last resort, and coupled with this phrase, another clause specifically mentioned "Shipwreck and other accident" as being outwith the contractor's responsibility. It is also probable that no other shipowner was now very anxious to compete with the Allans. So far, the difficulties and deficiencies of the route had baffled the best navigators of the day and even the Commissioners of Public Works admitted that progress in lighthouse building had been very slow. But 1862 passed without accident to the mail steamers, and it began to look as if better times might be ahead.

One of the great advantages of steamships and railways at this period lay in the fast transmission of news stories, an operation which had been speeded up with the introduction of the electric telegraph. But the trans-Atlantic telegraph cable was as yet unsuccessful, and it would be another four years before the *Great Eastern* landed the western end triumphantly at Heart's Content in Newfoundland. In the meantime newspapers often headed their stories by the name of the mailboat which had brought the news from Europe: shipowners were under considerable pressure and much competition to supply this demand. Among arrangements made to ensure the prompt receipt of foreign news, Associated Press News stationed a dispatch boat in Newfoundland with the object of meeting the mail steamers off Cape Race so that telegrams could be sent ahead to contributing papers throughout North America. To James and Bryce Allan in Glasgow and Liverpool, each of them with years of personal experience as St. Lawrence shipmasters, the idea seemed sound enough, provided that masters were left with the final authority to meet or not to meet according to the weather. The firm of J & A. Allan in Glasgow therefore issued a fleet memorandum on the subject:

> If you find no ice in the way, and can approach Cape Race without running any risk, it will be desireable that you should call off that Point to land your telegraphic despatches. Don't run any risk however in order to attain this. It is only with daylight and fine clear weather that the thing should be attempted.
>
> Please exercise great caution in approaching ice. It is not desirable to go into it if it can be at all avoided.
>
> At the date of our last advice the ice bridge still held fast at Quebec. We hope it will have disappeared before you arrive. You will learn at Father Point the state of the River above Quebec. If you reach that Point or Rivière du Loup and cannot proceed further, you will of course land your mails and send them up by railway in charge of the purser or some other responsible person.

Captain McMaster received this letter as he took over a new command, the RMS *Norwegian*. He was usually the first to be appointed to a new ship and he had left his familiar *Anglo-Saxon* in the capable hands of Captain Burgess, who had sailed before him, in receipt of a similar memorandum. McMaster had a safe and prosperous voyage and duly arrived at Quebec to find that Burgess had not been so fortunate.

Sailing from Liverpool on 16th April 1863 in the Denny-built *Anglo-Saxon*, Captain Burgess was pleased to find himself in command of a fast and popular ship. The *Anglo-Saxon* had succeeded in cutting her record passage of 1857 to 9 days 5 hours in 1859. With such a vessel there was no difficulty in filling every berth: when she cleared from Londonderry with emigrants for Canada-West, there was a total of 445 men, women and children on board, including crew.

They had bad luck in approaching Newfoundland for the Associated Press rendezvous. Whether or not Captain Burgess had actually sighted Cape Race is not known; but at 11 am on 27th April he was steaming in dense fog at reduced speed with double lookouts when there came a cry from the forecastle of "Breakers ahead." Almost immediately the *Anglo-Saxon* struck on a rocky shore. Putting his engine to full astern Captain Burgess was unable to get her off and she finished up wedged securely forward but afloat aft. She was obviously badly damaged. Visibility was reduced to a matter of yards: all that could be seen was rocks under the bows and a swell relentlessly rolling in from sea.

Burgess was a brave and resourceful seaman. In a very short time he had put a man ashore and had rigged a hawser to the rocks with a travelling block and basket. Starting with women and children, two or three at a time, the captain then had time to look around, size up the situation and do what he could to speed up evacuation. For the moment it seemed as though the stricken ship would hold for a few hours, but she was grinding ominously and water was rising in the berth decks aft. Boats were lowered and women and children left the ship, the lifeboats being ordered to stand off as it was too dangerous to attempt to beach them in the breakers. So far everything was under control.

Suddenly the vessel slipped off the rocks, with a lurch to port. Topmasts and yards began to crash down among the crowded decks and boats. As the cold ocean surged to and fro amidst the jumble and confusion, the chief officer was among others who managed to jump clear and were picked up. A lady passenger remembered afterwards that Captain Burgess had helped her into a boat, but when she looked round he was attempting to regain his place of duty on the bridge. With scores of male passengers, he went down in the vortex of his ship as she slipped off the rocks and sank.

The boats hung around, picking up survivors as best they could. But soon they had to look after themselves, somehow clawing off that fatal shore. Hours later they were found by rescue craft fifteen miles up the coast. The place where the *Anglo-Saxon* stranded is known as Clam Cove, about four miles or so to the North of Cape Race. Lloyd's agent at Quebec reported that 227 persons lost their lives, but a later count is believed to have reached 238.

When the news reached Hugh Allan at Montreal, a ship was at once despatched to Newfoundland to lift the survivors. At this period of suffering and anxiety it was inevitable that complaints should be made. In fact an acrimonious press correspondence ensued in which an army officer, Captain Stodhart who was stationed in Montreal, accused the Company of failing to provide onward expenses for his widowed sister who had survived her husband in the disaster. Eventually it was proved that the Company had in fact sent Captain Stodhart to Newfoundland in the relief ship to meet his sister, thereafter offering free passage to Montreal or Halifax for both, or alternatively a free passage back to England for the lady. It was all that could be done. Half a century later some of the *Titanic*'s passengers were stranded without a penny. Shipwreck was an Act of God: those who travelled by sea did so at their own risk, as they had done since the beginning of time.

Meanwhile spring slowly changed to summer, a season which brings little relief to navigators. They must make the ironbound coast of Canada all but blind, in fogs which last for days. Montreal and Quebec papers continued to use the heading "From Cape Race, by the Associated Press News yacht . . . " and liners continued to make the rendezvous. But Captain McMaster, the veteran of them all, had his own particular rendezvous to keep. At that time Andrew McMaster had been no less than eighteen years in command of St. Lawrence traders, both sail and steam. There can be no doubt that he knew the route as well as any man alive. Since 1845, when as master of the barque *Rory O'More* he first came in contact with Edmonstone & Allan as his Montreal agents, he had won the confidence of the Allans. He had made a fine start as captain of the *Indian* when on that record run to Gibraltar and the Crimea. Now 55 years of age, and at the peak of his long career which had taken him all over the world from his native Stranraer, it was his turn to lose a ship. In one way his luck held, in that there was no loss of life; and like Ballantyne and Graham he continued in the Allan service afterwards.

It happened very simply, at 7 am on Sunday 14th June 1863, when he piled up on St. Paul's Island in the *Norwegian* during dense fog. The weather was calm and all passengers were able to get ashore to the Humane Establishment. This was a small building stocked with provisions, provided by the Canadian Government for emergency use by shipwrecked survivors. Under Mr. Campbell, superintendent of the rescue staff and lightkeepers, 59 cabin passengers and 271 emigrants were cared for until they could be taken off the island in the relief steamer *Queen Victoria* from Quebec. Hoping against hope that his ship might be saved, Captain McMaster, once his passengers were safe, devoted his energies to salvage, but it was not to be. The *Norwegian* was all but on her beam ends, port side up and hard aground on unforgiving rock. Before long she flooded and eventually went the way of her sisters on other obstructions in the St. Lawrence.

Once more the newspapers were full of letters about disaster to the Allan Line, including a glowing testimonial from some passengers who praised the "thoughtfulness, diligence and promptitude" of Mr. Dolan, the chief steward. For the master of the *Norwegian* they had harsh words, accusing him of neglecting to save emigrants' belongings. However regrettable this might have been, these steerage passengers were themselves saved by McMaster's prompt and seamanlike actions. The mail was also recovered.

By this time even editors were beginning to run out of effective comment, or at any rate out of suggestions. The Quebec *Morning Chronicle,* praising Captain McMaster's long and honourable record as a seaman, had to fall back on the opinion that " . . . there would almost appear to be a fatality attending Messrs. Allan & Rae's line of steamships." They also took the opportunity to hope that it would not bring unfavourable notice to shippers and shipowners of the perils of the St.

Lawrence route. They need not have worried. Most shipowners running to Quebec were in the squared timber trade, a traffic notorious for casualties at sea, where old and worn-out sailing ships, of modest value were covered by insurance. This, in fact, was the main reason for their presence in Canada.

Although this long series of disasters occurred mainly in the Gulf of St. Lawrence, the dangers of fog were very real elsewhere. One more similar casualty must be recorded, this time at Portland, Maine. It happened in the winter of 1864 when the Denny-built *Bohemian*, Captain Robert Borland, became a total loss. Leaving Liverpool on 4th February Borland had a tiresome passage across the Atlantic in foul weather. He was overdue when he arrived off the harbour entrance at eight in the evening of 22nd February. The wind had died down but a heavy swell remained under a deceptively calm sea. When the lighthouse on Cape Elizabeth was sighted between fog patches, speed was reduced and Captain Borland closed the land while waiting for his pilot. Suddenly the *Bohemian* bumped over a rocky shoal before sliding across into deep water again. In the miserably poor visibility Borland had misjudged his distance off the land. With a large hole in the bottom, the ship was turned towards the beach. But with machinery spaces flooded, she settled down in about four fathoms when still two hundred yards from the shore. The upper deck was above water but the vessel would not lift on a rising tide and it was decided to abandon ship. Tragically, one boat capsized with the loss of twenty Irish emigrants; but most passengers reached safety. Captain Borland and his officers remained with the ship until the following day when the mail was recovered.

This accident was particularly hard on the master, for Borland was a good officer with a fine record. He was thirty-nine at the time and had previously commanded the *Anglo-Saxon* and *North Briton*. On six occasions during his career as master in the Allan Line he had been presented with trophies by appreciative passengers, these ranging from a telescope to a silver tea service, all of course "handsomely engraved." Gifts of this nature serve to emphasise the conditions of mid-nineteenth century steam navigation when safe arrival was still a matter for congratulation. The commanders of liners were in a position of immense prestige, but they carried their professional honour in their hands: a stumble could ruin them. Borland had his world in front of him till 8 pm on 22nd February 1864. Eleven years previously, after voyaging all over the world, he had married Miss Anne McArthur, daughter of the harbour-master at Bowling on the Clyde. The loss of the *Bohemian* affected him deeply and he died at the early age of forty-five.

Although the Allan Line suffered occasional losses in later years these were few. The Company established a fine record of safety for the remainder of its existence. The wreck of the *Bohemian* marked the end of the period of tragedy and disaster which darkened the early days of the Allan Line. They had to overcome fair criticism, and the feeling that luck had been against them. But Hugh Allan's dictum that they must look to their own techniques for improvement, however noble, was only partly true. Two of the directors had themselves had long experience in command, and all were thoroughly on top of their jobs. In their selection of shipmasters to command the mail steamers, there can be no doubt that the Allans did so in the tradition of personal knowledge instilled by Captain Alexander Allan since the days of the little *Jean*.

In retrospect we can see that errors of judgment in one form or another accounted for these accidents. But human judgement is only as good as the information on which it is based. Here we have the key to what happened. There were, at times, very few facts on which to calculate a safe course. Lighthouses and buoys were still few and far between. Sounding machines of primitive type were in use, but the technique of taking a line of soundings with the deep sea lead involved stopping the ship and drifting in a process which, at best, yielded a very few uncertain facts on which to plot a course. The magnetic compass was as yet an uncertain instrument, liable to deviations from iron in the ship. Steamers carried their standard compass up the mast, or on a pole, where it would be least affected. Apart from magnetic errors due to the ship, other deviations were due to mineral deposits not far beneath in the shallow waters of the St. Lawrence.

Tradition remained strong. For years to come, the master lived aft where the discomforts from a racing screw in a seaway were intense. In the prolonged fogs and blizzards to be expected between Newfoundland and Montreal, the demands of navigation exacted a heavy mental concentration from officers who were already tired from the movement of the ship and the bitter cold of an Atlantic crossing. The bridge of ships in those days was entirely open, a feature which would seem to be a reversion when we consider the *Dumbarton Herald*'s eulogy on the wheel shelter on the poop of the *Canadian* and *Indian*. Seamen of the time might have denied that exposure to the weather would have a bearing on their navigational efficency, for they took immense pride in their manly endurance, as they did in more professional attainments as navigators: but a realistic appraisal must take this into account.

However much the Allans put safety above everything else in their standing instructions to masters, however sympathetically they dealt with victims of error, however much they equipped their ships with the best appliances of the day – and they did all these things – the fact remains that the mail steamers had to make time if the Company was to remain in business. Sandy Allan in the *Jean* or the *Favourite*, James in the *Canada*, could afford to shorten sail and heave-to till daylight. Bryce in the *Albion* was forced to accept imprisonment in the ice with whatever patience he could muster. The commanders of the Royal Mail steamers had no such option.

Above all the "Dangers and accidents of the sea" were always present, as they always will be. From all these points of view it may be safely affirmed that in the middle of the nineteenth century the St. Lawrence Route to Canada was the most demanding of any regular steamship service in the world.

CHAPTER SIX

The Railway Rumpus

"How wisdom and folly meet, mix and unite:
How virtue and vice blend their black and their white;"

R.B.
Sketch inscribed to the Rt. Hon. Ch. J. Fox Esq.

By dogged perseverance, the Allan Line survived the dangers of the sea in the fifties and sixties. But other troubles threatened from this long series of shipwrecks. In 1861 adverse public opinion focussed on the mail contract. As we have seen, this came to nothing: in fact some newspapers missed the whole point of the problem, none more so than the *Daily British Whig* of 16th November that year:

> We have the right to give our opinion: and that opinion, plainly spoken, is that until paddle wheel steamships are substituted for screw steamers the Canadian Line of steamships never can be either safe or profitable.

This extraordinary view, doubtless based on a false conclusion from the popularity of Cunard's paddlers on the ice-free New York route, shows how little the safety issue was understood. In fact, by the late sixties, the Allan Line was both safe and profitable. As Hugh Allan's affairs prospered, he built *Ravenscrag* on the slopes of Mount Royal and was widely regarded as the wealthiest shipping man in all Canada – and a business leader of the first importance. But prosperity also had its dangers, although of another kind. Sudden squalls would blow up from differences between Hugh and Andrew in Montreal and their brothers in Liverpool and Glasgow.

A second danger had arisen from earlier proposals to sell the steamships outright. It was complicated by a difference of opinion as to which group of brothers was to have the controlling interest. Captain James Allan, who was head of the firm in Glasgow, had put his son R.G. Allan into the Liverpool office to follow in the footsetps of Uncle Bryce. Writing to his father on 4th January 1864, R.G.Allan commented from the third generation of shipowners in this remarkable family:

> Since I was in Glasgow I've somewhat changed my mind about the advisability of selling the steamers and if we can get £750,000 for them I think the best thing we can do is to sell them and go into sailing ships, even altho' it did break up our present business.

Two years later differences between partners separated by the Atlantic again threatened to break up the business. This time Hugh Allan was making a bid for tighter control of the entire group. Of this episode R.G.Allan, in a letter dated Liverpool, 26th February 1866, confided once more to his father:

> This nastiness of Uncle Hugh seems to be kept up much longer than is warranted by any provocation which he may have received, or rather fancy he received. But when he actually proposes a separation he shows he is very determined and may wish to carry it out. When he sees that Uncle Bryce will stand or fall by you he may change his mind. But the fact of his having proposed such a thing as separation shows that it is not desirable to continue business relations with him, if we can better ourselves. If a separation is to be effected it seems that either you must buy him out or vice versa. If sufficient money can be raised the former course seems the best for we would then have more thorough command of our present trade instead of having to seek a new one. It is at present a good one, and there are reasonable prospects of it continuing so, so that it is not a thing to be lightly cast aside. Were Uncle Hugh's shares held on this side the proportion of commissions to be divided abroad would be much less and the return for the outlay increased to a certain extent in that manner . . . What I have wished to urge is that the idea of being bought up by Uncle Hugh is much less desirable than that of buying him up, for the latter would ultimately be the most profitable, not to mention the fact of our thereby retaining the very profitable agencies which we at present

possess. If things remain as they are so much the better, but if Uncle Hugh puts you in the position of having to chose between two evils, I believe the least would be to buy and the greatest to sell.

Whatever 'nastiness' had been imputed to Uncle Hugh, he was a far-sighted man with ambitions which were yet to be made clear. However, for the time being, things remained as they were and James and Bryce managed to restore good relations and avoid a schism.

But no business can stand still, family or otherwise. To prosper it must change with the times or go under; and of the latter alternative Hugh Allan had no intention. Perhaps changes pending in Canada were less apparent, viewed from Britain; but Hugh Allan sensed a third danger for the Company from the proposed Pacific Railway. With the opening of a circuitous route across the North American continent in 1869, by way of the Grand Trunk from Canada to Chicago and thence by Union Pacific to San Francisco, the Allan Line had begun to take a few trans-Atlantic passengers who were either crossing America or en route to the Far East by whatever shipping might be available on the Pacific. In fact, a sketch map on an Allan Line sailing notice of the period shows such an arrangement. If Canada were to build a trans-continental railway, and if the railway company puts ships on the Pacific, they might well find themselves in an impregnable position for carrying freight and passengers half round the world. This was something which had better be looked into.

By 1871, with the accession of British Columbia into the Confederation of Canada, the decision to build the railway had been taken. Under the terms of union the Canadian government was bound to start construction within two years, simultaneously from east and west of the Rockies, and to complete the line within ten years. Viewed from Hugh Allan's point of view, whoever controlled the railway might eventually control the sea. If the Allan Line were to survive as a healthy family legacy, and already it represented the cumulative efforts of three generations, he must have a controlling interest and Montreal must be the focal point.

The power behind the Pacific Railway scheme flowed principally from one man, Sir John A. Macdonald, the Prime Minister of Canada. He was, of course, well known to Hugh Allan; not only from long association with government mail contracts and the building of light-houses on the St. Lawrence, but as the man whose statesmanlike judgement, limitless energy and messianic faith were committed to the Pacific Railway as a necessity of his fledgling Confederation. There had also been a more private relationship in the world of money. Indeed, as President of the Merchant's Bank Hugh Allan had offered to help the great man and Macdonald had taken him up:

Private   Ottawa,
                                                  Sept 29th. 1869

My Dear Mr. Allan,

    Some time ago you were kind enough to promise to submit my propositions to the Board of the Merchant's Bank for their favourable consideration. It is of importance that the matter should be settled. I cannot adjust my account with the Bank of Upper Canada until I settle with you. The Trustees of the B.U.C. commenced an action against me some time ago but have not proceeded with it as yet. I imagine that they will be obliged to wind up the trust so soon as the award is made between the Provinces of Quebec and Ontario. Should they get judgement against me I shall be unable legally to carry out the proposition I have made to you.

        Trusting to your kind aid in this matter, believe me,
        My Dear Mr. Allan,

        Yours faithfully,
        John A. Macdonald

In due course the Merchant's Bank did give their "kind aid" – on the usual secure precautions – and Macdonald was once more solvent.

Some time after this transaction, Hugh Allan got in touch with the Prime Minister with a proposal to form a Pacific Railway Company. He was not alone in making proposals. A Toronto group, headed by David Lewis Macpherson who had helped to finance the St. Lawrence & Atlantic Railway which had connected Montreal to Portland in 1853, and who had since been heavily involved in the Grand Trunk Railway, was also interested. The problem was how to raise money for this enormous scheme. Hugh Allan knew that it could not be raised in Canada, nor even in England; and that American capital would have to be attracted to have any hope of progress. That Macdonald was then prepared to consider such a scheme is certain from his letter to Hugh Allan dated Ottawa, February 3rd 1871. It was couched in familiar terms as between men who knew each other:

I received your telegram about the proposed company for the construction of the Pacific Railway. The government is in no way connected with any proposed company or companies. Besides the one that you mention Mr. Waddington, formerly of British Columbia, has given notice of his intention to apply to the Legislature for an Act. We will not in any way connect ourselves with any company; in fact we consider it premature, until the sanction of the Legislature is obtained to the junction of British Columbia, to take any steps at all.

The whole matter will be brought before Parliament next session; meanwhile I see no objection to the capitalists of Canada or England (or of the United States for that matter) joining together and making proposals for the construction of the road. It will be for Parliament at the proper time to decide as to the mode in which the railway can best be built with a view to public interests.

With Macdonald's blessing thus given to a wide range of possibilities, Sir Hugh Allan went ahead. His immense prestige was enhanced by his knighthood in the summer of 1871, an honour which, in his unique position as shipowner with an eye to railways, added to the general confidence. He was sixty-one at the time and in good health. Keeping in mind the unprecedented nature of the Canadian Pacific Railway, one wonders whether it ever occurred to him that the anticipated duration of two years for preparation and ten for the completion of the line would inevitably take him to that stage in life when most men lose their ability to handle crushing responsibilities. If so, he showed no outward sign except, if anything, a strengthening of will and a determination to crown his success in shipping by addition of the railway. The two systems would unite to form the greatest transportation system in the world. It was both a logical move and a dazzling prospect.

Meantime Waddington, who as it turned out was not to be taken seriously, had proposed to the government in Ottawa that the railway should be financed by American capital under a scheme which would have laid the rails south of Lake Superior. The route would thus lie in United States territory, while joining Canadian routes both east and west. This came to nothing. Waddington died in obscurity two years later. But the Toronto group, under D.L.Macpherson, was an entirely different kind of company, and a rival to be taken with the utmost seriousness.

Apart from the fierce rivalry of entrepreneurs competing for profits expected to arise from colonization by railway in an empty land, three other issues deeply affected the course of events. These were nationalism, which in effect meant anti-Americanism; the rivalry between Montreal and Toronto for financial supremacy; and the political power necessary to pass legislation. By this last process, Parliament would grant huge sums of money and vast tracts of land to the successful promoter. Without success in harnessing all these forces it was impossible for any group to gain the necessary influence and beat off rivals. The key word was "influence": and to gain it, whether financial, political or commercial, every prominent figure in that period of Canadian railway politics used every means at his disposal. There were many incentives: there was no income tax, the electorate was largely politically ignorant and highly partisan; elections themselves were corrupt; and members of Parliament and even Ministers, because of small remuneration, were susceptible to constant pressure from promoters with money to burn. Within this framework, interested parties knew the unwritten rules of the game, and some personal friendships survived extraordinarily hard knocks in the process.

The first issue was nationalism. Although Waddington's scheme had come to nothing, he had aroused the interest of American promoters, among them George W. McMullen, who with Sir Hugh Allan visited Ottawa in October 1871 to sound the Prime Minister on the possibilities. McMullen was Canadian-born but had gone south in his youth, taken root in Chicago and prospered as a railway promoter. Nothing came of this meeting – Allan made no proposals and Macdonald signified no intentions. However in December Hugh Allan and his American associates agreed to form a company with a view to getting the Pacific charter. Alarmed by this initiative from Montreal, deeply suspicious of American influence in Allan's scheme which it was feared might result in the line dipping south to the United States side of Lake Superior, the Toronto group also applied for the charter.

Thus in 1872 two Acts of Incorporation were passed, one for the *Canada Pacific Railway* under Sir Hugh Allan of Montreal, the other for the *Interoceanic Company* under D.L.Macpherson of Toronto. In the spirit of Macdonald's letter to Allan that" . . . the Government is in no way connected with any company . . . " Parliament passed another Act by which either of the two incorporated companies, or an amalgamation of both, or if necessary a new company in the event that agreement could not be reached, would be given the contract with a subsidy of thirty million dollars and fifty million acres of land. Clearly the hope of the Government was that the rivals would meet on common ground. Negotiations to this end were conducted in Toronto by J.C.Abbott, who was Sir Hugh Allan's lawyer and a director of the *Pacific Company*, but they fell through on the question of the presidency. For Sir Hugh Allan with his steamship interests at stake, this was of particular importance. Rightly or wrongly, he was determined, above all else, that he would be President of the Pacific Railway.

While affairs were at this interesting stage, the first Parliament of Canada was dissolved and a general election called. For anyone hoping to build the trans-continental railway the return of Macdonald's government was imperative. The *Interoceanic Company* already had influence in Ottawa through Macpherson, who was a senator. For Hugh Allan's company, dependent also on the strongest political representation, it was important that the member for Montreal East, Sir George Etienne Cartier, should hold his seat. Cartier and Allan knew each other very well. In their youth, the one as a "Patriote" and the other as a soldier of militia, they had experienced the 1837 Rebellion from opposite sides. Since then Cartier had risen to dominate Quebec politics and, by his success in bringing his Province into Confederation and his vigorous promotion of economic growth in Montreal – including support for Allan in founding the Montreal Ocean Steamship Company – had achieved stature as a catalytic figure in the great compromise on which Canadian survival is based. His influence in the Macdonald government was immense and he controlled Quebec patronage at all levels.

Although Cartier was thought to favour Allan, he was also the solicitor for the Grank Trunk Railway of which Macpherson was a director. From Allan's point of view, therefore, Cartier was to be encouraged in one direction but watched in another. The Grand Trunk Railway at that time ran from Levis to Sarnia and was the main artery connecting Upper Canada to the sea. There had been talk of the Grand Trunk going in for steamships on the Atlantic and, always sensitive to the relationship between sea and rail, Allan had advocated the building of alternate railways as a measure of self protection for his own steamship company. This system, to be known as the *Northern Colonization Railway* from Montreal to Ottawa, and the *North Shore Railway* from Montreal to Quebec, was intended to reach Toronto from whence it would be a natural link to connect the new Pacific Railway with the port of Montreal independently from the Grand Trunk. In promoting this line nothing could be achieved without extensive support from the electors of Montreal East and the villages along the proposed route. Here, also, it was in Allan's interest to ensure the return of Cartier to the Government front bench in Ottawa. Throughout his life Sir Hugh had shown an acute awareness of the advantages accruing to a combined management of steam services by rail and sea. If, in the conditions of his day, this was seen mainly from a monopolistic point of view, it is worth noting that the key to transportation a century later is the "intermodal" concept.

At this point, for the only time in his life, Sir Hugh threw himself into a frenzied political activity, a situation made possible by his experience buying wheat as a young man and his proficiency in French. He stumped the riding on Cartier's behalf, making speeches, holding meetings with influential people, hoping that Cartier's influence in the Government would be brought to bear. But just as Allan had reason to doubt Cartier's ability to do this, because of his Grand Trunk associations, Cartier on his part had reason to doubt whether Allan's support would be acceptable by Grand Trunk investors. It was an anxious time but relief came with an unexpected message from the Prime Minister. By this time Macdonald was anxious to settle the railway business because of the coming election and, as both Allan and Macpherson were obdurate over the presidency, he came down in Allan's favour. Doubtless the Prime Minister wished to buttress his Quebec influence through Cartier, but also he was desperately in need of election funds and Allan was the most likely source of help. The ground was anything but secure under his feet as Macdonald sent the following telegram to Cartier:

26th July 1872
Have seen Macpherson. He has no personal ambition, but cannot in justice to Ontario concede any preference to Quebec in the matter of the presidency, or in any other particular. He says that the question about the presidency should be left to the Board. Under these circumstances I authorize you to assure Allan that the influence of the Government will be exercised to secure him the position of president. The other terms to be as agreed on between Macpherson and Abbott. The whole matter to be kept secret till after the elections. Then the two gentlemen to meet the Privy Council at Ottawa and settle the terms of a provisional agreement. This is the only practical solution of the difficulty, and should be accepted by Allan.

(signed) John A. Macdonald

Cartier's relief was short-lived. The stakes were exceedingly high; if Allan had to pay to keep in the game he wanted assurance beyond the suggestion that the question of the presidency should be left to the Board. The Board of Directors of the amalgamated company was yet to be formed and they might well elect Macpherson, or anyone else for that matter. On 30th July, after another discussion, Cartier went further than Macdonald. He made an offer to Allan that the *Canada Pacific Company* should again take the initiative in attempting to form an amalgamation; in which case, he wrote:

. . . If the *Interoceanic Company* should not execute such an agreement of amalgamation upon such terms, and within such limited time, I think the contemplated arrangement should be made with the *Canada Pacific Company* under its charter. I might add, that as I approve of the measures to which I have referred in this letter, I shall use my best endeavours to have them carried into effect.

This was near enough to Sir Hugh's expectations; but all depended on Cartier's re-election, a possibility of which there could be no guarantee. Privately, Sir Hugh thought that Cartier's chances were slim. To make his position entirely clear, Allan therefore got in touch again with the Prime Minister to ask for his concurrence. Macdonald was by then in a very difficult position, he had gone as far towards Allan and Quebec as he felt he could, and with an election to fight in his own riding of

Kingston there was no time for further negotiation. He therefore told both Allan and Cartier that the matter must remain as stated in his telegram of the 26th. This being the case, Sir Hugh accepted the fact that he had pushed the matter of his presidency to the limit for the time being, and he withdrew Cartier's letter of the 30th.

Now came the *quid pro quo*. Cartier asked for $100,000 but increased this somewhat in a letter the same day:

Montreal, 30th July 1872

Dear Sir Hugh – The friends of the Government will expect to be assisted with funds in the pending elections, and any amount which you or your Company shall advance for that purpose shall be recouped to you. A memorandum of immediate requirements is below.

Very Truly yours
(Signed)
Geo. E. Cartier

Now wanted.

Sir John A. Macdonald	$25,000
Hon. Mr. Langevin	15,000
Sir G.E.C.	20,000
Sir J.A. (add'l)	10,000
Hon. Mr. Langevin	10,000
Sir G.E.C. (add'l)	30,000

This frank document had been preceded by others. On 26th July Macdonald had wired Abbott from Kingston:

I must have another $10,000, will be the last time of calling. Do not fail me. Answer today.

To this Abbott replied "Draw on me for $10,000." In the end it was all in vain for Sir George Cartier, who lost his seat; and only just enough for Sir John A. Macdonald, who was returned to Parliament but with a reduced majority for his Conservative Party.

Meanwhile the real loser was Sir Hugh Allan, and his backers, who were out of pocket for these and other election expenses. These were estimated to come to $350,000, expended as bribes in one form or another by politicians and their agents and as stock to some influential supporters. Whatever might be thought of the process morally (and it was regarded in much the same light as company donations to political party funds today), it was recognised as a gamble. Nobody really thought for one moment that promises to recoup were other than a sop to a prickly conscience.

Having paid his way thus far in the election lottery, Allan now had to assess the chances of the ticket he had drawn. Macdonald's Government was again in power, and the Prime Minister was personally devoted passionately to the Pacific Railway. Most politicians and a host of prospective contractors were looking forward to the start of construction. But the big question remained: who was going to get the charter? Although it had been promised to Sir Hugh, the fact remained that both he and Senator Macpherson were presidents of companies which existed only as legal entities. Despite efforts to bring them together, the deadlock remained. The issue of nationalism had been simmering for a long time: now it boiled over.

Public opinion on American participation had hardened since February 1871 when the Prime Minister had written that he saw no objection to the capitalists of the United States. In the meantime however, Allan had acted on this opinion and had put up the money, along with his American backers, to be used in Canada for raising "influence." By introductions from McMullen this had come from Jay Cooke, the banker behind the Northern Pacific Railroad. Throughout the entire episode this company was seen by many as the wolf ready to pounce on Canadian sheep. One such contribution, typical of others, was acknowledged thus:

New York, April 1st 1872

G.W. McMullen Esq.
Canada Pacific R.R. Ex. Committee:

Dear Sir – We have today received of you your drafts on various parties to the amount of $50,000 which sum we credit to the Executive Committee of the Canada Pacific R.R. Association, subject to the draft of Sir Hugh Allan.

Respectfully,
(Signed)   Jay Cooke & Co.

By July it was apparent to Allan that no Canadian politician, then as now, could retain his seat on a policy of American predominence on the board of a Canadian utility company. Discreet financing was perhaps acceptable, but not to the extent of outright control. Yet the money had to be raised somehow. In a letter dated 1st July 1872 to General Cass, who was another Northern Pacific man, Sir Hugh confided:

. . . A very formidable opposition was organized in Toronto which, for want of better, took as their cry 'no foreign influence' – 'no Yankee dictation' – 'no Northern Pacific to choke off our Canadian Pacific' and others equally sensible.

So much effect however was produced both in and out of Parliament by these cries and the agitation consequent on them that after consulting Mr. McMullen I was forced unwillingly to drop ostensibly from our organization every American name and to put in reliable people on this side in place of them.

This was done. The prospectus of the Canada Pacific Company was issued under the names of a Canadian directorate. Whatever comfort McMullen may have wrung from the word "ostensibly," he was soon disillusioned:

Montreal, 24th October 1872

Dear Mr. McMullen,   No action has yet (so far as I know) been taken by the Government in the matter of the Pacific Railroad contract. The opposition of the Ontario party will, I think, have the effect of shutting out our American friends from any participation in the road and I apprehend that negociation [sic] is at an end.

It is still uncertain how it will be given (the contract) but in any case the Government seem inclined to exact a declaration that no foreigner will have directly or indirectly any interest in it. But everything is in a state of uncertainty and I think it is unnecessary for you to visit New York on this business at present or at all till you hear what the result is likely to be.

Public sentiment seems to be decided that the road shall be built by Canadians only.

Yours truly,
(Signed)   Hugh Allan

In a final exchange of letters McMullen wrote again on 6th November in plaintive mood:

... I think you could have it arranged as we have several times talked, i.e. the stock held by you subject to private arrangement with the others. And whatever street rumour may say of public opinion, I should judge that this would do all that is needed.

But it was not to be. In reply Sir Hugh could only surmise, "You know as much about the Pacific Railroad contract as I do, and that is not much."

Events now took a different turn. Armed with the entire correspondence with Sir Hugh Allan, McMullen came to Ottawa and, on 31st December 1872, saw the Prime Minister and read to him the more embarassing letters and telegrams. Claiming that his American associates had advanced some $400,000 to the Canada Pacific Company in the belief that the Government had backed Sir Hugh Allan officially, McMullen complained that in fact he had been thrown overboard by Allan and that therefore the Government should now rescue him. On 23rd January 1873, in company with two more irate Chicago promoters, McMullen repeated the story with the threat that Allan's ships would be seized in United States ports before taking him to law. Macdonald could only protest, which he knew was not entirely the case, that Allan had gone ahead on his own and that therefore action at law was their only redress. At the conclusion of this extraordinary interview one of the Americans said to the Prime Minister:

> You must distinctly understand that we do not come here for the purpose of blackmailing you or blackmailing the Goverment, but for the purpose of stating our case.

To Sir John A. Macdonald, faced with calamitous possibilities, it must have seemed that of the many misunderstandings brought to his notice that day, this was farthest from the truth and by far the most threatening.

For the Prime Minister the problem was to sweep it all under the rug before the Opposition got hold of the story. Sir Hugh Allan was about to sail for England to invite British capitalists to replace the ousted Americans. Revelations would undoubtedly damage that prospect which, in any case, was not of the best. Abbott was hurriedly deputed to negotiate with McMullen in this delicate matter which, however much the Americans might protest to the contrary, reeked of blackmail.

On 25th February 1873, just before Sir Hugh sailed for England, the Prime Minister was informed that McMullen's demands, which had been stretched to the limits of his fertile imagination, had been whittled down to $37,500. Of this $20,000 had been handed over in cash with the balance by Allan's cheque deposited at the Merchant's Bank in a sealed envelope. The deal had been concluded with a neat safeguard in that another envelope, containing the entire collection of damaging letters, was lodged in Abbott's desk with instructions that, ten days after the end of the Parliamentary Session, McMullen would get the cheque and Sir Hugh would recover his letters. It might have worked, had it not been for an unsuspected twist.

The Opposition had indeed got hold of the story and the storm broke in Ottawa on 2nd April 1873, at the opening session of the new Parliament, when Lucius Seth Huntingdon, member from a Montreal riding, moved a resolution calling for a committee to enquire into the whole business of the railway negotiations. A Royal Commission was appointed in August and the "Pacific Scandal" came to light. It filled the papers for weeks and was preceded by a nocturnal visit which might have come straight from the pages of Sherlock Holmes. No sooner were Sir Hugh and his legal adviser out of the way in England than the envelope of letters in Abbott's desk was stolen from that apparently secure bottom drawer, almost certainly by Abbott's confidential clerk who promply left town. McMullen had no need of Sir Hugh's cheque; he already had the $20,000 in cash and had sold the letters to the highest bidder.

Perhaps the best comment on the Royal Commission was in a newspaper cartoon entitled "Whitewash and blackwash." It showed the aggrieved parties vigorously applying tar to one side of a bust of the Prime Minister while the Commissioners slobbered whitewash on the other. It was near enough the truth. Sir George Cartier died in England before the enquiry opened, Huntingdon decided that it was safer to skirmish from the floor of the House rather than to give evidence, and McMullen wisely decided to ignore a summons and remain outside Canada. Sir John A. Macdonald, Sir Hugh Allan and the Hon. J.C. Abbott were of course the star witnesses, and they stepped with care which was exceeded only by that of the Commissioners. Nobody disturbed the tightrope more than was necessary to make an interesting act. The Commission came to no conclusions but the record remains in letters and telegrams, in the voluminous files of the Macdonald papers and in the transcript of the hearings, all of which may be seen in the Public Archives of Canada. To this day eager researchers burrow with all the expectations of fundamentalists seeking truth from the remoter reaches of the Old Testament, and with results as varied.

After the enquiry Macdonald resigned. With the fall of his government, the Pacific Railway scheme was buried for the time being.

Since 1873 historians have heaped condemnation on Sir Hugh Allan. To many Canadians he is known only for his part in this disastrous affair. In this he has been done less than justice, and his conduct should now be re-examined in the light of the possibilities open to him under prevailing conditions.

Canada was virtually an empty land and governed by a system which, for all the apparent safeguards of its British parliamentary ways, had more in common with the eighteenth-century ways than with modern administration, and it was greatly influenced by American style frontier politics. In the first flush of enthusiasm for railways everybody expected to get rich quickly, be they politicians, contractors or settlers. Every proposition was received with the fervour or condemnation associated with outright gambling. Every decision by government was regarded as a favour by those likely to benefit, and every favour had its price. Politicians paid for votes, contractors paid for contracts. Both paid for the newspapers, which were highly partisan. Sometimes they used their own money, sometimes they used the money of others committed to their cause.

Of necessity, promoters fertilized the ground with money. If they lost, it was all part of the game; and many of them did lose. If they won, and a few of them did win, the way was open to fame and fortune to a degree hardly to be imagined today. There can be no doubt that Sir Hugh Allan wanted to build that railway in which, apart from more general considerations, he knew that the future of the Allan Line was at stake. As a Canadian of his generation, he saw this as part of the expanding British Empire. On this question of nationalism he was a realist and a businessman. From his trading position with United States, it is unlikely that he felt bound by the flag to a greater extent than would the chairman of an international consortium today when it came to raising money. Although, from his evidence to the Royal Commission, he considered himself worth some five or six million dollars, comparatively little was available in actual cash. In 1873 the population of Canada was small, Canadians had no money; but by comparison, the population of the United States was active, expanding and wealthy. British railway investment was cautious. Much later when Macdonald, the greatest gambler of them all, was attempting to drum up British capital, Sir Charles Tupper related of him in *Recollections of Sixty Years,* that Sir Henry Tyler, then President of the Grand Trunk Railway, gave this chilly warning:

> . . . If you omit the clause providing for a line round the North Shore of Lake Superior to Western Canada, I shall be pleased to lay the matter before my Board of Directors. Otherwise they would throw it in the wastepaper basket.

So much for the British attitude.

There can be no doubt that all concerned with the abortive Pacific Railway acted on rules, or rather lack of them, forced on the situation by such considerations as these. Sir Hugh Allan asked for the charter to build the railway, and also for its Presidency. Macdonald promised both. Macdonald and Cartier asked for political funds: Sir Hugh Allan provided them. Abbott, who knew everyone worth knowing – he was the most sought after corporation lawyer in Canada – gave much advice, was privy to all the secrets, and prospered. Looked at from this point of view, and accepting the fact that railways, partisan influence and politics were inextricably mixed, it is not surprising that even Sir John A. Macdonald, with his unique qualities, was unable to pull things together until 1881, when he was able to scale unprecedented heights of vision and bravado with a successful Pacific Railway bill. The fact is that Canada was not ready for the Railway in 1873, and it is doubtful if

116

it could have been carried through. A decade later, even the heroic financing of the CPR was barely able to carry the day. One fact is certain; whatever the attitude to the United States, it was the constructional genius of an American railroader, William Van Horne, that eventually gave Canada her transcontinental line. As for the financiers of the CPR, many of them came from the same Scottish heritage as Allan and made their fortunes by comparable methods. As already noted, Sir Hugh Allan was over sixty when he first became involved; the great men of the CPR were younger.

History had made more of the "Pacific Scandal" than was really warranted. Tupper called it the "Pacific Slander." If nobody came out of it with credit, most managed to survive and some continued on their way to the pages of history. Change came slowly: as late as 1891, when Sir John A. Macdonald was fighting his last election in the year of his death, he received a series of letters from George Stephen of the CPR pointing out that, considering the million or so contributed by the Company to Conservative Party funds since 1882, there might have been a better return. Sir John Abbott became Mayor of Montreal and succeeded Macdonald as Prime Minister of Canada; having counselled Sir Hugh in the abortive Canada Pacific scheme, it was he who had counselled the CPR in its opening years. Donald Smith, whose only part in Sir Hugh Allan's scheme was to appear on the list of directors of the reconstituted Canadian Board, lived to drive the last spike of the CPR and to become Lord Strathcona.

Of McMullen it might be said that his was a classic case of *caveat emptor.* He was no babe in the wood at railway promotion, and he went into it with his eyes open. He knew the rules and, for the most part, his money went down the drain. Not that he had not been warned: for at one stage Sir Hugh told him bluntly that " . . . I think you will have to go it blind in the matter of money – cash payments – I have already paid $8,500 and have not a voucher and cannot get one." It is difficult to work up much sympathy for McMullen.

Sir Hugh seldom referred to the matter afterwards. He had told the Royal Commission that he gave political funds in proportion to his wealth as did every other man of business. He would have contributed regardless of the outcome of negotiations for the charter which, in any case, he considered already settled because of Macdonald's promise. He made no comment on his relationship with the Americans but, as it turned out, he was dealing with the hard core of the railroad gamblers. His private correspondence was frank to the point of recklessness, a neglect equalled only by Cartier and Macdonald. It may have been that, as President of the Montreal Telegraph Company, Sir Hugh felt that he had a secure channel of communication by wire but, apart from this, everyone committed themselves to paper, pen in hand.

Many people wondered what he really felt about the events of 1873. One of the few to ask point-blank was William Smith, Deputy Minister of Marine and Fisheries, who was periodically invited to dinner at *Ravenscrag*. Smith was another Scots Presbyterian who had spent most of his life in Canada and, like Sir Hugh, he was regarded as a hard-driving man, of few words. From long association with the Allans on shipping matters he knew Sir Hugh as well as anyone outside the immediate circle. On one such occasion, putting his Doric camaradie to the test, Smith took the opportunity to ask his host whether he ever regretted his involvement with Macdonald. There was a pregnant silence as both men savoured their port in front of the library fire while Sir Hugh carefully considered. "Mebbe," was all that he said before changing the subject.

The relationship between the principals in this episode may have seemed bitter to many at the time; but in fact they knew each other too well for their personal feelings to be greatly disturbed. Years later, we get another glimpse of the Prime Minister and Sir Hugh Allan when they were rumbling down to Halifax together on the Intercolonial Railway. It is recorded that conversation, laughter and reminiscence flowed as smoothly as Sir John's brandy.

After the Railway Rumpus, Sir Hugh Allan devoted himself to his shipping business and to family affairs, following both with his customary energy and enthusiasm. At this period the Allan Line had over twenty steamships on the Atlantic and a fleet of splendid iron clippers earning handsome profits all over the world in the last supremacy of sail on the long voyage routes, their combined tonnage amounting to some 100,000 tons. As we shall see later, the Company forged ahead in this period, which culminated in the building of the *Parisian,* 5,000 ton flagship of the mail steamers, which set the pace in the St. Lawrence trade for years to come.

Lady Allan died in 1881 and her sister, the wife of Hugh's brother Andrew, died about the same time, a bitter blow to the brothers. Family mourning was lengthy and restrictive in the social sense; but within a year the passenger list of the *Peruvian,* sailing from Quebec on 7th October 1882, was headed by the name of Sir Hugh Allan and followed by his daughters Edith and Mabel and his sons Bryce and Arthur. It was time for the girls to "come out" into society and for all to visit their cousins in Scotland. It was a happy family voyage in the old tradition. There were forty passengers in the cabin: it is an interesting sidelight on the period that seven of them were clergymen. One wonders who read prayers on the first Sunday at sea: the bishop, Captain Ritchie, or Sir Hugh Allan?

On 9th December 1882 Sir Hugh Allan died suddenly while in Edinburgh. The holiday was of course cut short and the party returned to Canada with their father's body. It must have been a subdued voyage for all on board. December in the Atlantic is rough and cold, but perhaps there was a certain poetic justice that the great shipowner should make his last voyage westerly on the route which he and his family had done so much to conquer. Very early on Christmas Day, as the people of Halifax were still asleep, the RMS *Sarmatian* made her landfall at Chebucto Head, steamed slowly past McNab's Island into harbour, and secured alongside the Allan Line berth with her colours at half mast.

The principal Canadian newspapers published column after column on his life and work. The *Montreal Gazette* referred to Sir Hugh as the "Foremost commercial man in Canada," and even the *Toronto Mail*, not to be outdone, ran a black headline "Canada's foremost Merchant Prince." The *New York Herald* devoted two columns to his obituary, as did the papers in east coast ports where the blue-white-and-red houseflag was as well known as the Royal Mail pendant.

It was an age which wallowed in gloomy ceremonial at death and, inevitably for a prominent person, this was lengthy and public. According to the newspaper reports of such affairs, the civic funeral of Sir Hugh Allan in Montreal was exceeded in dolorous splendour only by the obsequies for Sir George Cartier himself, a ceremony which must be unique in the annals of Canadian funerals.

CHAPTER SEVEN

The Blessings of the Land

"Farewell, Old Scotia's bleak domains."

R.B.
The Farewell

The death of Sir Hugh Allan was a severe blow to the Company, for he had an unrivalled knowledge of the shipping business and had personally selected and trained many of the staff, both afloat and ashore. Despite the manificence of *Ravenscrag* and *Belmere*, and the opulent style which people associated with the few estates of this kind in Canada, Sir Hugh retained to the last the simple personal characteristics of his Ayrshire heritage. He worked extremely hard, had an encyclopedic knowledge gained in an exacting school, and could show any man his job. His brother Andrew succeeded to the direction of affairs in Montreal and the Allan Line continued to play an outstanding part in emigration from Britain to Canada.

In 1872 the Allan Line published *Practical Hints and Directions to Intending Emigrants,* a booklet modest enough in size but in other ways less restrained. "Which is the best field for emigration?" ran its opening announcement, to be answered in the very next paragraph which, in bold type, was headed "THE DOMINION OF CANADA":

The climate of this vast country is hotter in the Summer and colder in the Winter than western Europe; but it is healthy and favourable to the growth of a hardy and industrious population which, although at present under four millions, has laid the foundation, under the British flag, of another great North American Confederation where people, lightly taxed, live happily and contented on land which they can call their own, and under just and equal laws, fairly and honestly administered.

This glowing report, quoted in the handbook by a delegate sent to investigate the prospects for settlers coming from Working Men's Societies in England, forecast that Canada could support a population of 150 million – a century later we have just passed the twenty million mark. But, allowing for the boundless optimism which characterized the flow of people from the Old World to the New, and without which few of them would have had the courage to start, tales of the "Golden West" were far from illusory. There was land, land in abundance; and with the passing of the *Dominion Land Act* of 1872 160 acres of it, a "quarter section" as it was called, was available free to anyone who would build a homestead and settle. Between 1870 and 1914 some four million emigrants came to Canada. From 1885 when construction of the CPR reached Manitoba and Saskatchewan, and from 1886 when the line was laid right through to British Columbia, the West became accessible and captured the imagination of land-hungry Europeans. Apart from homesteaders heading for the Prairies, eastern Canada, which had already assumed its characteristic pattern of mixed farms, steam sawmills and small towns by the railway track, took thousands of masons, carpenters, miners, bricklayers, mechanics and general labourers who, in a constant stream, added their multitudinous skills to the empty reservoir of the New Dominion.

To complement this land settlement policy, the Canadian Government established Immigration Officers in Britain and Europe through whom they offered assisted passages to selected applicants. The Allan Line made sure that this policy was accompanied by equal coverage of information on how to get to Canada, and their advertisements appeared in countless local newspapers from Scandinavia throughout Europe to the remotest parts of the United Kingdom. A typical notice in the *Ardrossan and Saltcoats Herald* advertised "the best and cheapest routes" to all parts of the Dominion and the United States by the mail steamers of the Allan Line, commencing with special rates for the first railway journey to the ship at Glasgow or Liverpool, and ending with arrangements for travel by strange sounding "colonist cars" from the port of disembarkation in North America to the Pacific coast if need be. To illustrate the efficiency of the Allan Line coverage, this newspaper,

121

with a readership restricted mainly to that part of Ayrshire which was the home of the Allan family, listed no fewer than nine passenger agents, among them bank managers and small business men. One of the agents was the local Registrar of Births, Deaths and Marriages, a familiar official to healthy young parents, whose otherwise bleak government office walls offered an ideal setting for colourful messages of hope from a new land. With fares at six guineas for adults, three for children under eight, and one guinea for infants, these announcements of weekly sailings must have had an instant appeal to many working families of ambition.

The Canadian Government distributed official leaflets through the Immigration Offices but these did not always have the coverage of private enterprise Allan Line advertising which was greatly in demand. One irate gentleman, Mr. A. Styleman Herring of St. Paul's, Clerkenwell, London, who was one of many public spirited individuals attempting to offer hope to the overcrowded masses of the big cities, wrote a letter to the *Montreal Gazette* of 8th April 1871 complaining that no government pamphlets had been received in England for the ensuing season and that, despite a marked increase in emigration clubs and societies, the movement was falling behind. He added: " . . . If the Allans had not issued 100,000 pamphlets matters would have been worse."

Since first commencing regular sailings with the steamships *Canadian* and *Indian* the Montreal Ocean Steamship Company had undoubtedly brought order and efficiency to the previously chaotic emigrant business. The old sailing packets had, of course, disappeared almost overnight with the advent of steam; but early steamships, such as the *Sarah Sands* which had unsuccessfully tried to forestall the Allan Line, had been little better for food and accommodation and were equally haphazard administratively. In 1856, for example, the *Montreal Gazette* reported that "misery and starvation" had been caused by the Quebec agents for the *Sarah Sands* when they refused to honour through tickets purchased in England for Detroit and Chicago. Of recent years somewhat similar misunderstandings and even fraudulent transactions have been in the news, in connection with travel by chartered aircraft. Whereas today the worst that can happen is a few hours of delay and frustration or the price of a regular ticket for instant release, passengers stranded in the mid-nineteenth century were really up against privation and want. This kind of thing was a vicious evil, which sometimes ended in death from starvation and exposure. In one particularly sad case the Montreal police found a woman and child on the waterfront, recently off some ill-found vessel, lying dead in the gutter under a blazing noonday sun. Immigrants stranded without friends or resources then faced a hazardous time.

By the seventies the Immigration Officers had put an end to this kind of thing, but, according to the Allan Line booklet of 1872, the government agents " . . . Will not assist anyone who loses his time by staying in the city, unless detained by sickness or some other good reason." There was then no unemployment insurance benefit, but there was a social conscience. Steerage passengers in the Allan Line were warned that:

> The chief qualifications required for an emigrant are sobriety, industry and perseverance. Possessed of these, no one need despair of making a happy and comfortable home in the Dominion of Canada.

If this advice was tendered in the moralistic tone of the period, particularly when offered to the working classes, at least Hugh Allan had found it to be true. Tens of thousands of families, both before and since, have had reason to agree.

Most ships in the height of the season carried three classes of passenger, steerage, intermediate, and cabin. Steerage accommodation was more or less communal and by the seventies was little different from that originally offered in the *Canadian* and *Indian*. Families kept together but otherwise the sexes were separated. As the booklets took care to point out, the wants of "female passengers and children" were carefully attended to by stewardesses. This was an innovation for steerage and intermediate travellers. Intermediate accommodation cost three guineas more than the steerage fare but offered more privacy and better service. Whereas the steerage passengers had to provide their own bedding, plate, knife, fork, spoon and water-can – all of which could be purchased in Glasgow and Liverpool from standard outfits – the intermediate passengers had something approaching the equivalent of the modern tourist and were supplied with everything.

Food in the steerage class was wholesome, if somewhat monotonous to the modern taste. For many passengers of the period it was probably as good or better then anything in their experience because, in the first place, it was regular and cooked. The day started with fresh-baked bread from the galley, salt butter, porridge and molasses, with lots of coffee. As milk could only be had from the cow, and as one or two cows at the most were all that could be carried even on the best ships, there was none for the steerage. For one o'clock dinner, the main meal, there was soup, meat and potatoes or fish, with a variation each day. For six o'clock there was a plain supper of bread, biscuit and butter, and tea. Biscuit, of course, meant sailor's hard tack, square pantiles of incredible toughness which are not without appeal to sea appetites and sound teeth. On Sundays, always a special day at sea, there was pudding for the steerage passengers as there would be for the crew. Food was brought to the berthdeck by a steward, emigrants lining up with their plates and pannikins to be served.

In this way steerage passengers were treated with as much consideration as conditions would permit. Although the accommodation was a tremendous improvement on the cramped tweendecks of a sailing ship, where even fresh water was a luxury, the iron steamships of the seventies had severe limitations. Usually, even in summer, the Atlantic is an uncomfortable place to say the least; in bad weather a small steamer with her hatches and scuttles closed was anything but pleasant. The emigrant deck was crowded by modern standards. In bad weather when passengers were worn out with the constant rolling of the ship, there was small comfort. The stuffy atmosphere, compounded by smoky oil lamps and the nausea of seasickness, was relieved occasionally by draughts of cold air accompanied by dollops of sea-water, which somehow found its way down whatever ventilator could be trimmed to the wind. Often the entire crossing would be like this. It was a nightmare for passengers who had never seen anything bigger than the village pond, and a miserable time for the stewards who, come what may, had to cope with frayed and frightened humanity in unfamiliar surroundings. Anyone who served in the Navy in Atlantic escort ships in the Second World War will have some idea of what it was like to emigrate a century ago – except that, in any corvette or frigate, food, ventilation, heating and even bedding were better than in the narrow gutted steamships of the early Allan Line.

Occasionally, and perhaps inevitably, some ships fell below an acceptable standard. The situation came to a head in 1883 when complaints reached the pages of the *Montreal Witness* in accounts of filthy ships and incivility to passengers. As a result of these allegations the Montreal Ocean Steamship Company took the *Witness* to court in an action for libel, but lost their case. Press comment was unfavourable as, apart from the evidence presented, it was felt that the Allan Line were under government mail subsidy and should therefore have been particularly careful to provide universally high standards. Much was also made of the fact that the Allan Line conducted their case under evidence by commission, a procedure which judges quite naturally dislike; but as immigrants able to provide evidence for the Company were scattered throughout the Dominion, their testimony was taken locally by the Commissioner of Oaths. It was probably no mere coincidence that this case arose within a year of Sir Hugh's death. It is most likely that his eagle eye was greatly missed around the waterfront of Montreal. Many a chief officer had looked up from his duty to find a stocky, bearded figure of a Scots shipowner standing beside him on the crowded decks. Whatever the circumstances may have been, the case provided a clear warning to the Company that the travelling public, whether steerage or otherwise, were passengers to be cared for. This policy, a tradition seldom broken since the days of Sandy Allan and his sailing packets, was never again seriously called into question.

Sometimes steerage accommodation in the tweendecks was arranged by the erection of portable bulkheads which were put up by the ship's carpenter in Liverpool. They were later dismantled in Canada if necessary, for the loading of eastbound cargo. This sounds a lot worse than it actually was. In fact, without their knowledge passengers in some Atlantic liners travelled in this way right up till recent years. To the eye of a landsman, the neat white painted partitions and unfamiliar bunks, one above the other, afforded a better cabin than sea stories had led him to believe.

Although steerage and intermediate passengers filled the majority of berths, particularly westbound, the Allan Line always enjoyed the patronage of regular first-class travellers in both directions. These might range from the Governor General or the Prime Minister, through officials of one kind and another travelling on duty, to ordinary people of modest means. There were even a few wealthy globe-trotters who, even then, were beginning to set a trend. In 1871 the cabin fares from Quebec or Portland to Liverpool ranged from $70 to $80 according to the location and type of cabin; the rates were slightly less to Glasgow. There was a sliding scale by which children under twelve were charged at the rate of $6 for every year of their age, so that a youngster of eleven paid nearly full fare while a baby in arms travelled free. Many passengers in the first class brought their servants or perhaps a nanny for their children, who would turn the adjoining cabin into a nursery in the Victorian tradition. Servants were carried in the cabin for $50, a pleasant support for the steward and a reminder of home; but their meals were taken at a different sitting when the second table in the saloon would be graced by valets and ladies' maids.

Individual cabins in the seventies were much as they had been in the original Denny steamships. Most of them had two berths, one above the other placed fore and aft for comfort, their length fixing the room at seven feet three inches between the adjoining bulkheads. Outside cabins had a round brass scuttle which was always kept closed at sea. Otherwise light came from an overhead decklight and by means of an oil lamp which was mounted in gimbals. Hot water for personal use was brought in a copper can by the steward, and was often in limited supply. It was tipped by the user into a folding wash-stand with mirror and glass rack above and waste can below: this shared with the inevitable settee the distinction of being the most familiar item of nautical furniture until modern plumbing. The general effect, which was cosy in a cramped sort of way, was enhanced by bunk curtains and settee cover in matching velvet. The whole decor was set off by polished mahogany and brasswork, contrasting with white enamel on the deckhead above. Underfoot, a square of carpet or cocoanut matting was placed on the carefully scrubbed and whitened deck planking. As for toilets, there were separate washrooms adjacent to the ladies cabin and the gentlemen's smokeroom, but nothing *en suite;* and as yet, no baths.

In reasonable weather, first-class passengers enjoyed their trip. For many of them, people of settled position unclouded by the anxieties of emigrants, the easy ways of shipboard society provided a welcome and exciting change in life. There was an air of wonder and mystery about the sea which, associated now with regular passages, good food and attentive service to complement agreeable society, had banished the hardships of old. If the captain was a personality, which many of them were, he set the tone of the voyage. If he were dull, and long years of loneliness left their mark on many shipmasters, the social pattern tended to revolve round the doctor, officially known as the ship's surgeon. The doctor was an officer of importance; he could order medical comforts for the relief of emigrants and dispense his sympathy in the best bedside manner to the more interesting ladies in the first-class. Most seagoing surgeons were fresh from university, unmarried, and a source of interest to mothers and daughters. A few remained at sea for years but these tended to become rather eccentric.

The chief engineer also had his circle of devotees. A trip through the engine and boiler rooms with attendant hazard by nearly vertical iron ladders, elevated gratings and strange blasts of warm steamy air was pleasantly exciting for young mixed company. In a comfortable aroma of cylinder oil, passengers would be impressed by the rythmic wonder of shining rods on the most powerful machinery of the age, the marine steam engine.

The other officers, except for casual encounters, saw little of the passengers and were not encouraged to mix. As they lived in remote parts of the ship, their watchkeeping duties accentuated a tendency to retire into the private world of seamen.

One of the better known masters of the Allan Line in the seventies was Captain Joseph E. Dutton, Lieutenant Royal Naval Reserve, for many years commander of the RMS *Sardinian.* It was the period when "muscular Christianity" had a popular appeal, a philosophy which Captain Dutton embraced with all his not inconsiderable strength. Divorced from the ecclesiastical orthodoxy of the established church-goer on shore, he had found at sea the opportunity to bring his religion to a high pitch of personal evangelism. He had been known to have three additional services on Sundays, one in the forecastle at seven a.m. for the crew, ten o'clock in the steerage for the betterment of emigrants, and another in the chartroom during the first dog-watch for the spiritual navigation of his officers. Not unnaturally the sailors called him "Holy Joe," a sobriquet which was earned indeed. He baptized seven of them, by total immersion, at the Olivet Baptist Church in Montreal. To such a man, after half a lifetime of isolation in sailing ships, the command of a fine Atlantic liner brought also the delights of a captive audience of educated people. Divine service in the first-class saloon on Sundays marked the high point of his week: on one occasion, when the passenger list included eighteen clergymen on their way to a religious conference, Captain Dutton preached a highly Biblical three-decker sermon to the defenceless clerics.

A charming vignette of a cabin passage by Allan Liner in 1878 has survived in the diary of Miss Jean Glen-Airston, of Owen Sound Ontario, who left home with her father that year to visit her Scottish connections. It was the fashion for young ladies to keep diaries and scrapbooks and Jean's was in the best tradition. Not long out of school, her simple style of writing is compressed into lines of hairlike delicacy in a tiny leather-covered notebook not much bigger than a box of matches. It was her first venture into the grown-up world.

William Glen-Airston and his daughter boarded the *Sardinian* at Quebec on 20th July after a train journey from Owen Sound by way of Toronto. The Grand Trunk train was crowded and they were unable to get a seat in the Pullman. But Quebec was a wonderful scene of bustle after the pastoral life at home, enlivened for Jean by a visit from the Governor General and Lady Dufferin, who were then in residence at their favourite quarters in the Citadel, and had come down to the ship to say farewell to Sir Francis Graham, a cousin of Lady Dufferin's, who was returning to England after fishing and shooting in Canada.

Leaving Quebec at noon on Saturday in a stiff breeze, the *Sardinian* was bucking her way down the Gulf on Sunday as Jean wrote in her diary " . . . Went to church – very rough – many sick." In the saloon Captain Dutton had a smaller congregation than he would have liked. Swaying easily to the roll of his ship, he intoned "O Eternal Lord God, who alone spreadest out the Heavens and rulest the raging of the sea . . . Preserve us from the dangers of the sea . . . that we may return in safety to enjoy the blessings of the land." Doubtless there were those to whom the *Form of Prayer to be used at Sea* took on a hitherto unsuspected reality as, dodging icebergs in patches of fog, the *Sardinian* cleared the Belle Isle Strait while her passengers began to sort themselves out.

This process was greatly helped by the Captain who, nothing if not sociable, held his kettledrum every afternoon at three. This was a popular tea party on a pleasantly large scale at which everyone came to know

127

everyone else. There was Miss Graham – no relation to Lady Dufferin's cousin Sir Francis – whose father was Captain John Graham of the Allan Liner *Moravian*, now at sea westbound. He had been acclaimed for devotion to duty as "A noble British seaman" seventeen years ago when the second *Canadian* was lost in the ice in those very same waters. Then there was Mr. Tobin, of whom it is recorded that at supper he had consumed "Salt herrings and sardines, bread and butter, and lemonade," Miss Cuff of Toronto, "Who is a great talker," Mr. Brock – "Awfully handsome" – who played and sang at the piano, and the ship's doctor, who was slightly disappointing because he "Looks a good deal like Mr. Williams only not half so nice." The Baker family, Mr., Mrs. and Miss, were nautical enthusiasts who towed the breathless diarist from stem to stern of the *Sardinian*. "Saw all the engines and fireplaces," wrote Jean. After climbing to the bridge to see a four-masted sailing ship through the telescope, down they went to the steerage. Miss Glen-Airston, accustomed to life in a spacious brick house gracing 37 acres of rolling country near Owen Sound – now the Golf and Country Club – was not at all impressed. "30 to sleep in one little room," she wrote, leaning heavily on her pencil.

The days passed pleasantly and quickly. In the evenings Mr. Brock's recitals worked up boisterously to *Auld Lang Syne*, before concluding with *God Save the Queen*. One afternoon, while a few dutiful passengers were dozing through the Commander's lecture on the *Tabernacle in the Wilderness*, they were thankful to be wakened with the news that the *Moravian* was in sight and coming up fast, and that a string of coloured bunting straining at her flag halliards conveyed a loving message from a master sailor to his daughter. It was all very thrilling, as colours were dipped in salute and, with a final, deep-throated blast on their steam whistles, the ships reeled past at full speed to disappear in the ocean void.

A few days later, approaching Londonderry on a fine morning with a head wind, it was perplexing to admit that there were "Such a number of young gentlemen on board." Unfortunately the doctor had failed to qualify as one of them, being "Not very nice" and "Too big for his boots." He had stood on his dignity at the familiar greeting "How goes it Doc? and the consensus was that he disliked Canadian girls. Miss Cuff was all for showing the doctor "How a Canadian girl can go," but apparently it was all talk.

After the Grand Tour of Scotland Miss Jean and her father embarked for Canada a few weeks later, boarding the Allan Liner *Austrian* at Glasgow on a wet and windy September morning. The travellers had been up at four as the brougham called at Carlibar House in the green fields of Renfrewshire at Barrhead. But a discerning young lady with experience of who's who on shipboard was not too tired to notice a distinct improvement in Allan Line medical officers. There were only 28 passengers in the cabin, and not many in the steerage, so that young Doctor Shaw's duties were light enough to permit of an introduction to Miss Glen-Airston of Owen Sound. He had not long graduated from Glasgow University; and a confidential notation ran, "Had a long talk with the doctor – a very nice fellow."

By mid-Atlantic there had been time to look around, to enjoy a polite stroll with the captain and a longer one with the doctor. In this ship the master had not shared Holy Joe's concern for the spiritual welfare of his officers to quite the same extent, the fourth mate putting his dog-watch to good use by inviting young ladies to tea. On the 26th, with a Miss MacLachlan who appeared from nowhere, there were more walks with the doctor, culminating in "Some singing behind the wheelhouse." It was very cold as they sighted the coast of Newfoundland but three young people right aft were cosy enough as they watched the taffrail rise and fall to the glorious ocean while porpoises gambolled in the wake. Nearer Montreal kindly Mrs Newport, who occupied a neighbouring cabin, issued motherly invitations to stay for a day or two at her house – the ship would be in port, she knew – and a last walk with Dr. Shaw did not include Miss MacLachlan. In the privacy of her cabin Jean confided to her diary that "The water looks lovely at night, especially behind the wheelhouse; remained about two hours – Dr. Shaw is very agreeable, sweet and nice and handsome, a most charming companion – sorry when tea-time came." Holy Joe would have been pleased at their conversation which apparently took a religious turn, for the very last entry in the diary is an interesting riddle:

Why is a kiss like a sermon?Because it consists of two heads and a very close appreciation.

On arrival at Montreal Dr. Shaw was persuaded to sit for his portrait to William Notman, the foremost photographer in Canada. He sits easily enough, upright in a straight-backed chair, with an air of modest confidence which would not pass unnoticed in Owen Sound, where an impatient young lady was bubbling over with anticipation. But it would never do for people of good family to rush things. There were more voyages to Scotland when Dr. Shaw set up his professional plate in Glasgow a couple of years later.

One such voyage was distinguished by the presence of the Lyceum Company on a North American theatrical tour. No captain would allow such an opportunity to pass without their inclusion in the traditional charity concert usually held on the last night at sea – certainly not

Captain James Wylie, Commodore master of the Allan Royal Mail Line. Favourite benefactors included the Liverpool Seamen's Orphanage which, considering that over 3,000 British seamen lost their lives every year in the seventies, was a worthy cause. As their Prospectus put it:

> A very large number of these children have lost their fathers by the perils of the sea in crossing the Atlantic . . . and no more fitting tribute of gratitude can be shown to the Almighty Hand, who brings the ship in safety to her journey's end, than by helping to support the children who are left fatherless by the necessities of the seaman's life.

Small wonder that some seamen, such as Captain Dutton, found a deep and abiding faith in religion. On the practical side, and the Victorians were very practical, the Orphanage supplied liners with blank forms which, with appropriate insertion by hand, could be made up into entertainment programs:

RMS .... *Parisian*
Date............................... 27th September 1884

Oh who will aid the Sailor's Orphan Child?
We will, whose names are on the other side.

There followed eighteen signatures of performers who, under the chairmanship of the *Parisian's* medical officer, offered items ranging from songs, recitations and humorous recitals to a rendering of Richmond's Address to his Soldiers. These were given with self-conscious feeling by amateurs in the presence of famous actors and actresses, and with appropriate reticence by charitable professionals. The program is signed by Ellen Terry and George Alexander among others, Mr. Alexander autographing Miss Jean Glen-Airston's copy with a cheerful remembrance of a pleasant voyage in the *Parisian,* " . . . Not a little of which was due to the bright, pleasant and pretty ways of Miss Glen-Airston. May we soon meet again."

By this time Jean Glen-Airston had almost a proprietary interest in the Allan Line: it is fitting that her romantic shipboard encounter ended in a happy marriage. Dr. and Mrs. William J. Shaw settled in Govan where they became well-liked. Tragically, tuberculosis, the scourge of city life in Scotland at the period, carried off Dr. Shaw within a few years. He died of "consumption," probably contracted tending his patients in the crowded tenements of shipbuilding Glasgow. Jean returned to Canada with their son, living in Owen Sound until she died in 1935.

Meanwhile in Montreal Sir Hugh's death brought other changes than his brother Andrew's succession to the firm of H & A Allan. Of Sir Hugh's three sons, Alexander, the eldest, was not cut out for business.

He had been settled at Brockville in Ontario where he married Miss Eva Travers, daughter of the bank manager. Their home at 112 King Street, a graceful, white-painted frame house of the ornate style then in fashion, stands among lawns and shade trees today as it did then, although the family has long since died out. Sir Hugh's youngest son, "Master Arthur" of the *Peruvian's* passenger list on that fateful journey to Scotland before his father's death, was yet a schoolboy. As it turned out he never had the chance to show what he could do, as he died accidentally in a fire some years afterwards.

It was on his second son, Hugh Andrew, that Sir Hugh pinned his hopes. Born in 1860, he had already entered the firm after a very different type of education from the village schooling which had nourished his father. Following a thorough grounding at the up-and-coming Bishop's College at Lennoxville, in Eastern Townships of Quebec, he had been sent to Paris for finishing. But 'Old' Andrew, as we must now call him, also had a growing family in his house in Peel Street – among whom his son, Hugh Andrew, who was a year or two older than his cousin of the same name, was already in the firm. To avoid confusion which might otherwise arise, and there was never any in connection with their heritage, Sir Hugh's second son changed his baptismal name to Hugh Montagu Allan.

Montagu Allan, as he was usually called, fell heir to the property of *Ravenscrag* on the understanding that he would eventually succeed to the business. He was twenty-one at the time, an athletic young bachelor who rode to hounds with the Montreal Hunt, loved games and athletics, and was popular in society. He was already involved in a multitude of business concerns as well as the immediate family connection with shipping. It was a prospect requiring rather a different outlook from the earthy, hard-driving genius who had built them up. It was one thing to make a fortune in the great days of the entrepeneurs, quite another to expand it, or even to hang on, in the face of ever-increasing competition. But all this lay ahead. In October, 1892, when Hugh Montagu Allan married Marguerite Ethel MacKenzie of Montreal, the Allans of *Ravenscrag* were beginning a new period: they would be at the centre of social life in eastern Canada until the death of an entire lifestyle in the changing world of the nineteen thirties.

CHAPTER EIGHT

Twenty Knots to Canada

"Wi' wind and tide fair i' your tail,
Right on ye scud your sea-way;"

R.B.
Address to the Unco Guid

In 1883 the tide of emigration was running strongly. That spring the *Glasgow Herald* advertised that:

The best routes to all parts of America are those of the Allan Line, by which there travelled to America in 1882 no less than 55,215 passengers. The splendid steamers of this line (the longest established on the Atlantic) have acquired a reputation for comfort, speed and safety. A special feature of the line is the accommodation provided for and attention bestowed on the intermediate and steerage passenger.

This volume of passenger traffic, greater than that of any other British company, had not been achieved without energetic and capable management. Competition had attracted other shipowners since the Allans had finally demonstrated that steam navigation to the St. Lawrence was both practicable and profitable.

The first competitor was the Inman Line, which in December 1867

had been awarded the British mail contract for service between Queenstown and Halifax in place of a lapsed Cunard contract. The Inmans
owned the Liverpool company which had built the first really successful
iron screw steamer on the North Atlantic – the *City of Glasgow* so much
admired by the Allans when contracting with Denny for the first
Canadian – and the Inman entry to Halifax was potentially a threat. This
was overcome in 1871 when the Allan Line wrested the Halifax contract
from Inman and opened a new service from Liverpool by way of
Queenstown to Halifax, Norfolk (Virginia) and Baltimore.

Direct sailings from Glasgow had started in 1861, a service which
from 1870 called at St. John's, Newfoundland in August and September.
In 1873 the Newfoundland commitment was switched to the Liverpool
and Baltimore service which was fortnightly in summer. In winter the
Newfoundland calls were made by feeder service from Halifax, with the
wooden screw steamer *Newfoundland* of 900 tons, built at Quebec with
machinery made on the Tyne. Sailings were fortnightly, ice and weather
permitting; fares from Halifax to Newfoundland were $20 cabin, $15
intermediate and $6 in the steerage.

This gave the Allan Line a stronger footing in Halifax. The footing
became even firmer after 1876 when the Intercolonial railway to Montreal was completed. But the Canadian railway was nearly twice as long
as the line from Montreal to Portland through Maine – an important
factor when trains ran at thirty miles an hour. The earlier line continued
useful for much of the British mail to Canada, as well as being a handy
transhipment point for Boston and New York.

At the British end of the service London mail went to Northern
Ireland by rail and fast cross-channel steamer. Allan liners, from Liverpool or Glasgow, connected with the mail train at Moville, a convenient
place near the mouth of Loch Foyle, which saved the ship from going
right up to Londonderry. By a similar time-saving arrangement at the
Canadian end, Allan liners bound for Montreal stopped briefly in the
open roadstead of Rimouski. Here the bags were put ashore by tender
for dispatch to Montreal by Intercolonial.

In 1872 another competitor joined the fray, the Liverpool and Missis-
sippi Steamship Company. This firm later became the Mississipi and
Dominion Line and eventually, as the White Star Dominion Line, it
became a formidable rival. Like the Inman Line the the Dominion came
into the Canadian trade after doing well elsewhere. Since 1870 they had
been running to New Orleans but had been persuaded by a group of
Montreal shippers to open additional sailings to the St. Lawrence. This
was a direct frontal assault which the Allans were loth to suffer without
retaliation, but their counter attack was unsuccessful. It was opened in
November 1872 when the *Peruvian* sailed from Glasgow and Liverpool

for New Orleans. Unfortunately, the second sailing, a month later, came to grief. The *Germany*, which was a vessel originally ordered by other owners and taken over during building by the Allans, was wrecked near Bordeaux, where she was to complete loading before departure for New Orleans. Having made their gesture, and being short of ships in the meantime, the Allan Line withdrew from New Orleans. It was realized, however, that something of the kind would be necessary to employ surplus Canadian ships out of season, should they ever have enough. By similar reasoning the Dominion Line found the St. Lawrence to be attractive in the summer slump to New Orleans, and they continued to prosper in both trades.

Another competitor was the Canada Steam Shipping Company, originally founded at Montreal in 1867 with a small fleet of iron sailing ships. It was too late for sail to be profitable in the St. Lawrence – to make reasonable passages they had to take a tug from the Gulf, a trip which was costly – and before long it was realized that either they must go into steam or face bankruptcy. After flirting with chartered steamers by way of experiment, they took the plunge and built the iron screw steamships *Lake Nepigon, Lake Champlain* and *Lake Megantic* which made their debut in 1875. Within a year these vessels were sailing to Baltimore in competition with the Allan Line. Within two years they were running to Portland in winter. Known as the "Beaver" Line because of the emblem on their houseflag, the Canada Steam Shipping Company survived on the North Atlantic through many changes, until in 1899 it was taken over by Elder Dempster, who in turn were absorbed by Canadian Pacific in 1903.

In meeting these challenges the Allans were persistent but, of necessity, cautious. Experience had taught them to be wary of mail contracts which at times had placed unreasonable penalties on delay. To this extent the Canadian government had influenced the years when shipwrecks came in awful succession. Politicians naturally wanted a good service, and within the limitations of a new country with more land then money they were prepared to pay for it. But the coal bills for fast ships were gargantuan, while the size of their bunkers cut into earning capacity. If, in the uncertainties of political life, the mail subsidy should be withdrawn, the Allans might be left with hopelessly uneconomic tonnage at a time when competition was growing. With this in mind, they built a number of interesting if not spectacular ships, and modernized others. By this thrifty policy the Allan Line steadily increased its share of the available business and although threatened by others of like mind they actually strengthened their position.

Among additions of the seventies, the *Sarmatian* has been mentioned as the ship which returned Sir Hugh's body to Canada in 1882. Built by

Steele of Greenock in 1871, the *Sarmatian* was the first of the fleet to have a compound engine. This type of engine, although powerful, was disappointing in coal consumption because of an unusually complicated arrangement with four cylinders in horizontal and vertical pairs. Nevertheless, as the best Allan liner up till that time the *Sarmatian* made a great impression. Like many Allan ships she was designed for Admiralty use in time of war. With a speed of 14 knots she was chartered for tooping in the Ashanti War of 1874 where she came to official notice as the fastest transport in that African campaign. Because of these virtues she was chosen to convey royalty to Canada when the Marquess of Lorne and Princess Louise relieved the Dufferins at Government House in Ottawa.

Their arrival was treated with even more than the ceremony usually accorded to the Governor General. When the *Sarmatian* anchored in Halifax Harbour on 25th November 1878 a chilly afternoon was enlightened by a brave show of flags and the stirring sound of musical salutes from the flagship of the Royal Navy, HMS *Duke of Edinburgh.* The Commander-in-Chief in his barge, escorted by the boats of the squadron, went to the mail steamer to receive her distinguished passengers for a state landing. When the young couple set foot on Canadian soil – he was thirty-three and she was thirty – they were welcomed by Sir John A. Macdonald, who stood alone "Pale but erect" as the papers recorded. He was recovering from an exhausting political campaign climaxed by his re-election as Prime Minister of Canada. It was on this journey from Ottawa by Intercolonial that Sir John's exhaustion had been alleviated by a favourite palliative as he and Sir Hugh Allan rehashed the railway rumpus of 1873. The great shipowner was not to be left out in paying respects to the new Governor General and his elegant wife, who was a daughter of Queen Victoria. Sir Hugh was gratified to find that it had been a highly successful voyage; Princess Louise was delighted with the *Sarmatian* and travelled in her whenever the opportunity arose.

With the success of the *Sarmatian* the company returned to Steele for a larger model, which sailed her maiden voyage from Liverpool to Quebec in October 1872. This was the *Polynesian,* a ship with a peculiar fascination for thousands of people who came in her to make their homes in North America. She had one outstanding characteristic, never to be forgotten to this day – her propensity for rolling. All steamers of the period were lively at sea, but the *Polynesian* would "Roll on the wet grass," as sailors said. This attribute promptly brought the nickname "Rolling Poly." One seafaring Allan, recalling the days of his youth when sailing from the Clyde to Boston, remembered that she "Started her gyrations off Ailsa Craig and didn't stop until she was off Marblehead." In 1893, after an extensive refit, the *Polynesian* was renamed *Lauren-*

tian, mostly probably in an effort to conceal her well known antics from prospective passengers. It was a change of name which did nothing for a change of heart, and "Rolling Poly" she remained until the end. But her luck held and, although wrecked near Cape Race in 1909, there was no loss of life.

In addition to this building program the Company refitted some existing ships which, well-built and maintained, were worth considerable expenditure without running into the cost of new construction. In some cases this involved ship surgery by which the hull was cut in half and, with addition of some fifty feet of new middle body, was rivetted up again to form a longer vessel. This improved propulsive efficiency and increased carrying capacity. Further economies resulted with the installation of new boilers and compound machinery. In 1875, when the *European* entered a Birkenhead drydock on a falling tide, the surgical treatment was applied as first aid. Despite the protests of her captain the dockmaster insisted that the vessel should enter – a decision which was within his responsibility from the moment when the first lines were passed ashore and the ship was squared up for the keelblocks. As the captain had feared, the *European* grounded on the sill of the dock gate and, as the tide ebbed, she broke her back. Many weeks later she came out with a stretched hull and a new compound engine.

By the mid-seventies the Allan Line had enough ships to cope with the Canadian trade at the height of the summer season and some to spare in winter. Among interesting developments at this period the Allan liner *Caspian* brought the first frozen meat into Liverpool, a consignment of 12 tons which foreshadowed new ways. But opposition was hard on their heels and when, also in 1874, the Donaldson Line began to dabble in the St. Lawrence, the Allans once more looked southwards. Whether or not subsequent developments were in direct retaliation, the Donaldson Line was a progressive Scottish company not to be ignored, and they had been trading to South America since 1858.

In October 1876 the *Glasgow Herald* carried an unfamiliar Allan Line sailing notice under "Steamers to the River Plate." Although this service was managed from Glasgow, and the Montreal office had no direct part, it must be seen also as complementary to the Canadian trade. Both services left Glasgow from Plantation Quay – a name recalling Scotland's brief West Indian prosperity – and from their office which had now moved to 70 Great Clyde Street, the firm of J & A Allan made a good start by shipping to Monte Video and Buenos Ayres. Captain James Allan had retired and it was Alexander, youngest of the five brothers, who now governed the firm. His partner was Nathaniel Dunlop, who had risen steadily by ability. As confidential clerk to James in 1853, he had handled the Denny contract for the building of the first

Canadian. By coincidence Mr. Dunlop started the South American run with the third *Canadian,* at that time only three years old. At last the ill-luck which dogged the name would surely be broken! It was, but only by a second chance not vouchsafed to either of her unfortunate predecessors. Returning from Canada to take up the River Plate loading berth, the *Canadian* stranded off Larne in the early hours of 18th September 1876. Fortunately Captain MacLean had realized his danger at the last moment. The engineers were frantically responding to "Full astern" as the vessel struck; after a few days the *Canadian* was refloated without serious damage. At the subsequent Board of Trade enquiry the master was found to have made an error of judgement, but was not otherwise censured. Typical of the good relationship between the Allan Line and a trusted officer of fifteen years service, it was Nathaniel Dunlop whose testimony in favour of Captain MacLean influenced the court to disregard this unfortunate professional lapse. On 13th November, the *Canadian* opened the South American run from Glasgow as advertised.

As an interesting sidelight on the St. Lawrence trade, the report of this enquiry notes that the *Canadian* was valued at £80,000 and that she had 1,700 tons of cargo including lumber, general merchandise and 100 head of cattle. There were 69 in the crew, 5 cattlemen and 18 passengers. To modern eyes it is perhaps strange that passengers should be carried with cattle but, before the advent of modern food production meat on the hoof went a long way to supplement the British market. In a typical season 150,000 head of cattle, sheep and horses left Montreal. Cattle pens on deck were as familiar a sight as containers today. As for the passengers, they were used to animals and expected to find them at sea as elsewhere.

With the success of the *Canadian* running to Monte Video and Buenos Ayres, it was fitting that an Allan liner built for the Canadian trade should be named *Buenos Ayrean.* This remarkable ship, built by Denny in 1880, was the first Atlantic liner to be built of steel, as distinct from iron. This innovation brought high strength and ductility, with predictable and uniform standards of quality, to the basic shipbuilding material. It enabled ships to be lighter in weight, with correspondingly greater earning capacity. Aesthetically the *Buenos Ayrean* was an ugly duckling compared to the swan-like Denny ships of old, but times were changing. With her heavy superstructure and straight stem the profile looks severe; it looks even stranger in Denny's original rigging plan, which shows three widely-spaced masts carrying barque rig.

With options available in South America, the Allan Line could now respond boldly in the St. Lawrence. Although the fleet had been modernized, competitors were running much the same type of ship and the time was ripe for the Allans to introduce a vessel which would outclass the opposition. With assurance from the Canadian government that the mail subsidy would be continued, it was decided to build a large ship able to lift a big cargo on moderate draft, while appealing to passengers with a speed and standard of comfort never previously available to Canada. This concept was brought together in preliminary designs by Mr. Wallace, engineer superintendent at Liverpool under R.G.Allan, in the last specification to benefit from the experience of Sir Hugh. The final technical design came from the board of A.C.Kirk, a prominent marine engineer who was engaged as consultant. Kirk had been the first to introduce the triple-expansion engine, when working with the famous engineer John Elder of Glasgow. He was now the senior partner in the historic firm of Robert Napier & Son. Robert Napier had died in 1876, honoured as the patriarch of Clyde marine engineers; but he had trained some of the best men in the industry since the days when he built the first Cunarders, among them Kirk. It was therefore no surprise when Napier's yard got the order for the new Allan Liner.

Nine months later, on 4th November 1881, there was a fine gathering of Allans on the launching platform, but only two of the original brothers. Bryce had died in 1874 after laying out the property of Aros at Tobermory on the Island of Mull – a beautiful estate which he never lived to enjoy. James died three months before the launch after retirement to his Skelmorlie mansion, whence he could see the familiar blue-white-and-red houseflag passing to an fro against the backdrop of the Argyll hills and the Firth of Clyde. Andrew remained in Montreal and it was Sir Hugh who came to Scotland to preside with Alexander from the Glasgow office and his nephew R.G. Allan from Liverpool. The *Glasgow Herald* reported that Alexander's daughter Janie "Cut away the vessel" and that Mrs. Houston Boswell – Sir Hugh's daughter Phoebe – named the new ship *Parisian*.

There were the usual complimentary speeches by owners and builders, interesting among other points for Kirk's authoritative remark that the Allans had introduced the "Flush or covered upper deck" to Atlantic liners with the *Hibernian* of 1861. This arrangement, commonly known as the "Spar deck" had been at the back of Sir Hugh's mind since 1839, when he nearly perished in the old *Liverpool*. An Atlantic gale had filled her decks to the top of her high bulwarks; in 1865 the British liner *London* foundered in the Bay of Biscay with heavy loss of life from the same cause. By then it was clear that the type was dangerous, but under existing tonnage rules shipowners were penalised for the spar deck. The Allans persuaded the British Board of Trade to exempt such space from tonnage, thereby producing a strong financial inducement to build safer ships.

The *Parisian* had also profited from the antics of the "Rolling Poly" in being the first liner to have bilge keels, appendages projecting for some two-thirds of the length of the ship, which did help to dampen the roll. In replying to these compliments, and particularly to the part of the Allan Line in pioneering steel construction, Sir Hugh was in great form, remarking that:

> In the first place, as in the *Buenos Ayrean,* the material is steel; the best, and like most things that are the best, the dearest they could build a ship of.

It was the first time that the old man had seen the launch of an Allan liner, and the last.

In February 1881, as squalls of snow swept down from the "Sleeping Warrior" as she passed Saltcoats, the *Parisian* made 15 knots on her trial run under Captain Wylie. All the top shipping people were on board – including from Canada Mr. Smith the Deputy Minister of Marine and Fisheries – to witness the pride of the Allan Line at sea. Kirk had fitted her with four double-ended marine boilers supplying steam at 70 pounds per square inch to a three-cylinder compound engine of Gothic proportions which proved to be magnificently reliable. The *Parisian* completed 150 voyages without serious trouble. In appearance, the *Parisian* was distinguished by two funnels and four masts, heavily rigged in the fashion of the time with yards on the foremast and the main. Structurally she had double bottoms and ten watertight bulkheads, which added emphasis to Mr. Kirk's remark that his creation was "The largest steel merchant ship afloat."

After her maiden voyage to Boston, the *Parisian* entered the port of Montreal for the first time on 10th May 1881. On the following day, although the reporter was writing bilge about his keels, the *Montreal Gazette* announced her as "The largest vessel, with one exception, plying between Britain and North America." This account stated that:

> The saloon is amidships while on all other vessels it is aft. This prevents the pitching of the steamer being noticed at all and as the patent rollers with which the ship is furnished prevent any rolling, it is claimed that meals can be taken with as much comfort as on shore. Another noticeable feature is the addition of a promenade deck being nine feet above the spar deck. The saloon is elegantly furnished, a particular kind of leather is used in the decoration of the pillars and sides; the chairs are of walnut, the floors of oak and ash. A large music room or library overlooking the saloon is a very agreeable inovation on the old plan.

The public filed round her in droves, marvelling at innovations which included the sailors' "forecastle" right aft among the steerage passengers, paying 25 cents to charity for the privilege.

The Company was not long in bringing out a magnificent coloured lithograph of the *Parisian*. Over the caption "Allan Royal Mail Line," it is a classic advertisement of instant appeal. Few people then went to sea for pleasure and on the Atlantic they were only too well aware of peril; what they wanted was confidence. Looking at this picture of the great ship slicing easily through a lumpy sea under steam and sail, prospective passengers could see at a glance that they would reach Quebec, Halifax, Boston or Baltimore – or anywhere else for that matter – without the slightest trouble.

Despite the success of the *Parisian* the prospects for a heavy investment in more ships of the type were uncertain. Competition was held at bay for the moment but the Canadian government, fired by the progress of fast liners with the mail to and from Britain and New York, were rapidly coming to the view that Canada should be similarly served. This was all very well but with the difficulties of navigation on the St. Lawrence route and the transient nature of the mail contracts, the Allan Line might well find themselves repeating their early difficulties if they took the plunge. To make matters worse other shipowners were hovering around, some of them with more hope than experience. One powerful group without any sea-going ships posed the greatest threat of all. This was the Canadian Pacific Railway Company, which in 1881, the year before Sir Hugh's death, had revived old fears in the possibilities of their charter. This, in the *Statutes of Canada,* 44 Victoria Cap 1, empowered them to:

> ... Acquire, own, hold, charter, work and run steam and other vessels upon any navigable water which the Canadian Pacific Railway may reach or connect with.

As yet they had made no oceanic use of these powers, but their existence was in everyone's mind in the ensuing decade.

In July 1886, in addition to calling for tenders for a mail service of 15 knots with ships similar to the *Parisian,* the Canadian government tacked on a flier inviting bids for 16, 17 and 18 knots. In no time at all someone had coined the phrase, "Twenty knots to Canada." For the time being the Allans were able to hold their own, but they were understandably reluctant to venture into anything faster than the *Parisian.*

Despite misgivings about high speeds the Allan Line tendered for a service to average 17 knots at sea, a realistic proposal which would have cut the time from Moville to Rimouski to 5 days and 16 hours. Unfortunately for the Allans, and indeed for Canada, the slogan "Twenty Knots" was cleverly used by a London shipping group, Anderson & Anderson. They tendered for ships capable of steaming at 20 knots. In

140

Atlantic conditions this maximum would be necessary for any vessel hoping to average 17 knots at sea and it is doubtful whether the London offer would have been any better than the guaranteed speed of the more cautious Allans. But the damage was done. The very mention of 20 knots in the specification fired the government with enthusiasm and they closed with the offer. Perhaps to Sir John A. Macdonald's surprise, months of correspondence went on without official confirmation and on 6th March 1889 the Prime Minister sent a wire to the Andersons summarizing his position:

> Govt. propose one hundred and four thousand (pounds) and outside mail earnings . . . vessels not less than 6,500 tons, first class equipments, perform voyage speed 20 knots in moderate weather – steamers sail from Southampton or Plymouth to Quebec or Halifax and back, visit Canadian ports only . . . answer quickly

Again there was a long delay. When the Andersons' telegram came on 12th October 1889 Sir John must have been astonished and dismayed:

> With regret we surrender to you the Atlantic contract you placed in our hands as we can no longer reckon on the cordial cooperation of the Canadian Pacific Railway, Sir George Stephen having intimated that he has ceased to take an interest in our scheme.

The fact was that the Andersons had counted on CPR financing. To Sir George Stephen, President of the CPR, and to Sir Donald Smith, his cousin, who was a director, the Anderson scheme began to be seen in another light. They backed off at the last moment. In a letter to W.C.Van Horne, the CPR general manager at Montreal, Sir George Stephen wrote on 14th October from London:

> I send you a copy of a letter which I have received from Andersons' and a copy of reply to same.
>
> In an interview I had with them, they were almost rude in urging that Sir Donald and myself were bound, in fairness to them, to subscribe our promised £50,000 apiece to their scheme, even if the government finally decided to compel the Company to stop its trains at Saint John. I was annoyed at what appeared to me to be their unreasonableness, and told them that, if they approached the question in that frame of mind I would not discuss the matter with them; that nothing would induce me to interest myself in an enterprise the benefits of which would go to the Grand Trunk, to the entire exclusion during the winter months of the CPR.
>
> The impression made upon my mind by the interview with them is that they feel themselves utterly unable to float the scheme without

active influence and cooperation of Sir Donald and myself. In fact it looks as if they could do very little themselves, either directly or indirectly – financially I mean – and you will observe from the tone of my reply to them that I pretty plainly hinted that, in surrendering the contract to the Govt., they acted hastily and as if they were anxious for a pretext for the course they say they have pursued. How all this will end I do not know. I am afraid, if Andersons fail, the whole scheme will fall through. It seems hopeless to persuade the Allans to provide such a service as is required. They seem to have a hankering after something betwixt and between that would be, in my judgement, a failure from the outset. If the Allans only had the pluck to offer to supply the service provided by the Anderson contract, I should be less concerned about the failure of the Andersons.

Well might Sir George Stephen write "If only" to Van Horne. There were a number of "Ifs" besides the "Pluck" of the Allans; the policies of the CPR, well illustrated here, were extremely far-sighted. It was to their advantage at this stage to let shipowners compete for the doubtful profits of the "Fast Line." Perhaps, at the back of Sir George's mind, was the thought that if the Allans or the Andersons built new ships, despite the mail subsidy they still had to compete for freight with other established lines such as the Dominion, Donaldson and Beaver. In the end, CPR might pick up the survivor on favourable terms. But the Allan Line, privately financed and conservatively directed, was in no mood to risk its existence. One other interesting point emerges from the above letter – the continuing railway influence. In 1889 the CPR were completing their short line to the coast from Montreal to Saint John, N.B. with a view to encouragement of that port in winter. The Intercolonial Railway to Halifax, although much longer, was a government line likely to be supported at any cost by subsidized shipping using Halifax. Thus the projected 20 knot service would be of small benefit to the CPR. The probability is that this, as much as anything, influenced Sir George to hold his hand on the Atlantic.

If the CPR was cautious for the moment on the North Atlantic, they had already exercised their shipping option on the Pacific. In 1886, no sooner had the railway been completed to Port Moody than Stephen chartered a sailing ship, the barque *W.B.Flint* for an experimental voyage from Yokohama to Vancouver. This turned out well and in the following year Canadian Pacific went into shipping in earnest by inaugurating a regular service between Vancouver, Yokohama, Shanghai and Hong Kong using the former Cunard liners *Abyssinia, Parthia* and *Batavia* under charter. In 1888 three more ships were chartered and the Pacific service was intensified.

In July 1889 the CPR was awarded the (British) mail contract across the Pacific on condition that they should build three 18-knot steamers to provide a monthly service under subsidy of £60,000 a year. This was the beginning of the "All Red Route," a dream which had been simmering in mercantile, Admiralty and Imperial minds throughout the eighties and was now approaching reality under the moguls of the Canadian Pacific Railway. It had also been in Sir Hugh's mind in 1873 when he struggled for the railway charter, and there was a touch of unconscious irony about an advertisement which appeared in the *Glasgow Herald* of 9th March 1891, immediately under the usual long list of Allan Line sailings on the Atlantic:

ROUND THE WORLD FOR £120
Tours arranged by
CANADIAN PACIFIC RAILWAY
Starting from Liverpool per
RMS *Empress of Japan* in April
RMS *Empress of China* in May

This was a wonderful stroke of business. Sailing from England in the new white *Empresses* on their maiden voyage to take up their station, passengers could circle the world by sea and rail always, except for the homeward run across the Atlantic, under the colours of the CPR. Its houseflag – three red and three white squares in a chequer pattern – would soon become as familiar to seafarers as the Allan tricolour. When the first *Empress* was commissioned under the chequered flag, someone asked Van Horne whether there was any special significance to his design, "Three of a kind" perhaps? Van Horne retorted that "Three of a kind" was not a good enough hand and if that had been the intention nothing short of a "Straight flush" would have been good enough for the CPR.

The construction of the three *Empresses* encouraged proponents of the Atlantic "Fast Line" and, as early as 1889, the Canadian Government asked their designer for a comparable specification suitable for completion of the China mail and trans-Canadian railway by an Atlantic link. The key figure here was Archibald Bryce Douglas, managing director of Vickers, Sons and Maxim at Barrow-in-Furness, who was something of the same type as A.C. Kirk, designer of the *Parisian*. Whether or not Douglas would have been successful as a ship operator he was at the peak of his career as a naval architect when he took the *Empress* contract to Vickers, and these efficient and beautiful ships fully justified his reputation. In these circumstances it is probable that his Atlantic mail contract would have materialized, had it not been for Douglas' untimely death on 5th April 1891 following a stroke. He had been attending trials of the *Empress of Japan* on the Clyde measured mile.

Although the Allan Line were not overtly enthusiastic about the "Fast Line" concept, which they thought to be too much of a gamble, they could not afford to be left out of the running. In 1892, they put in a bid for a 20-knot service for a subsidy of £5,000 per round voyage or £260,000 a year. This was done only at the insistence of government: the Allans pointed out that they would much prefer to establish a 16-knot service for $750,000. Whether unluckily or otherwise, this 20-knot scheme was defeated by a lower tender from Furness of West Hartlepool whose price was £200,000. In his *History of the Canadian Pacific Line* Frank C. Bowen says of this episode:

> ... The (Canadian) Post Office were delighted at the idea of knocking £60,000 off the Allan offer until they discovered that Furness insisted on a four per cent guarantee on a capital of a million and a quarter (pounds)

With the collapse of this negotiation, the Allan proposal was allowed to lie dormant, probably with the acquiescence of the Company. Considering the vacillating actions of the Canadian Government the Allan Line could be excused for a reluctance to invest in new and costly ships of uneconomic speed. So far, tenders had been offered by shipbuilders of high technical reputation and by other groups distinguished mainly by hopeful financing, but nothing had been heard from experienced Atlantic shipowners such as the Donaldson or Dominon Lines. This point of view was emphasized in 1893 when yet another scheme, equally sterile, came from Robert Napier & Sons for an improved *Parisian* of 18 knots.

The problem was mainly economic, but not entirely so. In an editorial of 18th October 1892 the *Montreal Gazette* noted that:

> The scheme put up by Messrs. Anderson of London fell through from inability to complete the necessary financial arrangements. . . . The later effort in which Mr. Bryce Douglas, as representative of a shipbuilding company, was concerned also failed to mature; and the terms proposed by the Allan Company in response to the call for tenders are understood to be considerably above the sum the Government felt warranted in asking Parliament to vote.
>
> Our dispatch from Washington yesterday contained particulars . . . of a (New York) contract for vessels of the highest speed, probably more than twenty knots, and the subsidy to be paid is $1,250,000 for two trips weekly each way. Now it must be obvious that if the United States Government deems the expenditures of a million and a quarter

dollars yearly to obtain an independent fast service, money well invested, Canada must be prepared to hold out larger inducement. . . . Nearly forty years ago the Old Province of Canada appropriated $225,000 in encouragement of a steamship service to the St. Lawrence, a sum afterwards increased, and if the small population of Ontario and Quebec at that time found the investment of this money profitable, assuredly the Dominon of today can well afford to pay a liberal sum for the pride and profit of an Atlantic service unsurpassed in any part of the world.

Pride or profit? Pride was involved in envy of the United States but there was a heavy financial risk and, despite improvements in pilotage and lighthouses, some navigational hazard. These were not to be compared with the risks facing Sir Hugh and his brothers at the founding of the Montreal Ocean Steamship Company when they built the *Canadian* before they knew about the subsidy, but perhaps something of that spirit had died with the Old Man. Perhaps also the crash of his railway hopes in 1873 had warned the Allans that never again must they go in deeply.

Meantime Imperial authorities were disappointed that the Canadian Government had been unable to round out the China Mail contract with better service on the Atlantic. The Allan Line, prevented from modernizing their fleet, carried on at 15 knots with a subsidy of $125,000 little more than a tenth part of the United States subsidy. While matters were at this stage another hopeful entrepreneur came on the scene, this time from Australia. He was James Huddart, who owned a line of steamers sailing from Sydney to Vancouver. Huddart succeeded in negotiating an agreement with the Canadian Government by which he would supply four 20-knot ships for a subsidy of $250,000 a year. Despite apparently favourable terms, this arrangement also came to nothing, partly because the St. Lawrence shipping community took care to point out that Huddart lived on the other side of the world and that he had no experience on the Atlantic. In the long run he too was unable to find the money.

These abortive negotiations, characterized by random and almost desperate approaches from the Canadian Government, were extremely frustrating to the Allans. Starting under Sir John A. Macdonald, scheme after scheme rose and fell after his death in 1891, carrying on under his successor Sir John Abbott – of railway memory – and into Sir John Thompson's ministry of 1892. The "Fast Line" policy was firmly rooted in Conservative hopes and it continued with increasing momentum as a result of the Ottawa Conference of 1894. This great meeting, attended by representatives of Australia and New Zealand as well as Britain, met under the aegis of the Canadian Government to discuss preferential trade within the Empire, including the "All Red Route." Among various resolutions it was noted that:

> The Conference learns with interest of the steps now being taken by Canada to secure a first class mail and passenger service . . . it regards such an uninterupted through line of swift and superior communication between Australasia and Great Britain . . . as of paramount importance to the development of intercolonial trade and communications, and to the unity and stability of the Empire as a whole.

Sir MacKenzie Bowell succeeded Thompson as Prime Minister in December 1894, and still the Conservative hopes rolled on. By this time the British government were anxious to close the gap in the Empire lifeline. On 21st November 1895, the Colonial Secretary wrote to the Governor General, Lord Aberdeen, outlining proposals on steamship policy arising from the Ottawa Conference. It was a long letter, advocating the 20-knot service and for the first time offering British assistance with the Atlantic mail subsidy provided that the Canadian Government speeded up the transcontinental railway. Doubtless this raised an eyebrow or two when it became known in the CPR boardroom at the Montreal Windsor Station. The Colonial Secretary's letter swept on to a firm conclusion:

> . . . Your Government should publically invite tenders for a fast service between Canada and this country such as is indicated in the Resolutions of the Conference. When the result of this invitation has been received it will be possible to ascertain with greater accuracy than at present, how far the new line is likely to be successful, and what conditions as regards subsidy and other points will be necessary and Her Majesty's Government will also be in a better position for deciding as to the extent of the assistance which they would be justified in contributing.

> > I have the Honour to be,
> > My Lord,
> > Your Lordship's most obedient humble servant,
> > (Signed) J. Chamberlain

Thus Joseph Chamberlain, ardent advocate of Imperial togetherness, placed the influence of Lord Salisbury's Government behind the Canadian Conservatives in their tortuous passage to the "Fast Line."

On 29th February 1896 the Canadian Government invited tenders once more, this time for a weekly service with four 20-knots ships of at least 8,500 tons which were to be built to Admiralty requirements as auxiliary cruisers. Canada offered a subsidy of $750,000 to which Britain added a further $350,000. Mails were to be landed at Rimouski for Quebec in summer and at Halifax in winter. The Allan Line submission was the only one to meet the terms of the specification and three others were rejected. With everything settled the contract was sent to the Governor General for formal signature. But it was too late.

In July, while the document remained unsigned, the Tupper government fell. The Conservatives were swept out of office and the Liberals came in under Sir Wilfred Laurier. Among Conservative debris the mail contract went down the political drain. Despite a continuation of parliamentary and shipping enthusiam, and despite a great surge in immigration, the magic moment had passed and it would be another decade before the "Fast Line" came anywhere near fruition. It was not for lack of trying by the Allan Line in the end.

CHAPTER NINE

High Noon

"As the day grows warm and high,
Life's meridian flaming nigh,
Dost thou spurn the humble vale?
Life's proud summits would'st thou scale?"

R.B.
Written in Friar's Carse Hermitage

The concept of "Twenty knots to Canada" was a mirage, but while politicians and the public continued to lure shipowners as far as they could be persuaded in that direction, solid progress was made in the world of ordinary commerce. For most passengers a day or two here or there was of small importance. For some the comforts of the voyage were exchanged all too soon for the harsh realities of their first winter on the windswept prairie. Shippers of cargo were more concerned with regularity, reliability and reasonable freight rates than they were with speed. On all these counts they were well served by the Allan Line which, in the eighties and nineties, expanded to provide a coverage which has never been exceeded before or since.

Under "Old Andrew" and his nephew Montagu in Montreal, Alexander who was the survivor in Scotland of the original five brothers, and Captain James' son R.G. Allan who had succeeded his Uncle Bryce in charge of the Liverpool office, the business became one of the top half-dozen shipping companies under the British flag. It was predominant in cargo liner services to Canada and South America. Among the waterfront public the Allan Line was known as a versatile company in which the bread-and-butter steamer trade on regular routes was complemented by profits which could still be picked up by sailing ships on more speculative freights. The wooden sailing ships of Sandy Allan had given way to iron clippers which maintained his tradition as a training ground for apprentices and junior officers who wished to make a career in the Company. Sometimes these vessels loaded from Glasgow or Liverpool on the regular North American berth, but as competition forced sail from the Atlantic the Allan houseflag would be seen on the long voyage trades – coal from Britain to almost anywhere, steel rails for South America, India or Australia – with homeward cargoes of lumber, grain, jute, wool or other bulk commodities according to circumstances.

The Allan family governed a world-wide shipping network from their offices at Glasgow, Montreal and Liverpool, with agents in half the principal ports of the world. Unfortunately for the historian, almost the entire collection of official correspondence was destroyed by fire in the bombing of Liverpool and Glasgow during the second world war. Occasional documents have survived, among them.personal letters which might have come straight from the pages of Galsworthy. Apart from family news, this interchange kept up to date on what was happening in the world of shipping – on "Allan 'Change" one might almost say. In a typical note written by Captain James to one of his sons in '68, pleasure at arriving back in London after a leisurely trip to the South of France is heightened by snippets of news about the ships:

> We had a very rough day yesterday to cross the Channel and almost everyone suffered from sickness. I am glad to say that I escaped entirely but Eleonora felt very ill . . . The McMillans of Helensburgh have also gone to Cannes . . . I find the *Iona* and *Albion* have arrived here two days ago, I paid a visit to them today . . . I see by a letter that the *Strathblane* was launched two days ago and that the *Prussian* will be launched tomorrow; also the *Moravian* is bringing the 100th Regiment and is to land them in Glasgow where she will embark the 25th and land them at Birkenhead. I am only picking up news bit by bit about our vessels and I cannot say anything about the facts at Quebec. I see however that the *Gleniffer* has got to Glasgow and is loading for New York.

Two years after, on 1st March 1872, another Allan communication is pure Forsyte. Captain James in Glasgow had written to his son R.G. Allan in Liverpool about a young man, John Graham, who had asked for the hand of his daughter in marriage. Robert replied from his office at 19 James Street:

My Dear Father,

I have your letter of yesterday on the subject of John Graham and Mary. The attentions of former to latter have for the past months been very noticeable, and James informed me the other day that things had culminated in the present position.

I am sure that with John Graham for a husband Mary would be very well off. His family you know to be respectable, and he is very well liked personally by all his acquaintances, myself included. His temper and general disposition are I understand unexceptionable and I think we might pretty confidently assume that his financial position is such as to enable him to keep Mary comfortably. I know he is a partner in McFie & Sons and has been so for about 6 years. But as to his share, or what he gets out of it, I have no more knowledge than I have of Wm. MacFie himself. I do not like to question Mr. MacFie on the subject and there is no one else I could get the information from. But there need be no doubt that financially his position is good.

Altogether, as I said before, I think Mary would be very well off with him, and I will be glad to hear that you have sanctioned the engagement – one which I think might be said to have prospects of happiness for both.

Believe me, My Dear Father,

Yours affectly.
R.G. Allan

It is pleasant to record that the engagement was sanctioned with full approval and that the "good prospects of happiness" were indeed fulfilled.

With the widespread nature of their business the Allans operated feeder services as necessary for their ocean routes. We have already mentioned the *Newfoundland* which collected passengers for St. John's from the mail steamer at Halifax, and there were a number of inland water steamboats on the upper St. Lawrence connecting Montreal with the Great Lakes. At the European end the steamship *Sweden* was put into service about 1870 for the convenience of Scandinavian emigrants who were brought to Hull before crossing England by train to join their ship at Liverpool. These vessels were tributaries to the main stream of Allan Line passenger traffic but one interesting paddle steamer stands alone. This was the *Ivanhoe* in which Alexander Allan, a strict teetotaller, was one of the principal shareholders. Launched at Glasgow in 1880, the

Ivanhoe was put into service as a "dry" ship to clean up drunkenness on day excursions in the Clyde, an engraved plate on the water fountain informing the thirsty traveller that he might go farther and fare worse. For seventeen years these principles of business were faithfully maintained until, after purchase by the Caledonian Railway Company, the usual bar services were installed. For many years afterwards a handy silver-mounted pocket vessel of unobtrusive shape was known to Glaswegians as the "Ivanhoe" flask.

In 1883 the Allan Line became London agents for the Twin Screw Line which ran from London to New York. This agency enabled them to look into the prospects for a direct Canadian service, and an experimental sailing was made in March of that year by the *Hanoverian* to Halifax. In 1884 two ships were put on the London berth, the *Lucerne* and *Norwegian,* a service which was increased by a third ship in 1885 when fortnightly sailings from London went to Quebec and Montreal instead of Halifax.

Encouraged by their London business to Canada it was thought that there might be an opening from there to South America, a scheme which was tried in 1886 with the *Phoenician* and *Grecian* to the River Plate. This was unsuccessful and in 1887 the South American service from Glasgow, which up till that time had been seasonal, was strengthened by withdrawing the London ships and putting on a monthly sailing from Glasgow to the River Plate. This year-round schedule required new tonnage and the opportunity was taken to introduce the first triple-expansion machinery in the fleet on this long run where economy in coal consumption was of the utmost importance. Two ships were built, both from D. & W. Henderson of Glasgow, the *Rosarian* and *Monte Videan.*

The fortunes of the Allan Line were now at high noon and, from the point of view of ship management, Glasgow was the focal point of administration. Their office at 70 Great Clyde Street, handy for Plantation Quay and the Customs House, was now too small and it was decided to move away from the dock area into the centre of Glasgow, a move which was resented by many of the old-timers of the Company. The new building in Bothwell Street, still standing, was the finest office block in Scotland and was described in the *Mercantile Age* of 1st August 1890 as:

> . . . French Renaissance style, freely treated with doorways handsomely carved with . . . A swallow and pigeon seen in flight, an allegory showing that speed, reliability and letter carrying are some of the most important features of the Line.

No sooner was the firm of J. & A. Allan safely installed in red sandstone magnificence in Bothwell Street than another expansion loomed up.

On 13th March 1891 the influential magazine *Engineering* carried a story on the trans-Atlantic trade in which it was disclosed that:

> The State Line Company of Glasgow has for some time been in a very depressed condition owing to losses incurred in the steam trade between the Clyde and New York, and latterly it has resolved to proceed to liquidiation. There is a belief however in other quarters that a good passenger business can be cultivated on that route now renounced by the owners of the State Line . . . Messrs. J. and A. Allan of this city have resolved to put a number of their fastest steamers on the same route.

Engineering was well informed. The Allan Line purchased the State Line for £72,000 which, even in 1891, must have been something of a bargain for six liners, even if the goodwill was of more doubtful value. Of the ships thus taken over, all named for States of the American Union, the *State of Alabama* and the *State of Pennsylvania* were sold and the others commissioned under the Allan flag.

Sailing advertisements in the *Glasgow Herald* of 6th May 1891 show the truly imposing service offered by the Allan Line at the highwater mark of their fortunes. There was a weekly sailing from Glasgow to Quebec on Thursdays, while on Fridays the weekly service to New York by the recently acquired State Line offered fares as low as seven guineas "With all the comforts of the first-class saloon." There was a fortnightly ship for Boston, leaving Plantation Quay every second Wednesday, with sailings also from Glasgow to Halifax and Philadelphia fortnightly on the Wednesdays between. The South American run to Monte Video and Buenos Ayres sailed monthly on Tuesdays. From Liverpool the fortnightly sailings to St. John's, Halifax and Baltimore also left on a Tuesday, and there was a weekly ship from there to Quebec and Montreal. In London the Allan Line office in Gracechurch Street handled a fortnightly sailing for Canada and the agency for the Twin Screw Line to New York.

Thus there was no lack of opportunity for sons and grandsons of the founders of the steamship business, and from Montreal and Boston to Liverpool, Glasgow and London there was closely knit family management. On the lighter side of their shipowning interests the Scottish Allans included enthusiastic yachtsmen. In February 1891 the yachting correspondent of the *Glasgow Herald* mentioned a fast centre-board yacht which was built for Bryce and Richard (sons of Captain James) as being the "Most staggering apparition the Clyde has enjoyed for a long number of years" while great hopes were expected from a 2½ rater building for Alexander's son Henry. These boats came from the drawing board of George Lennox Watson who was then rising to the peak of his career and was famous, on both sides of the Atlantic, for the grace and beauty of his steam yachts which were looked upon as the poetry of shipbuilding.

In June 1891 the steam yacht *Hermione,* built by Fleming & Ferguson of Paisley to Watson's design, was completed to the order of J. & A. Allan. She was a graceful and lovely little ship with the unmistakeable Watson trademark of nicely proportioned clipper stem sweeping into a classic hull, jet black above a white boot-topping, which terminated in a long overhanging counter. On trials she attained an effortless 15 knots from her "Patent improved quadruple engine" which ran as smoothly as a sewing machine. The *Engineer* of 12th June 1891 recorded that:

> The *Hermione* is a finely modelled steam yacht of 320 tons yacht measurement. Her saloons and owner's staterooms, which are below, are elaborately fitted in combinations of walnut, oak, olive and mahogany; the sidelights are covered with stained glass windows. On deck she has a smoking room and a chart room. The *Hermione* is schooner rigged, has a steam windlass, steam and hand steering gears, steam launch, distiller, Thomson's compasses and sounding machine, and all the latest and most improved yacht fittings.

The *Engineer* noted the satisfaction which was felt by Mr. Watson and the owners at the trial results. They had every reason to be pleased with G.L.'s beautiful creation: it was outstanding even among the fleet moored off the Royal Clyde Yacht Club at Hunter's Quay, adjacent to Alexander Allan's estate of *Hafton.* In summer the *Hermione* would cruise leisurely among the Hebridean Islands, where the family would enjoy that incomparable prospect safe in the knowledge that one or other of the Allan Line masters was on the bridge as a welcome respite from the rigors of the North Atlantic. It was a pity they did not have longer to enjoy the *Hermione*: Alexander Allan died in 1892 and some time after his death the yacht was bought by the Duke of Connaught. He had first met the Allans in 1869 as the guest of Sir Hugh at *Belmere* and would later return to Canada as the Governor General. In 1898, with the outbreak of the Spanish American War, the United States Navy were on the lookout for fast, light craft and they bought the *Hermione* from the Duke of Connaught. As the USS *Hawk* she was in action during the blockade of Cuba, during which she destroyed the enemy ship *Alphonso XII* by gunfire. Thereafter the *Hawk* served as a naval reserve training ship, latterly on the Great Lakes, until she was scrapped at Michigan City in 1940.

At this high point in their fortunes the Allan Line began to dispose of their sailing ships. Of these the *Saint Patrick* had the strangest history. Built by Stephens of Kelvinhaugh as the *John Bell* in 1854, she was bought by the Allans in 1862. At the time they were short of ships, and perhaps money. As the *John Bell* had been converted to a steamer by her previous owners she was going cheap. Under the name *Saint Patrick* she made a trio with the *Saint Andrew* and *Saint George* for the Glasgow to Quebec service which they had inaugurated in 1861. By 1875 she had outlived her usefulness as a steamer, but as the hull was in good condition the machinery was removed and the *Saint Patrick* reverted to a full-rigged sailing ship. She was afloat until 1905, latterly under the Italian flag.

According to Basil Lubbock, in his book *The Last of the Windjammers*, it was the durability of the *Saint Patrick* which influenced the Allans to go in for iron sailing ships as early as 1866 when many were being built of wood or were composite. Certainly the iron ship *Gleniffer*, launched by Barclay Curle for the Allan Line that year, brilliantly justified the policy. The best of the wooden sailing ships had been able to make three trips to Quebec "between the ice" but in 1871 the Allan flier broke the record by making four, a feat possible only by a superb shipmaster in a strong vessel. Very early in the season for those days, the *Montreal Gazette* of 24th April 1871 recorded her first arrival:

> The ship *Gleniffer*, Captain Jarman from Greenock March 23rd, passed Quebec at 4.30 this morning under sail on her way to Montreal with a fine easterly breeze.

To navigate the St. Lawrence River above Quebec, in the dark, with a square rigged ship under canvas, was a feat in the best Allan tradition.

In 1873 Captain Jarman again made news when he brought the *Gleniffer* into New York under dramatic circumstances. Two days out from Glasgow he had encountered Donald McKay's famous clipper *Flying Cloud*, reputed by some to be the fastest ship in the world, which had left Britain four days previously. It was October and, as usual in the Allan Line, the *Glennifer* had her short top-gallant masts up for the winter. The *Flying Cloud* passed her to windward with everything set. This was too much for Jarman, who promptly rigged topsail and t'gallant stu'nsails as the two separated. They fell in again off the American coast in a hard breeze; this time the *Glennifer* had the luck, being snugly rigged, for the *Flying Cloud's* upper yards carried away and Jarman swept in past Sandy Hook a half-hour ahead of his opponent after knocking two days off the *Flying Cloud's* passage. With the long family tradition of Sandy Allan and his sons James and Bryce behind them, the masters of the Allan Line sailing ships were the equals of anyone afloat when it come to windward work in the Atlantic.

This was confirmed by an unusual compliment in 1870 when Captain R.S. Tannock, master of the Allan Line ship *Abeona*, was invited to navigate the schooner yacht *Cambria* in a trans-Atlantic race against the *Dauntless*. Tannock won by two hours after 23 days constantly beating to windward, a thrilling finish to an exciting race which caught the fancy of the sporting world.

On eastbound passages in the *Abeona* Tannock rarely took more than 14 days and he had been kown to overhaul the mail steamers, not failing to show the end of a line over the taffrail as he passed to windward. Captain Tannock died at sea when homeward bound from India in the Allan Line four-masted barque *Glencairn.*

Among other beauties in that first wave of iron sailing ships the *Ravenscrag,* built by Steele of Greenock in 1866, recalls Sandy Allan's happy connection with that firm in the forties and was almost certainly named by Sir Hugh. Barclay Curle also built some fine vessels for the Allans, among them the *Strathblane* and *Glenfinnart.* Stephen's *Abeona* was generally considered to be the fastest in the fleet but they were all North Atlantic clippers and most were fortunate in the quality of their masters. Tannock had the reputation of being unbeatable in any of them. Sail-plans of all four of these ships have survived; from these it can be said, without any shadow of doubt, that in appearance as well as performance the Allan sailers were fine examples of the peak period of sailing ship design. Moderate tonnage, a sufficiency of good seamen, and a few brilliant masters of the art of sailing navigation, combined to make profits for careful owners. The last survivor was the full-rigged ship *Glenmorag,* which was sold in 1896.

With the passing of sail there was no longer a reason for the long red pendant which had hitherto been worn above the houseflag to distinguish steamers although the tradition remained for a while. Eventually they hoisted only the blue-white-and-red originally chosen by Sandy Allan. But although, in 1819, the Napoleonic *tricoleur* had an appeal for him it was, after all, the national flag of a proud maritime country. About the nineties the French Government raised objections to the Company's usage which, in any case, must have caused confusion. The colours were therefore reversed, a popular combination which, with various additions, was already in use by at least two other British shipping companies. However, so far as is known, the Allan was the only Line to wear the undefaced red-white-and-blue. The new houseflag became well known, particularly in Glasgow after 1892, when the Allan Line transferred their dock operation from Plantation Quay to the Prince's Dock, then being completed. There were seldom less than half-a-dozen houseflags to be seen in company over the sheds of the new dock which, as late as 1939, was still known to dockers as "The Allan Line Berth."

One of the more dramatic events of the nineties was the westbound voyage of the *Pomeranian* which left Glasgow for New York on 27th January 1893 " . . . As staunch and complete a craft in every respect as ever left port" to quote the newspaper. The *Pomeranian*, which was employed at the time on the State Line service, had been built by Earle of Hull in 1882, originally as the *Grecian Monarch* for the Royal Exchange Shipping Company, and was purchased in 1887 by the Allan Line. When first designed she was awarded the Gold Medal at the Shipwrights International Exhibition as the best design for a trans-Atlantic steamer which had been submitted. Her photograph shows her to have been a sturdy steamer of the period except for the bridge which appears to be perched on stanchions above a small deckhouse.

On Saturday 11th February, with a howling gale of wind and rain sweeping the Firth of Clyde, the pilot station was surprised to see the *Pomeranian,* stripped of everything from the foremast to the funnel, limping back to anchor off Roseneath. The weather delayed contact by tug and rumours began to fly. Most of them were true.

At 9.30 on the morning of 4th February, while slamming into a heavy sea some 1,200 miles to the west of Tory Island, the *Pomeranian* had been hit by a sea described as "The father of all waves." The bridge and forward deckhouse disappeared with an almighty crash, taking with them the second and fourth mates who were on watch, two quartermasters and two other seamen, together with four passengers who were in their berths. Captain William Dalziel was swept along the deck and so badly injured that he died soon afterwards, as did another passenger. In this situation, with the ship about to fall into the trough of the sea, which would probably have been the end, Chief Officer McCulloch dashed aft to the hand steering gear and managed to wear the *Pomeranian.* Running her off before the wind with careful judgment he was able to take stock. Twelve lives had been lost, the ship had no bridge, navigating appliances nor chartroom, and he was left with nothing but the after compass.

There was no panic. McCulloch's fine leadership as a "Calm, brave man" brought well-merited honours from owners and underwriters. Despite the prize-winning design which had excited the admiration of the Shipwrights – who should have known better – it was that weak bridge and flimsy structure which caused the casualties and nearly lost the ship. The public did not take this view, perhaps nobody did, and the fact that the *Pomeranian* had survived this terrible battering made her even more popular with passengers. Certainly McCulloch's conduct added to the confidence which travellers felt towards the Allan Line.

Up till this period the Allans had borne the entire financing of the Company through various partnership agreements but the scale of their operations and the growing need for replacement tonnage necessitated a major reorganization. On 19th June 1897, the formation of the *Allan Line Steamship Company Limited* was announced, with a capital of £650,000; the Chairman was Andrew Allan – "Old Andrew" of Montreal – whose Limited Company now financed ship ownership, the various agencies remaining under their previous titles. Some of the older vessels were sold and the opportunity was taken to buy three replacements from the Twin Screw Line, which had gone out of business. These were the steamers *Tower Hill, Richmond Hill* and *Ludgate Hill,* which were placed on the run from Glasgow to New York as the *Turanian, Roumanian* and *Livonian.* This was something of a windfall, but it gave the reconstituted Company time to plan for a more efficient fleet. Although they now dominated the Canadian trade the Allan ships were aging. While their 18-year old flagship *Parisian* was put in hand for complete modernization, some of the other ships were considerably older and beyond rejuvenation.

The first of the new program was the *Castilian,* a 7,400 ton singlescrew passenger and cargo liner by Workman Clark of Belfast, which was singularly unlucky. On the 11th March 1899, while returning to Liverpool from Portland on her maiden voyage, the *Castilian* was wrecked on the Gannet rock near Yarmouth in the Bay of Fundy and became a total loss, fortunately without loss of life. This was a shattering blow which must have brought to mind sad memories, the more so as the *Parisian* was in refit and the Company were short of ships. The former Cunard liner *Gallia* was therefore purchased to fill the gap. By a cruel irony the *Gallia* also stranded on her maiden voyage, near Sorel in the St. Lawrence in May 1899, and had to be scrapped.

But the century ended on a more cheerful note with the production of two fine Allan Liners, the *Bavarian* from Denny in August 1899, and the *Tunisian* by Stephen of Linthouse in April 1900, each being the largest yet launched by their builders. These two good-looking ships belonged to the twentieth century, marking a departure from sailingship thinking. Although by this time the older ships had been stripped of yards and sails, their configuration smacked of yesteryear. The *Bavarian* and *Tunisian,* on the other hand, had more in common with the type of intermediate liner to be found in ocean convoys in the Second World War than with their predecessors. They were almost identical in design, just over 10,000 tons, and with their twin-screw reciprocating machinery they made a full 17 knots on trial. With telemotor steering gear, extensive refrigerated space, good heating and mechanical ventilation, and a continuous supply of hot and cold fresh and salt water for domestic use, these ships were thoroughly up-to-date. From the best first-class accommodation on the promenade deck – which had sitting room, bedroom and bathroom *en suite* – to the four-berth emigrant cabins

157

with their spring mattresses, passengers could reach any part of the extensive public rooms without going on deck. At the conclusion of her second voyage the *Bavarian* went trooping to South Africa, as did the *Carthaginian* of 1884, but despite the great improvements in comfort of the new ship over the old, soldiers went to war slinging their hammocks in the tweendecks as they did until almost the last phase of military movement by sea. There was no other way to fit them in.

In June 1901 "Old Andrew" died, the last survivor of the original five brothers and the longest-lived. As a younger brother who had come straight from school into the office of Edmonstone, Allan & Co., he was overshadowed by Sir Hugh from the start. Perhaps inevitably, he lacked his brother's enormous vitality and drive. He did, however, guide the family business through years of counter-attack which followed his brother's phenomenal success, as he did in other activities as President of the Merchant's Bank and the Montreal Telegraph Company. "Old Andrew" was the doyen of the shipping community. As Chairman of the Montreal Harbour Commissioners he presided over a notable period of port development. With his death, there was a shift in emphasis from Montreal to Glasgow: Nathaniel Dunlop, who under James and Alexander had risen from principal clerk to deputy chairman, succeeded "Old Andrew" as Chairman of the *Allan Line Steamship Company Limited*. In Montreal Hugh Montagu Allan followed his uncle to the presidency of H & A Allan, and the mansion of *Ravenscrag* began a period when it became a centre of social and sporting life which was unique in Canada.

The new directorate were soon to be reminded that trouble was never far away on the Canadian route, first by the loss of the *Grecian*. This ship had come to public notice in July 1898 when she towed the battered sailing ship *Cromartyshire* into Halifax with survivors from the French liner *La Bourgogne* after one of the worst tragedies of the sea. Homeward bound to Le Havre from New York, the fastest ship of the *Compagnie Generale Transatlantique* was in collision with the *Cromartyshire* in fog off Sable Island. To the surprise of all, the liner sank with the loss of 580 lives after scenes of sheer horror, while the sailing ship remained afloat to rescue many survivors and be towed to port by the *Grecian*. In February 1902 the *Grecian* met her end entering Halifax Harbour, while under pilotage in a snow squall, and became a total loss, fortunately without loss of life.

A month later, on 7th March 1902, an obscure paragraph in the *Glasgow Herald* was headed 'ALLAN LINER OVERDUE'. This turned out to be the *Huronian* but as yet there was no alarm. The Bothwell Street office issued a statement reminding enquirers that probably she had broken a shaft and would turn up under sail – by no means an unheard-of incident. There was no radio to report progress as the *Huronian* made her way from Liverpool towards Saint John, New Brunswick, and two weeks later the official view was that there need be no undue anxiety for she was "An efficient steamer in charge of a capable commander." After 20 days of silence, "considerable apprehension" was coupled with the hope that she might be found on Sable Island, that graveyard of the Atlantic which had been reached by some survivors from countless ships stranded in surf and quicksand. This was checked without result, as was another report that Allan Line passenger bedding had been washed ashore near Halifax. The *Huronian* carried neither passengers nor bedding of that type and eventually the missing ship was given up. Her disappearance has never been solved. The *Huronian* remains the only Allan Liner to be lost without trace.

As 1902 came to a close there was increasing competition on all Atlantic freight and passenger routes, both to Canada and New York. This gave rise to mergers and rumours of mergers, and to some new developments. An announcement in the *Montreal Gazette* of 2nd October stated that the "Allan Liner *Ontarian* sailed from Glasgow to Montreal last Saturday and will be the first steamer to open the new South African service." This was operated jointly by Allan, Elder-Dempster and Furness Lines to Capetown, Port Elizabeth and Durban; it was soon to be abandoned in the face of other changes which struck nearer home. Of particular concern to North Atlantic shipowners was an announcement on 20th October that the American financier J. Pierepoint Morgan was behind a consortium of shipping companies, including the White Star, Dominion and Inman Lines, registered at Trenton, New Jersey, as the *International Mercantile Marine Company* with an authorized capital of $120 million. In the face of this the independent companies began to look for alliances and shippers wondered when freight rates would go up.

Van Horne of the Canadian Pacific had no intention of placing railway freight prospects at the mercy of an outside steamship consortium. He gave notice of long suspected intentions on 18th February when the *Montreal Gazette* quoted his remark:

As I have said before, Canada has for some years been raising the sides of her hopper without enlarging the spout . . . we are apt to get left out in chartering vessels when we need them most, so we propose to have our own.

On 24th February 1903, Canadian Pacific announced the purchase of fourteen ships, hitherto operating under Elder-Dempster Atlantic service, which would henceforth become the *Canadian Pacific Atlantic Line.* In describing this as "The most interesting commercial announcement of the year" the *Montreal Gazette* of 24th February reflected editorially that:

The action of the Company should have a good effect on the trade of the St. Lawrence and of Montreal. The road's interest will be to bring by its trains all the business it can get for its steamships, and by its steamships all it can get for its trains.

Canadian Pacific introduced three services from Montreal, weekly to Liverpool, weekly to Avonmouth for Bristol, and fortnightly to London.

The first ocean sailings were advertised to commence with the *Lake Champlain* from Montreal on 1st May, a date which she was unable to keep. On her way from Liverpool to take up this sailing, the *Lake Champlain* was held up for two days by ice in the Gulf and returned to Halifax where she disembarked Montreal passengers to connect by rail. She was late in proceeding up the St Lawrence but a few days later, on 5th May 1903, the *Montreal Gazette* was able to report:

> The C.P. Atlantic Line steamer *Lake Champlain*, Captain W. Stewart, sailed from Montreal yesterday afternoon at three o'ckock. The steamer has a large passenger list and a large cargo. The *Lake Champlain* is the first Atlantic liner to sail from Montreal for English ports this season and will be followed tomorrow by the Allan Liner *Corinthian*.

Sir Hugh Allan must have been turning in his grave.

far left: Robert Burns (1759-1796) from the portrait by Alexander Nasmyth.
(Courtesy, Scottish National Portrait Gallery)

left: Andrew Allan (1822-1901) photographed about the same age as Burns in the Nasmyth portrait; note the resemblance.
(Courtesy, Mrs. Sydney Dawes, Montreal)

Fairlie House, "Fairlie-five-lums", in 1971. The house was designed by Robert Adam and built in 1776. The Allans sheltered Burns on this estate.
(Courtesy, Mrs. Ingrid Pillans, Fairlie House, near Kilmarnock)

far left: Captain Alexander Allan (1780-1854) Sandy Allan was the patriarch of the Allan Line. From a portrait at *Neighbrook*.
(Courtesy, Richard Allan, Moreton-in-the-Marsh)

left: Jean Allan, *née* Crawford, wife of Sandy Allan and mother of James, Hugh, Bryce, Andrew and Alexander who founded the Allan Royal Mail Line of steamships. From a painting at *Hafton*.
(Courtesy, Miss Jean C. Allan, Hunter's Quay)

above: Sir Hugh Allan (1810-1882) second son of Captain Alexander Allan, in 1871.
(Courtesy, Notman)

right: Sir H. Montagu Allan (1860-1951) second son of Sir Hugh Allan. Taken in 1912 when Honorary Lieutenant Colonel of the Black Watch (Royal Highland Regiment) of Canada.
(Courtesy, Notman)

below: Children of Sir H. Montagu and Lady Allan at Montrose House, Cacouna, in 1902. Left to right: Martha (1895-1942), Hugh (1896-1917) who was killed in action, Gwen (1898-1915) and Anna (1900-1915) who were drowned in the torpedoing of the *Lusitania*.

above: Croquet at Belmere, Sir Hugh Allan's estate on Lake Memphramagog, in 1870. Prince Arthur of Connaught, then a lieutenant in the Rifle Brigade, sits at the table with Lady Young. Sir John Young, the Governor General and later Baron Lisgar, is standing behind and

above: Montrose House, Cacouna, on the south shore of the St. Lawrence, in 1902. Sir H. Montagu and Lady Allan's summer home is now a religious retreat. (Courtesy, Notman)

below: Sailplan of the ship *Abeona*, fastest of the Allan clippers, built by Stephen of Glasgow in 1867. (Courtesy, National Maritime Museum, Greenwich)

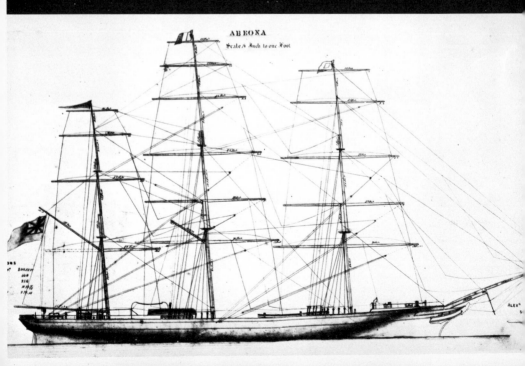

above: Wooden ship *Albion*, built by
Steele of Greenock in 1845. When under
the command of Captain Bryce Allan in
1847 the *Albion* was 72 days from
Greenock to Quebec of which 46 days
were fast in the ice.
(Courtesy, Richard Allan, Moreton-in-
the-Marsh)

below: Model of the brigantine *Jean*,
Captain Alexander Allan, which made
the first Allan sailing, from Greenock to
Quebec, in 1819.
(Courtesy, *Greenock Telegraph)*

right: RMS *Canadian*, first steamship of the Allan Line. Note the red pennant above the houseflag which was worn only by steamers.
(Courtesy, National Maritime Museum, Greenwich)

below: The Allan ship *Gleniffer* beating Donald McKay's famous clipper *Flying Cloud* into New York in 1873. When off the Ambrose Lightship the *Flying Cloud* lost her main t'gallant mast in a squall while the *Gleniffer*, with short t'gallants always used in winter by the Allans, was able to weather her opponent.
(Courtesy, D. Appleton & Co. New York)

below, right: RMS *Circassian* arriving at Montreal, probably on her maiden voyage in 1873. Note the tripod on the bridge which supported the standard compass high above magnetic deviation from the iron hull.
(Courtesy, Public Archives of Canada)

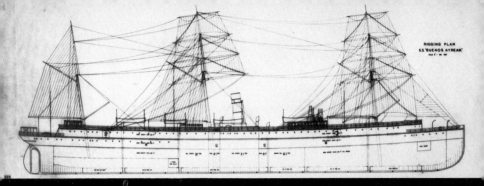

above: RMS *Buenos Ayrean,* first Atlantic liner to be built of steel. Denny's rigging plan of 1880 shows the transitional stage between sail and steam.
(Courtesy, National Maritime Museum, Greenwich)

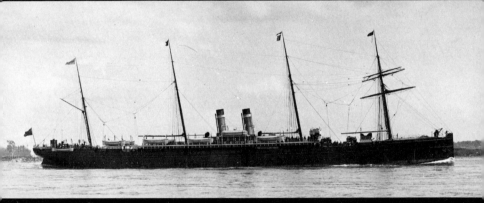

above: RMS *Parisian* in the St. Lawrence about 1890. Her appearance changed considerably with successive refits. She was the first large ship to be fitted with bilge keels.
(Courtesy, Notman)

below: German emigrants boarding an Allan liner at Liverpool in 1874.
(Courtesy, Public Archives of Canada)

top: The Allan Line terminal at Montreal in 1889.
(Courtesy, Notman)

middle: RMS *Pomeranian*. Note the flimsy bridge which was swept overboard with heavy loss of life in 1893.

left: Dr. William J. Shaw, surgeon of the RMS *Austrian* in 1878.
(Courtesy, Mrs. Glen Shaw, Burford, Ont.)

Above: Three stewardesses of the Allan Line. On the left is Miss Gunda Skarre who married George Jackson, Chief Engineer of the *Parisian*, who was one of three generations of Allan Line engineers.
(Courtesy, Mrs. Eva W. Davies, Liverpool)

Left: USS *Hawk*, formerly the steam yacht *Hermione* built for J & A Allan of Glasgow. Photographed under refit at Norfolk Navy Yard, Va., in 1900.
(Courtesy, U.S. Bureau of Ships)

Below: RMS *Virginian* passing Levis bound for Montreal. With her sister ship *Victorian* of 1905 the pair were the first turbine liners.
(Courtesy, Notman)

ENGINES OF STEAM-SHIP "PARISIAN."

Two Low-pressure Cylinders (each 85″ diam.), with one High-pressure Cylinder (60″ diam.) between them. Stroke of each Piston 5 ft. Steam Pressure 70 lbs. Condensing Surface 9624 sq. ft. Indicated Horse-power 6019.

THREE-CYLINDER COMPOUND INVERTED ENGINES OF STEAM-SHIP "PARISIAN,"
5359 TONS GROSS.
CONSTRUCTED BY MESSRS. ROBERT NAPIER AND SONS, GLASGOW, FOR THE
ALLAN LINE OF ROYAL MAIL ATLANTIC STEAMERS.

Compound engine of the RMS *Parisian*, 1881.
(Courtesy, National Museum of Science and Technology, Ottawa)

Triple-expansion engine of the RMS *Castilian*, 1899.
(Courtesy, William Lind, Johnstone)

Turbines of the RMS *Victorian* under construction at Belfast in 1904.
(Courtesy, William Lind, Johnstone)

above: Wreck of the RMS *Castilian* on Gannet
Rock Ledge, near Yarmouth N.S., in March
1899 when returning to Liverpool from Portland on her maiden voyage. No lives were
lost.
(Courtesy, Mrs. W. B. Hamilton, Seal Island,
N.S.)

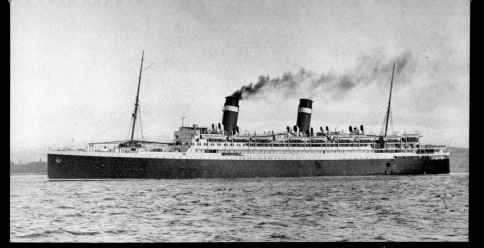

below: The last Allan liner afloat, the old *Virginian,* under the Panamanian flag as the *Homeland* shortly before 1955 when she was scrapped after half a century of service. (Courtesy, C. G. Brownell)

above: RMS *Calgarian* leaving the Clyde in 1914. (Courtesy, Miss Ishbel D. Crawford, Glasgow)

A piece of broken soup plate showing the
Allan Line badge which was embedded in the
cable of the *Empress of Canada* when weighing
anchor off Greenock in 1964. The fragment is
believed to date from 1860.
(Courtesy, *Greenock Telegraph*)

CHAPTER TEN

Indian Summer

"But pleasures are like poppies spread,
You seize the flower, its blooms are dead;"

R.B.
Tam O' Shanter

Despite the addition of Canadian Pacific to the St. Lawrence trade in the spring of 1903, initiative still lay with the Allans. The principal traffic was between Liverpool and Montreal, where the Allan Line had the largest number of passengers with Canadian Pacific second and the Dominion Line third. But when bookings from Glasgow were included, the Allan Line's share of business was almost half as much again as their nearest competitor. In the winter sailings, which since 1901 had been routed through Saint John, New Brunswick instead of Portland, the Allan Line was also well placed. To remain ahead, however, new ships were needed. The question was how many and how fast?

Canadian Pacific had not yet announced a building program – for the moment they were content to operate the 13-knot Beaver ships acquired from Elder-Dempster – but Canadian Government aspirations for the Fast Line indicated that the 17-knot *Bavarian* and *Tunisian* must be improved on. The Allan Line were by no means alone in their cautious

161

attitude towards the economics of speed and it is interesting that the Government were given independent advice from time to time. On 1st November 1901, a prominent and long established Montreal shipping agent, Robert Reford whose Company dates back to 1866, wrote to Lord Strathcona (Donald Smith of the CPR) about the prospects for an improved St. Lawrence service, sending a copy of this letter to the Prime Minister, Sir Wilfred Laurier:

> I very strongly advise against the Canadian Government being in a hurry in arranging a fast service. The shipbuilding trade of England is in a transition state, cost of building has been running up owing to demand for steamers to fill wants of the British Government for African business, freights have fallen greatly within the past six months, and the feeling amongst those best informed is that orders for new ships must greatly decrease owing to there being already an over supply of tonnage, and the fact that nearly all tonnage is being worked at a loss. This is expected to cause a sharp decline in cost of building steamers which well informed parties estimate at 30% or more within the next 18 months.
>
> It would be wretched policy for the Canadian Government to allow the Fast Line to be started with the millstone of excessive cost around its neck. It would be a burden it could never shake off and which would greatly mar its chances of success. The greatest care should also be taken in seeing that the steamers composing the Canadian Fast Line should be contracted for with thoroughly competent and honest builders, as well as at the lowest possible price, as want of care on these points may mean failure of the Line, no matter how good the Line's prospects in other ways might be.

In fact the "Wretched policy of the Canadian Government" did not, as yet, allow the Fast Line to be started and, despite Laurier's enthusiasm, it dimmed the prospects by being indecisive. However, although the mail contract and subsidy was a year-to-year arrangement, for what it was worth it remained in Allan hands. They emphasised their initiative in 1903 by ordering two new ships of superior size and speed. These were the *Victorian* and *Virginian,* launched in the spring of 1904.

As Robert Reford had remarked, the shipbuilding industry was indeed in a "Transition state," not only economically but because of fundamental technical developments. In these circumstances the Allans made a bold decision, shortly after construction had started, when they changed the original design – which had called for quadruple-expansion engines driving twin screws – to steam turbines with smaller and faster propellers on triple shafts. Although the Parsons turbine had been applied successfully in coastal vessels, and the steam yacht *Emerald* had

162

crossed the Atlantic without trouble, no turbine ships had as yet been laid down for Atlantic service. The *Victorian* and *Virginian* were 540-foot ships expected to have sufficient power for a sustained sea speed of 17 knots and, as the first of a new breed of liner, they excited the attention of the shipping and engineering world.

The contract for both ships was originally placed with Workman, Clark & Co. of Belfast. When the design change was made in October 1903, however, it was decided that early delivery was necessary if the full benefits of this new propulsion system were to be achieved. The contract was therefore split, the *Victorian* order remaining at Belfast while the *Virginian* work was transfered to Alexander Stephen & Son of Linthouse. This was facilitated by Charles E. Allan, a senior partner in Workman, Clark, who was a son of the late Alexander Allan of J. & A. Allan of Glasgow. Mr. C.E.Allan, who had been Technical Director of the Belfast firm since 1891, was a recognized authority on marine engineering and was responsible for many fine ships, including some for the Blue Funnel Line and the Royal Mail Company, in addition to Allan Liners. When he retired in 1921 the *Engineer* referred to Stormont Castle, "Mr Allan's magnificent Belfast residence," which is now better known as the seat of Government in Ulster.

As the first large turbine merchant ship, the *Victorian* raised doubts on her ability to stop and reverse with the required precision. In an official statement after the launch, Nathaniel Dunlop found it necessary to emphasize that Parsons had given special consideration to this, and that he had the confidence of owners and builders. There was a high-pressure turbine on the centre shaft which could not be reversed and was not used when manoeuvring. Steam was admitted to low-pressure ahead or astern sections of the two wing turbines for handling in the same way as a normal twin-screw ship. Despite the confidence of designers and builders it came as something of a surprise to masters and pilots to find that astern characteristics of the turbine were not to be compared with the stopping power of familiar reciprocating machinery. In all other respects the *Victorian* was brilliantly successful, her turbines working up to 12,000 indicated horsepower on trials in the Irish sea, giving a speed of 19½ knots at nearly 300 revolutions. This was the beginning of a new era, recognized in the pages of the *Engineer:*

Questions of durability and lasting efficiency are still, of course, matters for future experience to determine, but there seems at the moment every prospect of these points emerging triumphantly from the severest ordeal, while in respect of cost of manufacture and perfecting of detail every day should yield its quota of progress.

"Triumphantly" was the word. In June 1905 the *Virginian* was reported by the *Montreal Gazette* to have averaged 17.05 knots across the Atlantic. In August 1905 the same ship ran from Moville to Rimouski in 5 days, 20 hours and 22 minutes. For the first few months both ships were carefully handled but, as the machinery settled down to work, engineers became confident and opened the throttle to full and sustained power until, in June 1906, the *Victorian* steamed from Rimouski to Moville in 5 days and 5 hours.

Allan Line advertising made the most of their "New ocean triple-screw steamers" which were now approaching the Fast Line concept. An imposing painting of the *Victorian* at speed was flanked by more intimate views showing her three propellers, a source of comfort to timid travellers who could see all too well that she had one smokestack only, a deficiency known to deter emigrants in those days of multi-funnelled ocean greyhounds. For the benefit of apprehensive passengers unversed in the anatomy of the steam turbine, eulogies on quietness, comfort and speed were crowned by the surprising assurance that the new liners were also "odorless."

In fact they were well-appointed ships, carrying some 1,650 passengers on five decks, all of which were heated and ventilated on the thermo-tank system with individual cabin control. Intermediate passengers travelled in confort aproaching first-class standards in older ships – except for a certain condescension applied by some travellers towards second-class – while emigrant quarters with their four-berth cabins were greatly enhanced by spacious public rooms. To quote the sailing literature of the period:

> One feature of third-class accommodation deserves special mention. Hot water is provided, and is always on tap, so that "Lady thirds" who wish to dispense the kindly cup of afternoon tea to their fellow voyagers have always the means of doing so.

Despite the real improvements which placed the Allan Line with the best of the period, few tourists today would appreciate the sparse and "schoolroom" atmosphere which was considered appropriate to third-class accommodation. Emigrants were served their meals at table, the food was good, but the homely style of midday dinner and "high" tea was preferred to the sophistication of lunch and dinner. Space for the three classes of passenger was kept "Wholly distinct," but unaccompanied emigrant ladies with social aspirations were perhaps comforted by the many references to "Lady thirds," an honourable if bleak status to be compared with "Distressed gentlewomen" whose appeals were made in the columns of society papers. For those who could afford to travel in style, the first-class accommodation of the *Victorian* and *Virginian* offered the luxurious service characteristic of Edwardian hotels.

A new feature of travel in these ships was the *Allan Line Daily News,* a publication covering "The world's latest news by wireless from shore to shore." Since Marconi's historic trans-Atlantic radio transmission of 1901, the Canadian Government had established a chain of radio stations on the east coast, a facility which the Allan Line were quick to appreciate by equipping the *Parisian* with "Wireless" in 1902. The first regular Allan Line radio operator was William Davies of the Marconi Company who joined the *Parisian* in January 1903. The ship's newspaper, attractively produced and supported by luscious advertising from both sides of the Atlantic, featured Marconigrams from press agencies, stock market reports, and a selection of feature articles on the lighter side of travel. Passengers also enjoyed the convenience of sending and receiving personal messages and the wireless operator or "Sparker," tapping his morse key in transmission to the infinities of the air, was symbolic of the age. With their quickly-won reputation for remaining on duty in emergency, wireless operators had enhanced their new calling by adhering to the oldest tradition of the sea. If disaster should occur – and few passengers cared to think of it – the last resort was the lifeboats which, in those pre-*Titanic* days, were not necessarily sufficient for all on board. But strollers taking their constitutional round the boat deck of the *Victorian* or *Virginian* could take comfort from lifeboats made of "Seamless steel" and from two sets of the latest type of boat-lowering gear, the "luffing quadrant" davit.

As well as being the first turbine steamers on the Atlantic, the new Allan Liners were also the first to have triple screws, a feature which may have influenced the Canadian Government when awarding the subsidies of 1904-5. Under this arrangement the Company received £2,000 for each round voyage of the fast triple-screw *Victorian* and *Virginian,* £1,000 for the intermediate twin-screw *Bavarian* and *Tunisian,* and £500 each for the slower single-screw *Ionian, Sicilian* and *Pretorian,* also built in 1901. This arrangement was quickly put to use in advertising, which informed prospective travellers that the Allan Line was the only company "Under Government contract for conveyance of mails to Canada." This was a distinction which, from 1905, was extended to direct service between Canada and France by way of the London ships which henceforth called at Le Havre.

Nevertheless, and despite this air of confidence, there were signs of recession in the Indian Summer of 1905. Competition was increasing, costs were rising, and perhaps there were too many ships on the Atlantic. The lease of the New York pier used by the Allan Line ships from Glasgow expired that year, but the service had not been profitable of late, no effort was made to find alternative berthing, and with convenient rationalization the old State Line service was discontinued. But the most ominous news of 1905, announced in the *Montreal Gazette* of 6th January, was that Canadian Pacific planned to build two superior liners in opposition to the *Victorian* and *Virginian*. The original intention was to name them *Empress of Austria* and *Empress of Germany* but, whatever appeal this may have had for Teutonic emigrants, it was dropped because of the deteriorating international situation. With second thoughts on their imperial progress, Canadian Pacific forged the last link in their All Red Route by re-naming these challenging ships *Empress of Britain* and *Empress of Ireland*. Strangely enough, although they were bigger and more powerful than the latest Allan ships, Canadian Pacific hesitated about following the bold lead of the Allans in propelling machinery, and the two big *Empresses* came on the Atlantic from the Fairfield Shipbuilding and Engineering Company in Glasgow with two sets of enormous quadruple-expansion reciprocating engines, the last *Empresses* to be so fitted.

In January 1906, a few months before the *Empresses* came into service, the Allan Line were successful in securing a six-year contract which, it was hoped, would once more place them in the lead. In effect this was the culmination of nearly twenty years of indecision, frustration and disappointment in negotiation for the Fast Line. This contract was for a weekly service with four ships which would maintain 18 knots at sea under subsidy of £3,000 per round trip, with penalties for delays not due to stress of weather. With the advent of the radio stations and much improvement in St. Lawrence aids to navigation, such an arrangement had become a practical proposition compared to the contentious mail contracts of old, and the plan was to augment the *Victorian* and *Virginian* by construction of two new Allan Liners which would compete with the *Empresses,* a concept which required at least 20 knots on the measured mile. In the meantime shipbuilding costs had risen very considerably and the Allan Line were forced to rationalize their building program with a view to replacement of their older and slower ships. With this retrenchment Canadian Pacific's far-sighted policy and immense financial resources now began to pay off. There was only one thing to do, and the Allans did it, the two companies coming to an arrangement by which Canadian Pacific became sub-contractors to the Allan Line. It was the beginning of the end.

There was speculation in political circles over this arrangement and, in Ottawa, the government was questioned on placing the CPR in the position of sub-contractor. But the Allan Line was recognized as the senior company to engage in the Canadian Atlantic mail service, and the Minister of Finance told the House of Commons that the Government were satisfied with the arrangement:

It would be rather unfortunate that the Allans should be obliged to build two expensive steamers while these very fine Canadian Pacific

Railway vessels were available, and we are happy to find that the two companies came to an understanding. The result is that we have got on the whole a remarkably good service, not perhaps all that is desirable, but so much better than any service we have ever had before, that I think it has given a great degree of public satisfaction.

Despite this public satisfaction there were those who felt that the Government should have considered certain railway aspects which, as always, were associated with shipping policy. This contract again named Halifax as the winter port, and again the old bugaboo of the Government monopoly in the Intercolonial Railway was raised. For years the CPR, had tried without success to acquire running rights and it was argued that, consequent on their construction of the line to Saint John, their railway would suffer by sailing the two *Empresses* into Halifax. However Sir Wilfred Laurier stuck to his guns and in 1906, when he declared publicly that his ministry wished to save the rail freight, passenger and mail traffic for the government line, he was being refreshingly frank. As for the CPR, there was no need to worry. They could well afford to wait.

While the *Victorian, Virginian, Empress of Ireland* and *Empress of Britain* jointly fulfilled the mail contract from Liverpool, their owners were otherwise in direct competition for passengers and cargo on this fast route. Meanwhile the Donaldson Line, whose original South American service had been withdrawn within a few years of the Allan Line's challenge of 1876 to the River Plate, had made steady progress since their retaliation in the St. Lawrence. Thus in 1905, when Donaldson's began to make inroads on the passenger business, the Allan Line were influenced to replace their slower and older ships on the Glasgow run rather than invest in the Liverpool fast line. Indeed it was the Donaldson threat which largely influenced the Allans to economise by sub-contracting with Canadian Pacific instead of building two new turbine liners. The Glasgow challenge was answered directly by the building of the Allan liners *Grampian* and *Hesperian*, by Stephen of Linthouse and Barclay Curle of Scotstoun, respectively.

The trade from Glasgow to Canada did not require the speed necessary for the mail run from Liverpool. A comfortable ship which could average 15 knots in all but the worst weather was fully adequate, and an improvement on anything which had gone before. At that time the turbine was coupled directly to the propeller shaft, an arrangement which was suited to high-speed mailboats but which presented difficulties in slower cargo ships. The geared turbine, which overcame this difficulty, had not then been developed, so the new ships were fitted with conventional twin-screw triple-expansion reciprocating machinery. In the technology of the day it was a sound decision.

The first of the twin sisters was the *Grampian*, launched on 25th July 1907, by Miss May Allan, Now Mrs. May M. Last, who is the great-grand-daughter of Captain James. For the little girl who clutched her bouquet of flowers excitedly while a 10,000 ton ship, which she could practically touch, began to slide down the ways at her dainty command, it was a breathless moment, one never to be forgotten. But amidst the cheers and the bunting and the noise of that gathering momentum there may have been those among the launching party who wondered how long the Allan Line could last – and whether, if it came to the worst, they could get their money out on reasonable terms. If so they were remarkably prescient: for the *Grampian* and *Hesperian* were the last of the fleet to be planned, laid down and put into service under predominently family financing and control.

Great changes had taken place since 1897 when the Allan Line became a limited company rather than a partnership. All of the five brothers were dead and, although in Canada it was the sons of Sir Hugh and Old Andrew who ruled the firm, in Scotland associates of the founders were now predominant. The Chairman of the entire company, Sir Nathaniel Dunlop – he was knighted in 1907 – who had joined the brothers James and Alexander as a clerk about 1847 and had risen to succeed Old Andrew in the highest position, was due to retire. In the meantime another graduate of the Glasgow office, Colonel James Smith Park, who was prominent in Scottish military circles, had become an influential director. In Canada the key figures were Sir Hugh Montagu Allan – his knighthood came in 1904 – his younger brother Bryce James, and two of his cousins, Hugh Andrew and Andrew Alexander, who were sons of Old Andrew and were prominent in Allan Line affairs in Montreal and Boston.

About 1908 a meeting of the Scottish and Canadian directors was held in Montreal to determine the future of the Line. Facing growing opposition from Canadian Pacific and its enormous resources on sea and land, and with competition also from other North Atlantic companies typified by the Donaldson Line, it had become increasingly difficult for the Allans to hold their own on a broad front, never mind improve the position. If they wished to regain the lead they must finance at least another two turbine ships of the largest class which, now at the planning stage, must soon be built. The question was, what to do? Pull out now or attempt to carry on?

It seems likely that the meeting developed into a test of financial strength. If so the results were interesting and perhaps unexpected. The magazine *Canadian Railway and Marine World* carried this comment in December 1909:

Since the retirement of J. & A. Allan of Glasgow, Scotland, from any active part in the affairs of the Allan Line, a general transfer of shares has taken place, so that practically the whole are held on this side of the Atlantic. The list is as follows: – Sir H. Montagu Allan 15,727; H. A. Allan 14,132; B. J. Allan 14,580; A. A. Allan 14,698; J. S. Park 500; J. A. Spens and A. D. Wylie, one each.

This intriguing announcement, among others of the kind which appeared as titbits here and there in the shipping press, gave rise to rumours on the waterfront. It looked as though the Montreal Allans were in the driving seat. Certainly they held the majority of shares; everyone knew Colonel James Smith Park with his modest 500, and those in the know recognised Spens and Wylie with their single share. These were lawyers in Glasgow, Mr. Spens in particular was known far beyond the confines of MacLay, Murray & Spens in West George Street, a highly respected firm of Writers known to irreverent juniors of the cloth, with no more justification than any other nickname, as "Delay, Worry & Expense." Other rumours surmised that the Allan Line had been quietly taken over by Canadian Pacific, a report which was denied, or at least parried, by numerous highly-placed spokesmen over the next few years. In 1912 *Canadian Railway and Marine World* was particularly rich in denials. In October they wrote:

> Reports as to the amalgamation of the Allan Line with the CPR are met by the statement of Mr. G. Hannah, passenger manager of the Allan Line at Montreal, that he personally believes that the so-called fusion is a newspaper story, and that no official notice of it has been received at the Montreal office which would have been notified if it had taken place.

In November there was more speculation with the announcement that Sir Hugh Montagu Allan, B. J. Allan and J. Smith Park had retired from the Allan Line Board, and that the vacancies were filled, among others, by Sir Thomas Skinner, who was a CPR director. To add to the confusion various Canadian Pacific officials were elected directors of Allan, Brothers & Company in Britain. Developments 'of an extraordinary nature' were stated to be rumoured in Glasgow. In these circumstances the fine edge of the following denial, from the same paper, must have been blunted:

> In connection with the various rumours as to the acquirement of the Allan Line by the CPR which have had currency during the past two or three years, and which have been revived with continued persistency in the past few weeks, Sir Thomas Shaughnessy, President of the CPR, is reported to have stated that the arrangements between the

CPR and the Allan Line are the same now as they have been for years past, and that no change is contemplated in them.

In this, Sir Thomas was strictly accurate, if not illuminating. No change was contemplated, for it had been made over three years previously in a personal transaction. On 6th July 1909, a letter from F.E. Meredith K.C., acting on behalf of "Clients whose names are not disclosed," informed Sir Hugh Montagu Allan that:

> My clients are now ready to carry out the transaction that you have had under discussion with them during the past two or three months, namely to acquire all the capital stock of the Allan Line Steamship Company Limited, and to take it over as a going concern, free from debt, excepting ordinary operating liabilities, from month to month and except as hereinafter set forth, at the price of £1,609,000 . . . In addition to the above amount they are willing to pay £100,000 for the goodwill of the agencies on both sides of the Atlantic.

This letter of intent was put into effect by an agreement, dated at London, 8th September 1909, to which Mr. John A Spens and his clerk Andrew Hyslop were witnesses. It commenced as follows:

> Agreement between Frederick Edmund Meredith K.C., Montreal, acting and taking personal liability and burden for clients whose names are not disclosed (herein called the purchaser) of the first part and Sir Nathaniel Dunlop, Richard Gilkison Allan, Bryce Allan, James Alexander Allan and Henry Allan, Glasgow, Hugh Andrew Allan, Sir Hugh Montagu Allan and Andrew Alexander Allan, Montreal and James Bryce Allan, Boston (hereafter called the Trustees) acting jointly and severally for themselves and taking personal liability and burden on them for all others the present shareholders of the Allan Line Steamship Company Limited (herein called the Company) of the second part . . .

In one respect the *Railway and Marine World* was not quite correct. It forecast the "Severance of all Allan associations" with the Company's management. In fact, although the controlling interest passed to the Royal Trust Company, presumably on behalf of the "Clients whose names are not disclosed," members of the family continued to hold managerial positions, particularly in Montreal and Boston, for some years. From records of the Registrar of Companies in Edinburgh, Scotland, the financial position of the Allan Line Steamship Company Limited is made clear. Share transfers were completed on 11th November 1911, at which date the holdings were as follows:

Sir H. Montagu Allan, C.V.O.,	Montreal	500 shares	Shipowner
James Smith Park, M.V.O.,	Glasgow	500 do	do
Andrew Alexander Allan,	Montreal	500 do	do
Hugh Andrew Allan,	Montreal	500 do	do
Bryce James Allan,	Boston	500 do	do
Archibald D. Wylie,	Glasgow	1 share	Writer
John Alexander Spens,	Glasgow	1 share	do
H. Maitland Kersey, D.S.O.,	London	500 shares	–
The Royal Trust Company,	Montreal	57,637 do	–
Total		60,639 shares	

Major H. M. Kersey was a Canadian Pacific executive who thus acquired a status equal to the Allans in the financial structure.

The transfer of financial control was far from being the official demise of the Allan Line. This did not come about until 28th January, 1931, when a notice of dissolution appeared in the Register of Companies at Edinburgh. For years previously the Company had been nothing more than a legal entity retained only for accounting purposes. But the Annual Report of Canadian Pacific for 1931 shows that Allan Line deposits, amounting to nearly $8½ million, were transferred from reserve to the C.P. steamship replacement fund. The new owners had done well from the Allan Line which, after purchase and 22 years of corporate existence, left them with a tidy balance.

The 1914 War had much to do with this favourable financial position. Wars have always stimulated shipping, at least in the short run, and it was from profits earned in Napoleonic sea transport that Sandy Allan built the little *Jean* in 1819. Revenue from chartering the *Canadian* and *Indian* as troopers in the Crimean War helped his sons at a crucial stage at the foundation of the Montreal Ocean Steamship Company. In the Kaiser's War it would appear that Allan Line earnings went some way to augment the Canadian Pacific post-war building program.

The period from 1909 to 1931 was twilight for the Allan Line but as often at sunset there was colour and splendour. Certainly Canadian Pacific historians have given credit to the Allans as the lineal ancestors of that great enterprise in the shipping world. The prestige of the older company undoubtedly strengthened the new. In fact the epilogue is not the least important chapter in the story of *Ravenscrag* and the Allan Royal Mail Line. It is the climax.

EPILOGUE

ALLAN MEMORIAL

"Still my heart melts at human wretchedness;
And with sincere tho' unavailing sighs
I view the helpless children of distress."

R.B.
A Penitential Thought

Notwithstanding the confidential transaction of 1909, by which Canadian Pacific bought the Allan line, the two companies appeared to run in opposition; only those named in the transfer knew to the contrary. Partisans of the *tricoleur* and the chequer flag showed their loyalties by travelling in their favourite ships. Watchers in the St. Lawrence and the Mersey admired the aristocratic buff funnels of the *Empresses* and the familiar red-white-and-black smokestacks of the Allan Royal Mail Line. In company administration, members of both staffs may have been surprised at the ease with which economies were made by integration, first by uniting the supply departments, later by combining the offices of the marine superintendents. In numerous private lives, in Canada and in Scotland, life went on much as before.

Sir Montagu and Lady Allan were heirs to a rich tradition of hospitality by which *Ravenscrag*, the first and finest of the "Mountain" mansions of Montreal, with its acres of grounds, was the focus of social life. Every important visitor to Montreal was received there and an invitation to

Ravenscrag was socially coveted. In 1906 Prince Arthur of Connaught, son of the young Duke of Connaught who had been guest of honour in 1869 when three hundred of Montreal's elite danced till morning, was the guest of Sir Montagu and Lady Allan towards the end of his visit to Canada. On 9th May, in "Cold and wretched weather" as one observer noted, dinner at *Ravenscrag* was a warm gathering of fifty or so, after which the Allans took everyone to the Horse Show before escorting H.R.H. to the *Virginian* for a late supper. Amidst loyal toasts and farewells, the Royal Tour ended in the pride of the Allan Line.

Another interesting visit is recalled by a Notman photograph of 1907. It shows a distinguished group on the conservatory steps, the men in morning coats and high collars, the women crowned in the glory of wide hats with fruit, flowers and feathers in trimming of gorgeous profusion. Lady Allan sits in dignity on the step above her daughter Martha, a striking girl with the finest hat of all and an air of serenity far beyond her twelve years, while younger daughters Gwendolyn and Anna cluster with childlike eagerness on the lower steps. With Lady Allan sits His Imperial Highness Prince Fushimi of Japan, brother of the Mikado, while Sir Montagu presides from the top step with others of his family and the Prince's suite. It was an occasion to be remembered, a time when Sir Montagu offered the hospitality of *Ravenscrag* as a personal gesture for the honour of his country, a sentiment which Prince Fushimi recognised when he invested Sir Montagu, in a prandial interlude, with the Order of the Rising Sun.

Although *Ravenscrag* was the setting for many occasions of the kind, and successive Governor-Generals stayed there at one time or another, it remained essentially a private home where the Allan family enjoyed their friends. Sir Montagu was a keen sportsman, still remembered for the Allan Cup in amateur hockey, but best of all he loved horses. The *Ravenscrag* stables were noted for their thoroughbreds whose names, until fairly recent structural alterations, appeared above the loose-boxes. After the Montreal Horse Show, or at hunt breakfasts and other equestrian gatherings, the house and grounds would be alive with the presence of young men and women in hunting pink or black habits as they enjoyed the Allan hospitality. On winter afternoons the sleigh would be harnessed for the children and, on the annual procession of the Tandem Club, Sir Montagu would drive his sparkling turnout along Sherbrooke Street past the limestone mansions of Victorian Canada.

In summer the Allans left for the seaside. They had a glorious place at Cacouna, which was completed in 1901, a few miles east of Rivière du Loup. Here a superb framed mansion, white-painted and in classical style, looks across the blue of the Gulf to the mountain ranges behind the Saguenay. It stands there today, in outward appearance not greatly

173

changed, altered within to suit the needs of a religious retreat administered by the Capuchin Order. Young people still play tennis on the grass courts, the driveway still sweeps elegantly in a semi-circle from pillared iron gates, and the view from Lady Allan's bedroom, now enjoyed by the Father Superior, lacks only an Allan Liner hurrying upstream in the middle distance after dropping the mails at Rimouski. In the early years of the century Notman took photographs at Cacouna, among them a quartet in a spontaneous moment under the shade of the front porch. The four children of Sir Montagu and Lady Allan pause naturally on the steps, Martha with her intelligent searching gaze, young Hugh a round-faced, small boy in his white sailor suit, and Gwen and Anna in their summer frocks looking with eager anticipation beyond the camera. It is a poignant portrait of innocent childhood, the more so for the few short years vouchsafed to many of their generation.

Meantime the Allan flag was everywhere on the Atlantic, the numbers of emigrants began to be matched by eastbound passengers returning to renew family ties, and an increasing number of tourists. As always, passengers looked forward to the sea voyage which was still enough of a novelty to inspire the inevitable diary. In 1908 Mr and Mrs A.H.M. Bruce of Ottawa, with their children Arthur and Eileen, sailed to Glasgow in the *Grampian,* boarding at Montreal in baking heat which, in those days before air conditioning, was insufferable in the closeness of docks and grain elevators. But once in the Gulf, sea breezes and the pleasant anasthesia of shipboard routine began to work their timeless influence:

Sunday, 21st June '08:
Clear and very calm. Breakfast at eight, ship rolling slightly and breeze fresh. 10.30 am, service in the saloon . . . collection for the widows and orphans of sailors in Scotland . . . lovely afternoon . . . passed the *Victorian* bound for Quebec . . . Rose and the children enjoying the trip very much.

On the last night at sea passengers in the *Grampian* held the traditional concert, benefiting again the Scottish widows and orphans. Some of the audience entered into the spirit of Scotland too literally, making "quite a row" as they retired aft. Arthur Bruce had his own ideas on difficulties which might beset the Allan Line, noting the candid truth that:

After the ship passed Dumbarton the water rapidly became black and a short distance above and on to Glasgow the stench is simply disgusting. Why the Allan people do not land their passengers at Greenock is a puzzle and the direct cause, in my opinion, of their losing a large number of passengers.

174

Since then the Clyde has been improved out of all recognition, more than can be said for Montreal where oil and sewage combine to form pollution of the vilest kind half a century after Glasgow began to tackle the problem in earnest. As to the decline in passenger traffic, there was a slump in trans-Atlantic travel in 1908 which, according to a New York steamship agent quoted in the *Montreal Gazette* of 11th September that year, was down by thirty per cent. This state of affairs was attributed to financial uncertainty in general.

Although Glasgow interests in the Allan Line had passed entirely to Canadian Pacific, and the Montreal Allans remaining held only a small number of the total shares, it was Old Andrew's second son who became the last Chairman of the Allan Line, and his third son who became manager in Canada. In October 1912, commenting on Sir Montagu's retirement, the *Canadian Railway and Marine World* noted that:

Hugh Andrew Allan, who left Montreal a few years ago to take up his residence in London, England, will continue to act as Chairman of the Company, and Andrew A. Allan will represent the Board in Canada.

Hugh Andrew Allan had spent much of his business career in the Boston office, both he and his brother being trained and experienced in shipping. As with the sons of other prominent Montreal families, the brothers had been sent to Britain for their schooling, Hugh Andrew at first to Merchiston Castle in Edinburgh, and both eventually to Rugby where legends of Doctor Arnold and the adventures of Tom Brown lingered to make interesting schooldays. Hugh Andrew had been a partner in H & A Allan, he was a founder of the Shipping Federation of Canada, member of the Canadian Lighthouse Board, an ardent imperialist with enthusiasm for the Navy League, and a business leader whose influence on both sides of the Atlantic was considerable. As a shipowner he was progressive and it was generally held that his views had prevailed in the decision to pioneer the Parsons turbine in the *Victorian* and *Virginian.* When, in October 1911, it was announced that the Allan Line would build two liners of the highest class, those who knew the Chairman looked forward to something special. They were not to be disappointed.

These were the *Alsatian* and *Calgarian,* sisterships technically but differing somewhat in internal arrangement, which were intended to outclass the Canadian Pacific *Empresses* and to bring to the St. Lawrence route the luxurious standards of travel hitherto found only between Europe and New York. The pair were brilliantly successful and are acknowledged by all authorities to rank among the most attractive passenger ships of the early twentieth century, a period in which the Atlantic liner was approaching its zenith. The concept, which had been maturing in the Company for some years, was expressed in technical specifications originating from their chief naval architect, A.M. Gordon. Special attention was given to passenger appeal, the public rooms being decorated to the ideas of an interior design specialist, G.A. Crawley of Westminister. Both ships were built on the Clyde, the *Alsatian* by Beardmore at Dalmuir and the *Calgarian* by Fairfield at Govan.

At 600 feet on the waterline, the *Alsatian* and *Calgarian* were bigger than the *Empresses* and faster, achieving a service speed of 19½ knots at the full-load displacement of 22,500 tons. They had a flexible arrangement of turbines driving quadruple screws of which only the two inner shafts were used for manoeuvring. The port wing shaft was driven by a high-pressure turbine. There was an intermediate-pressure rotor on the starboard wing, while the two inners were coupled to the low-pressure turbines. They were, of course, coal-fired, burning 270 tons a day in six double-ended and four single-ended Scotch marine boilers under forced draft. In keeping with the Allan tradition of innovation, these ships incorporated a number of new ideas, among them the cruiser stern – which was the first to be seen on the Atlantic – and an exceptionally strong hull built to remain afloat with up to four compartments flooded. They had lifeboats for all on board, including the first motor lifeboat to be fitted with wireless on an Atlantic liner.

In appearance they were just right. They had a knifelike stem flaring into magnificent shoulders sweeping aft in a graceful sheer on which the superstructure sat with ease. Their two funnels, elliptical, slim and raking, were crowned to perfection with Admiralty cowls. The cruiser stern, another Admiralty feature befitting an auxiliary war vessel, sloped firmly out to complete an aristocratic profile. A vivid personal recollection of October 1929 is the *Empress of France* seen from the Blue Funnel Liner *Achilles* which encountered her at sea hurrying from Hong Kong to Liverpool by way of Suez. She was sighted ahead, at first a white mirage with curling bow wave in the blazing sheen of the Indian Ocean in the forenoon watch. But the Liverpool lookout man was not to be fooled and hailed the bridge with her original name. All eyes were on her as she drove closely past at over 20 knots. It was unforgettable. For the midshipmen it was a vision of youthful ambition, a dream of a ship to command.

Internally the new Allan Liners were equally impressive. In the magazine *Engineering* of 26th December 1913 the lounge is described as:

> . . . The finest room in the ship. It is almost exactly amidships on B deck – the highest deck with passenger rooms. For his inspiration in designing this lounge Mr. Crawley went to the royal apartments at

Hampton Court, for which Sir Christopher Wren was responsible. The roof, largely glazed, rises in the centre to a height of 18 feet and is carried on oak columns, beyond which are alcoves, with three great bow windows on each side of the ship. At the forward end is a handsome fireplace, and at the after end a mirror, both surmounted by carved trophies in the style of Grinling Gibbons, with paintings by George Lambert, the Australian artist.

Crawley went to immense trouble to authenticate the decorative style he used, going to Kensington Palace for the William and Mary motif for the *Alsatian's* library and writing room where bookcases were copied from those in the Pepys Library at Magdalene College, Cambridge. The smoking room, with its gallery and staircase, was Jacobean and included the replica of a chimney-piece in Old Place at Lindfield, a Sussex Manor house, with furniture reproduced from upright sofas in Knole House at Sevenoaks in Kent. Appropriately enough for Scottish traditionalists, Mr. Crawley did not forget the classical appeal of the Adam brothers, decorating his card room in the style so well exemplified at Kilmarnock in "Fairlie-five-lums."

Both ships sailed from Liverpool on their maiden voyages in 1914, the *Alsatian* to Halifax and Saint John in January, the *Calgarian* to Quebec in May. Allan Line brochures, superbly illustrated in colour, did full justice to the inauguration. Pains were taken to emphasize the merits of the cruiser stern which, reflecting that period of grave naval anxiety, may have imparted some comfort by reference to its "Warlike appearance" in addition to the peaceful virtues of strength, space and freedom from propeller vibration. First class fares varied enormously, according to the space and luxury provided. The single fare for one adult in the summer season ranged from £210 for the best suite on the bridge deck to £19 for the modest comfort of an inside berth on the shelter deck. For the first time "Motor cars" appear in Company literature, it being advised that passengers must have them crated and that freight rates would be quoted on application. Rates were quoted in sterling at five dollars to the pound.

It was a pleasant way of travelling. Some passengers took their servants but, as always, the brochure warned that servants were not entitled to sit at regular meals in the dining room. Families travelling first class could enjoy a well-earned rest with the assurance that their children would have special meals at separate sittings. Youngsters who aspired to dining *en famille* at the fashionable hour had to persuade their parents to pay full fare.

Apart from superb public rooms these ships gave every opportunity for different tastes. There was a fine gymnasium with everything from

177

the punch-ball to rowing machines. Perspiring bicycle enthusiasts could pedal like mad without moving an inch, encouraged by an enormous dial which crept round to register yards and even miles. For less active tastes there was the darkroom, where photographic snapshots could be developed, or the bookstall which was more than adequate for an hour's reading before retiring to deck-chair and steamer-rug. There were elevators at the main companionway by the purser's office, internal telephones throughout the ship, and the general effect was spacious, airy and comfortable. In the dining saloon, where passengers could sit unobtrusively at alcove tables or in larger groups as desired, the orchestra played in the musicians' gallery during dinner after which people wandered off to the smokeroom, for a rubber of bridge, or simply to indulge in pleasant conversation after the thrills of early cinema. Service was good, the liner steward of the day was acknowledged to be among the best personal attendants to be found anywhere and would invariably lay out his passenger's evening clothes, and there was an abundance of cooks from the world's best hotels. For those who liked to start the day with a brisk constitutional in bracing sea-air, the promenade deck offered some 400 feet of yellow-pine planking with the protection of bulwarks capped with teak rails.

Comparing this service with air travel today which, even in first class, is characterized by an uncomprehending tolerance of high-altitude flying in pressurized boxes with cramped seats, it is safe to assert that in every way other than elapsed time no vehicle can now equal the pleasure, comfort and dignity of an Atlantic voyage of 1914 in the *Alsatian* or *Calgarian*.

On the operating side, *General Regulations for the Navigation of the Company's Ships* provide an insight to life in a well-found Atlantic liner of 1913. All officers and senior petty officers were career men who rose by ability and satisfactory service under rules which were well understood. Apart from specific clauses dealing with primary technical matters, the regulations laid down standards of dress and deportment which applied to all from the Commander down. In keeping with the principles of the founders of the Line officers were warned to "Refrain from spirituous liquors while at sea" and not to smoke on duty at any time. Even the Commander, whose supremacy is constantly brought to notice, was enjoined to abstain from gambling and card playing. Doubtless rules of this kind were intended as a lever to be applied with common sense in the maintenance of discipline, but a glance at the accommodation plan of the *Alsatian* shows that the Commander was not expected to entertain lavishly in his own quarters which, although with day and night cabin appropriate to a ship of the size, opened off the officers' alleyway and were intended to be functional only. Safety of Life was the main theme

178

of the *Regulations,* followed closely by the comfort of passengers. They included for older vessels, this survival from older ways:

At sea in such ships as carry sail, every advantage is to be taken of the sails for the purpose of steadying the ship. When sail is carried at night, all gear must be kept clear and ready, and every precaution taken to reduce sail at a moment's notice.

It is unlikely that even the oldest Allan Liner carried sail in 1913 for topmasts and yards had been abandoned twenty years previously. But as long as a rag of a staysail or trysail remained in the bo'sun's store, the spirit of Sandy Allan lived on and no chances were taken.

It was an age which was rapidly drawing to a close. In the world of shipping some observers in 1913 thought they could see the hand of Canadian Pacific when the Allan Line South American service was sold to their old rival the Donaldson Line; but all such speculation was swamped in the onslaught of August 1914 and the dislocation of merchant shipping which immediately resulted. Three days after the outbreak of war the *Alsatian* was taken over by the Admiralty for service as an armed merchant cruiser, followed not long afterwards by the *Calgarian, Victorian* and *Virginian.*

The *Calgarian* was employed in blockading neutral ports to prevent the escape of German liners, first off Lisbon and later off New York, but as the war at sea settled down she became an escort vessel for North Atlantic convoys. Although ships of this kind were of little use in action, and suffered appalling casualties in both world wars, they filled an emergency role with distinction. In 1914 almost 50% of the world's merchant fleet flew the British flag, including 100 passenger liners of more than 10,000 tons with speeds up to 18 knots. Among 24 such vessels commandeered for naval service, the cream of the crop were assigned to the 10th Cruiser Squadron, an extraordinary group of ships which must be unique in having replaced major warships which were found to be hopelessly unsuitable for the job.

The 10th Cruiser Squadron, under Admiral de Chair with his flag in HMS *Crescent,* consisted of eight obsolete cruisers from the reserve fleet, all of which were over 22 years of age. They had been activated to carry out the Northern Blockade with the objective of preventing the passage of German ships from the North Sea by the Orkneys and Shetlands route. Experience in the fearful weather of the Northern patrol soon showed that these old ships could neither steam nor fight, despite the undoubted energy of their officers and men. After severe and continual storm damage they were paid off at Liverpool on 3rd December 1914. Meantime the liners had been refitting and, armed with 6-inch guns, HMS *Alsatian* commissioned at Liverpool before sailing for Scapa Flow to join the fleet as flagship of the reconstituted 10th Cruiser Squadron. On Christmas morning 1914, Admiral de Chair was piped on board at Scapa as his flag was hoisted at the main, the anchor was weighed, and the *Alsatian* proceeded to sea to join her consorts on Patrol 'A' which ran northwards from the Faroes to intercept ships bound to or from Scandinavia.

It was a thankless and hazardous task but at least these ships could keep the sea. Another of their advantages lay in the accommodation which, although it had been knocked about during conversion, was spacious compared to broadside messing in the old cruisers. The stokers fell heir to the second class smoke-room, the seamen having usurped the first class, and an article in the magazine *Sea Breezes* of August 1964 recalls that:

> The stokers' smoking room was one of the cleanest and best run of the lot in all the crew's section, the men taking a great pride in it, and having their own rules about using it, that no man should do so unless properly dressed in the rig of the day.

To appreciate this one should remember that the *Alsatian,* in common with the Grand Fleet, was still burning coal at the time and every pound of the 5,000 tons she carried in her bunkers had to be trimmed, fired and raked (and thrown overboard as ashes after burning) entirely by manpower. Liner firemen, as might be expected, were a breed all of their own whose contribution to maritime history is fundamental, unique and all but forgotten. The Liverpool-Irish fireman, generally acknowledged as the arch-type, had many virtues but the wearing of uniform was not usually one of them.

The officers and ships company included a few from the Royal Naval Reserve, although most RNR officers from the Allan Line were already in cruisers and destroyers by this time, and a number of men from the Royal Fleet Reserve, the balance being made up of merchant seamen under temporary engagement. Fortunately there were plenty of Scottish fishermen without whom, in high-sided liners, the boarding and examination of other ships would have been impossible. Life in an A.M.C. was often frustrating and uncomfortable – on one occasion the stately *Alsatian* was immodest enough to roll 25 degrees, flaunting her shapely bottom in a way unbecoming to an Atlantic lady. The 10th C.S., which included the Allan Liner *Virginian,* had a morale of its own and has earned a secure place in naval history.

By October 1917 when the Squadron was dispersed, the 10th C.S. had intercepted 8,905 merchant ships, sent 1,816 into port under armed guard for examination, and boarded 4,520 fishing vessels. At no time did the Squadron exceed 25 liners and ocean freighters, plus a few steam trawlers, its own losses by enemy action amounting to 12 ships and something over 1,000 lives. In enforcing the blockade these liners and trawlers played a vital part in Allied strategy. As in the Second World War, it was proved that in the long run sea power depends on merchant shipping and seamen.

The flagship of the 10th Cruiser Squadron came through the war safely but other Allan Liners were not so lucky. On 4th September 1915 the *Hesperian,* Captain Maine, on a normal voyage from Liverpool to Halifax with passengers and cargo was torpedoed by U-20 (a submarine to remember) with the loss of 32 lives when off the Fastnet. The *Carthaginian* was mined and sunk in 1917 as was the *Ionian;* the *Pomeranian* was torpedoed in 1918 only six weeks after the loss of the beautiful *Calgarian.* The loss of HMS *Calgarian,* Captain R.A. Newton R.N., was particularly unfortunate as she had almost reached safety at the time. On 1st March 1918, when escorting an eastbound Atlantic convoy into the Clyde, she was torpedoed by four shots in succession and sank quickly with the loss of 49 lives in the last and bitter phase of the submarine campaign.

The knockout blow for the Allan Line, although delivered in wartime, came not from the enemy but from Canadian Pacific. On 1st October 1915, following a meeting in Montreal, a new company was announced as "Canadian Pacific Ocean Services" which would take over both fleets. The chairman was Mr. G.M. Bosworth, who was Vice President of the CPR. The managing director of the new shipping company, to nobody's surprise, turned out to be Major H. Maitland Kersey, the CP nominee on the Allan Line board. Commenting on this merger the *Canadian Railway and Marine World* noted that:

> Under any circumstances other than those now prevailing it would have been a matter of universal comment, even in the daily press, that the Allan Line was to be, in fact, absorbed by its big ally the Canadian Pacific Railway Company. As it is, the news was published in a small paragraph and there, as far as the public interest goes, the matter seems to have ended.
> . . . The gross tonnage of the Allan Line was about 155,000 tons – excluding the lost *Hesperian* – whilst that of the CPR is about 239,000 tons, the united concerns thus controlling somewhere approaching 400,000 tons of first class steamships, many of which are modern passenger vessels.

The Allan Line, with its entire staff and assets, was officially transferred to Canadian Pacific on 16th July 1917 when Sandy Allan's flag was hauled down for the last time. For almost a century, in good times and bad, in peace and war, the Allan houseflag had gained the respect of those who knew the North Atlantic but its passing was hardly noticed in the maelstrom of the War. Afterwards people wondered what had become of the red-white-and-black funnels. In Glasgow, Montreal, Liverpool and Quebec the old name lived on for years in familiar dockside notices and fading advertisements peeling from rural railway stations.

The war years, which covered the demise of the Allan Line, were tragic for the family of whom many were on active service and some died. Sir Montagu and Lady Allan's family suffered grievously. Sir Montagu kept up the militia tradition in the Black Watch (Royal Highland Regiment) of Canada, of which he was Honorary Lieutenant Colonel by 1911. With the outbreak of war in 1914 he at once volunteered for service overseas, but at fifty-four he was too old to command the Battalion. In any case his immense capability in shipping was needed in Canada during the first hectic months when merchant vessels of all kinds were pressed into use. His daughter Martha, by then a spirited girl of nineteen, was studying drama in Paris as the Germans swept through Belgium. She came home to train as an army nurse before returning to France driving an ambulance which she bought with her own money.

About a year later, by which time Martha was nursing in a military hospital in England, Lady Allan decided to go there to provide a convalescent home for Canadian soldiers. Young Hugh was still at school but to keep the family together as much as possible it was arranged that Gwen and Anna would go to England with their mother in the expectation that Sir Montagu, to be sent to London on war business, would join them later. Accordingly Lady Allan and the girls went to New York where they had booked in the *Lusitania* for a quick passage. Sailing day must have been uneasy as passengers read a grim warning in their morning papers:

> Travellers intending to embark for an Atlantic voyage are reminded that a state of war exists between Germany and her Allies and Great Britain . . . and that travellers sailing in the war zone in ships of Great Britain or her Allies do so at their own risk.

> Imperial German Embassy,
> Washington D.C.
> April 22nd., 1915

Despite this notice most passengers remained on board and the *Lusitania* sailed as ordered on 1st May with 1275 passengers and 702 crew. The voyage was uneventful until they neared the Irish coast when wireless warnings of submarine activity were received. Passing through this area the danger appeared to be receding when Captain Turner closed the land to fix his position before altering course for Liverpool and reducing speed to 18 knots to catch a favourable tide on the shallows of the Mersey Bar. At 2 pm on 7th May, when 10 miles off the Old Head of Kinsale, the *Lusitania* was torpedoed by the German submarine U-20 under Kapitan-Leutnant Schwieger. She sank in fifteen minutes with the loss of 1198 lives.

The news reached Ottawa early the following day in a flurry of cables, from the High Commissioner in London to Sir Robert Borden, which included the following:

Prime Minister, Ottawa.

Harold Daly, Lady Allan and two daughters, Miss Braithwaite, Bob Holt and Orr Lewis reported safe. As we have many cable enquiries from Canada kindly notify public that we have sent a man to Queenstown to render all possible aid to Canadian passengers on board. Could you ascertain position and cable us.

Dominion.

Subsequent messages raised doubts about the safety of the girls although one report mentioned that they had been seen in a lifeboat. But among the Borden Papers in the Public Archives of Canada there is the message which destroyed that hope:

Prime Minister, Ottawa.

Griffith now at Queenstown. Telegraphs body of Canon Phayre, Winnipeg now identified. Lady Allan is considered to be holding her own splendidly. She is so badly bruised that nature of injury obscure but the feeling in regard to her is hopeful. One of her daughters was with Mr. Lewis but was wrenched from his grasp. The other was with her mother but he fears that both are lost. Lady Allan went to Dublin today.

Thus died the two little girls photographed by Notman on the porch at Cacouna. Gwen was sixteen and Anna a year younger.

In September 1915 Sir Montagu went to London as head of the Canadian Overseas Pension Board. Lady Allan opened her convalescent home for Canadian soldiers, provided at her own expense in the South of England, where Martha joined her in nursing.

Two years afterwards the war claimed the small boy in the sailor suit. On 6th July 1917, at the age of twenty, Flight Sub-Lieutenant Hugh Allan of the Royal Navy was shot down and killed while piloting a fighter aircraft on his first patrol over enemy lines. He is buried at Coxyde in Belgium where his brother officers placed a simple memorial on his grave. Today, in the library at *Ravenscrag,* a poignant scrapbook reminds the visitor of his death.

In the post-war years life at *Ravenscrag* was bravely resumed. Martha, by then a talented woman of many interests, took her place among the leaders of cultural life in Montreal and young people from all the arts and parts were especially welcomed. Sometimes, as had happened before the war when the Earl and Countess of Minto stayed there for a while, *Ravenscrag* became a second Government House. On occasion the Governor General in temporary residence would invite Sir Montagu and his Lady to the unusual experience of dining as guests in their own home. Once, when Lord Bessborough was there for a waiting week or two, the old house savoured the joy of new life when a son was born to the Bessboroughs in the nearby Royal Victoria Hospital.

In 1930 Martha Allan took over the stables for rehearsals of "The Perfect Alibi," first production of the Montreal Repertory Theatre which she founded. Among her own plays, "All of a Summer's Day" won the Sir Barry Jackson Trophy in the Dominion Drama Festival. She also wrote "What Fools We Mortals Be."

With the outbreak of the Second World War it was no longer desirable to keep *Ravenscrag* as a private home, Sir Montagu and Lady Allan donated the house and grounds to the Royal Victoria Hospital on the understanding that, whatever humanitarian use might be made of *Ravenscrag,* it would be called the "Allan Memorial." In 1942, with the death of Martha Allan at Vancouver, the memorial commemorated also the last survivor of the four Allan children. The transfer of the property took place in 1943 when Major James C. Routledge, who is Sir Hugh Allan's grandson and now farms Sir Hugh's estate of *Belmere,* handed the keys of *Ravenscrag* to Dr. D. Ewen Cameron who was Professor of Psychiatry at McGill University. Today the Allan Memorial Institute, which houses clinical, teaching and research activities of the Department of Psychiatry of McGill University, is known throughout the world.

Sir Montagu died in 1951, Lady Allan in 1957. Some will remember Sir Montagu for the Allan Cup in amateur hockey, others will think of the Marguerite Martha Allan Trophy in Canadian Theatre. In the shipping world the Allan Royal Mail Line has long ago earned an honoured place in history although, for most people, little now remains to bring this to light. The last Allan Liner to be afloat called at the Port of Montreal in the early fifties, unrecognized by all but oldtimers on the waterfront. Under the name *Homeland* the proud old *Virginian,* flying the Panamanian flag, was still a fine ship after half a century, a record surely unique among Atlantic liners when she was finally scrapped in 1955.

Of necessity *Ravenscrag* has been much altered internally and external additions have been made. Sir Hugh would feel at home in his library, which is the only room remaining as it once was, but he might have difficulty surmounting unfamiliar obstacles in ascending the square tower from which he watched the distant river for the smoke of his incoming mail steamer. His motto is still over the front door and, if epitaph there must be, what better than the prospect it suggests to those who enter seeking help? *Spero.*

APPENDICES

APPENDIX I

The Ayrshire Allans, The Burns Connection and The Founding of The Allan Line

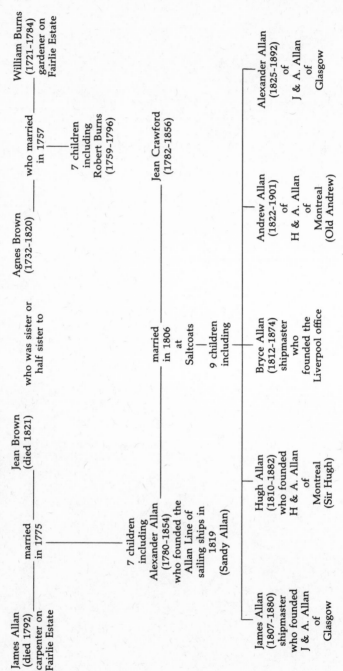

James Allan (died 1792) carpenter on Fairlie Estate — married in 1775 — Jean Brown (died 1821)

William Burns (1721-1784) gardener on Fairlie Estate — who married in 1757 — Agnes Brown (1732-1820), who was sister or half sister to

7 children including Robert Burns (1759-1796)

7 children including Alexander Allan (1780-1854) who founded the Allan Line of sailing ships in 1819 (Sandy Allan) — married in 1806 at Saltcoats — Jean Crawford (1782-1856)

9 children including

James Allan (1807-1880) shipmaster who founded J & A. Allan of Glasgow

Hugh Allan (1810-1882) who founded H & A. Allan of Montreal (Sir Hugh)

Bryce Allan (1812-1874) shipmaster who founded the Liverpool office

Andrew Allan (1822-1901) of H & A. Allan of Montreal (Old Andrew)

Alexander Allan (1825-1892) of J & A. Allan of Glasgow

These five brothers founded the Montreal Ocean Steamship Company in 1854 which became

THE ALLAN ROYAL MAIL LINE

APPENDIX II

Ravenscrag, Montreal and the Allan Memorial

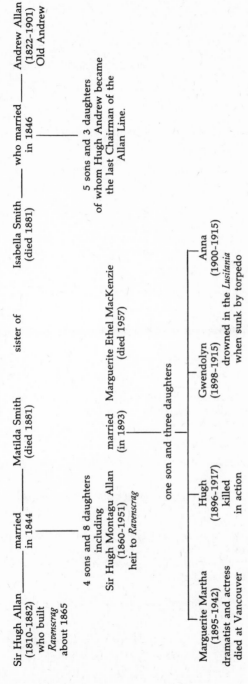

Sir Hugh Allan
(1810–1882)
who built
Ravenscrag
about 1865

married
in 1844

Matilda Smith
(died 1881)

sister of

Isabella Smith
(died 1881)

who married
in 1846

Andrew Allan
(1822–1901)
Old Andrew

5 sons and 3 daughters
of whom Hugh Andrew became
the last Chairman of the
Allan Line.

4 sons and 8 daughters
including
Sir Hugh Montagu Allan
(1860–1951)
heir to *Ravenscrag*

married
(in 1893)

Marguerite Ethel MacKenzie
(died 1957)

one son and three daughters

Marguerite Martha
(1895–1942)
dramatist and actress
died at Vancouver

Hugh
(1896–1917)
killed
in action

Gwendolyn
(1898–1915)

Anna
(1900–1915)
drowned in the *Lusitania*
when sunk by torpedo

The Allan Memorial Institute

In 1943 Sir Montagu and Lady Allan gave *Ravenscrag* to the Royal Victoria Hospital with the request that henceforth it be known as the *Allan Memorial Institute*. With the death of Sir Montagu and Lady Allan's family there were no male heirs of Sir Hugh. The *Allan Memorial Institute* houses clinical, teaching and research activities of the Department of Psychiatry of McGill University.

APPENDIX III

Chronology of the Allan Line

1819   Captain Alexander Allan, owner and master of the brigantine *Jean,* commenced regular sailings between Greenock and Quebec. Sailed from Greenock 5th June.

1826   Hugh Allan landed in Montreal.

1830   Captain Allan built his first full rigged ship, the *Canada.* His eldest son James became master of the brig *Favourite.*

1834   Captain Alexander Allan opened his first office in Greenock, replacing agents.

1837   The third son, Captain Bryce Allan, became master of the *Canada.*

1839   Hugh Allan became a partner in Edmonstone, Allan & Co., Montreal, and was joined by his younger brother Andrew. The firm became H & A Allan later.

1842   Captain James Allan retired from sea to open an office in Glasgow.

1846   James, with his youngest brother Alexander, founded the firm of J & A Allan, shipowners, in the Glasgow office.

1847   Nathaniel Dunlop, then a young man of 17, started employment in J & A Allan.

1853   St. Lawrence & Atlantic Railway opened between Montreal and Portland. The 5 Allan brothers, with 5 Canadian partners, raised capital to build steamships.

        Captain Alexander Allan, who was then 73, abstained.

        The first Allan Line steamship, the *Canadian,* was laid down at Dumbarton.

        Captain Bryce Allan retired from sea about this time and opened the Liverpool Office.

1854   Hugh and Andrew Allan, with other Canadian partners, incorporated the Montreal Ocean Steamship Company with powers to operate the vessels building in Scotland. The steamship *Canadian* arrived in Quebec on her maiden voyage.

1855   The Canadian Government awarded the Atlantic mail contract to Hugh Allan, Montreal.

1856   After an interruption due to the Crimean War, the Allan Royal Mail Line started regular sailings with four ships, fortnightly from Liverpool and Quebec.

1857   The Allan brothers bought out their partners and commenced weekly sailings.

1861   The Allan Line opened regular steamship service between Glasgow and Canada.

1870   Newfoundland was included in the Glasgow Service.

1871   Sir Hugh Allan of Montreal became interested in financing the trans-continental railway envisaged by Sir John A. Macdonald as the backbone of Confederation.

1873   After a bitter struggle which became a political storm, Sir Hugh Allan was unsuccessful in financing the Canada Pacific Railway. He foresaw that whoever controlled the railway might also control the sea routes to Canada.

1876   The Allan Line commenced regular sailings to South America.

1880   The Allan Line built the first steel Atlantic liner, the *Buenos Ayrean.*

1881   The *Parisian,* finest ship in the Canadian trade, came into service. She was the first liner to have bilge keels.

1882   Sir Hugh Allan died. His brother Andrew became senior partner and was known as 'Old Andrew'.

1886   The Canadian Pacific Railway was completed.

1891   The Allan Line opened Glasgow to New York service. The CPR were awarded the China mail contract and placed three *Empress* liners on the Vancouver to Far East service.

1896   The Allan Line sold their last sailing ship, the full rigged *Glenmorag.*

1897   The *Allan Line Steamship Company Limited* was incorporated with Andrew Allan of Montreal as Chairman.

1901   Andrew Allan died and his son, Hugh Andrew, became senior partner in H & A Allan of Montreal.

Nathaniel Dunlop, of the Glasgow office, became Chairman of the *Allan Line Steamship Company Limited.*

1905   The Allan Liners *Victorian* and *Virginian,* first turbine liners and the first to have triple screws, were built and created a sensation.

Canadian Pacific announced the building of the *Empress of Britain* and *Empress of Ireland* for their Atlantic service.

1906   The Allan Line, unable to finance additional fast ships, subcontracted with Canadian Pacific to place the *Empresses* in the mail contract.

1909 Sir Nathaniel Dunlop retired. Sir H. Montagu Allan of Montreal became Chairman of the Allan Line. Under a confidential agreement between Sir H. Montagu Allan and Sir Thomas Shaugnessy of CPR, Canadian Pacific purchased the Allan Line and its agencies for about $8½ million. Outwardly the two companies were in opposition.

1912 Sir H. Montagu Allan retired as Chairman of the Allan Line and was succeeded by his cousin Hugh Andrew of Montreal.

1913 Donaldson Line purchased the South American service of the Allan Line.

1914 The Allan Line Royal Mail Steamers *Alsatian* and *Calgarian,* fast quadruple screw turbine liners, were put into service between Liverpool and Canada.

1915 Canadian Pacific announced the formation of Canadian Pacific Ocean Services which would absorb the Allan Line.

1916 January 1st, C.P.O.S. came into operation as managers and agents for Canadian Pacific and Allan Lines.

1917 Amalgamation of the two companies was completed, thus confirming a state of affairs which had been in evolution for eight years. The Allan Line remained as a legal entity, without ships or real property, only for accounting and corporate purposes.

1931 On 28th January, the Registrar of Companies in Edinburgh noted the formal dissolution of the *Allan Line Steamship Company Limited.*

APPENDIX IV

Allan Line - Fleet List

(a) Sailing ships

Name	Tons	Description	Date and builder	Remarks
Abeona	979	iron ship	1867 Stephen Glasgow	Considered to be the fastest of the Allan Line clippers Sold to Andrew Weir 1900 lost off Cape of Good Hope
Albion	471	wood ship	1845 Steele Greenock	After many years of Allan Line service was believed to be afloat 1870 as a barque
Ardmillan (1)	987	wood ship	1855 Quebec	Built of oak, elm and tamarack. For many years in the Australian trade from Britain
Ardmillan (2)	1729	iron ship	1878 Dobie Glasgow	
Anglesea	913	wood ship	1855 New Brunswick	Liverpool to North America
Blonde	676	wood barque	1840 Montreal	Oak, elm and tamarack. Owned by Edmonstone and probably partly owned by Hugh Allan. Jamaica trader. Lost at sea 1849
Brilliant	428	wood ship	1834 Montreal	Owned by Paterson of Greenock, probably partly owned by Allan. Jamaica trader from Montreal. Lost at sea 1847
Britannia	419	wood ship	1845 Greenock	Liverpool Atlantic trade.

APPENDIX IV
(a) Sailing ships

Name	Tons	Description	Date and builder	Remarks
Brunette	676	wood barque	1840 Montreal	Wrecked on St. Paul's Island, Gulf of St. Lawrence, 1843
Cairngorm	1043	wood ship	1853 Quebec	
Caledonia	438	wood ship	1841 Greenock	Quebec trade from the Clyde
Canada	330	Wood ship	1831 Steele Greenock	Allan Line first full-rigged ship. Employed on Quebec and West Indian Atlantic trade as opportunity offered.
Catherine	687	wood barque	1850 Russell Quebec	
Cherokee	718	wood ship	1854 Steele Greenock	Employed Liverpool to India in the fifties. Later Liverpool to Newfoundland with salt, Newfoundland to Brazil with dried cod, Brazil to Liverpool with coffee and tobacco.
Chippewa	1072	wood ship	1863 Gingras Quebec	Later sold to R. Burns of Greenock
City of Montreal	1187	wood ship	1863 Paterson & Shaw Quebec	In Australian trade.
City of Toronto	696	wood ship	1855 Toronto	Oak and tamarack. Built for the Allans and brought from the Great Lakes to engage in the Liverpool to North America trade

Name	Tonnage	Type	Year	Builder	Notes
Dunbritton	1536	iron ship	1875	McMillan Dumbarton	By 1905 was sold to Andrew Weir and had been cut down to barque rig
Favourite (1)	296	wood brig	1825	Montreal	White oak and cedar. By 1845 was owned by J. Cullen of Port Glasgow
Favourite (2)	405	wood barque	1839	Montreal	Oak and hackmatack
Florence	960	wood ship	1857	New Brunswick	
Glasgow	347	wood barque	1836	Millar Edmonstone Montreal	Hugh Allan was part owner. Jamaica trader, lost on Sable Island, 1840.
Glenbervie	800	iron ship	1866	Connell Glasgow	Later bought by Bramwell & Gardiner
Glencairn (1)	949	wood ship	1850	Quebec	In the Australian trade
Glencairn (2)	1619	iron ship	1878	Dobie Glasgow	Converted to 4-masted barque by 1887 and reputed to be the smallest of the type. Sold to Thomas Law of Glasgow in 1895 and lost off the Horn in 1907
Glendaruel	1840	iron ship	1876	Barclay Curle Glasgow	
Glenfinnart	1601	iron ship	1876	Barclay Curle Glasgow	
Gleniffer	800	iron ship	1866	Barclay Curle Glasgow	1871 made 4 trips to the St. Lawrence between the ice including one passage of 15 days Quebec to Greenock. Sold to Nicholson & McGill in the nineties.
Glenmorag	1648	iron ship	1876	Dobie Glasgow	The last sailing ship of the Allan Line, sold in 1896

Appendix IV (Cont)
(a) Sailing ships

Name	Tons	Description	Date and builder	Remarks
Harlequin	702	wood barque	1851 Dubord Quebec	Clyde to Savannah trade
Iona	847	wood ship	1857 Quebec	
Jean		wood brigantine	1819 Gilkison, Thomson & Co Irvine	The first regular trader of the Allan Line. Under Captain Alexander Allan opened the business in 1819. Length 76' - 8" × breadth 22' - 6" × depth 13' - 4"
Marion	738	wood ship	1848 Russell Quebec	Employed Clyde to India
Medora	811	wood ship	1867 Barr Ardrossan	By 1887 owned by Lagergren of Stockholm
Minerva	1365	iron ship	1868	wrecked 1871
Mohawk	850	wood ship	1854 New Brunswick	
Montreal	506	wood ship	1848 Dumbarton	Liverpool to Montreal trade
Ottawa	492	wood ship	1851 Quebec	
Pericles	991	wood ship	1856 Miramichi	Liverpool to North America
Polly	710	wood barque	1845 Donaldson Quebec	

Name					Notes
Pomona	1252	iron ship	1867	Steele Greenock	
Ravenscrag	1263	iron ship	1866	Steele Greenock	Sold to Richardson of Swansea
Romsdal	1887	iron ship 4-masted	1877	Steele Greenock	The only 4-masted full-rigged ship of the Allan Line and one of the few ever built
Staffa	922	wood ship	1856	New Brunswick	
St Lawrence	578	wood ship	1852	Dumbarton	
Saint Patrick					See under (b) Steamships
Strathblane	1440	iron ship	1868	Barclay Curle Glasgow	
Strathearn	1784	iron ship	1871	Barclay Curle Glasgow	Noted as a fast ship in heavy weather; reputed to have sailed from New York to the Clyde in 10 days. Sold to Schramm of Hamburg and renamed *Henriette*
Thalia	472	wood ship	1840	Montreal	
Thistle	260	wood barque	1836	Montreal	

Appendix IV (Cont)
(b) Steamships

Name	Tons	Description	Date and Builder	Remarks
Alsatian	1848	steel turbine quad-screw	1914 Beardmore Dalmuir	First Atlantic liner to have cruiser stern 1914 armed merchant cruiser 1917 taken over by CPOS 1919 renamed *Empress of France* 1935 scrapped
America	1826	wood paddle sidelever	1848 Steele Greenock	Built for Cunard. Chartered by Allan Line in 1863 for temporary summer service to St. Lawrence. The only paddler to be employed by the Company on ocean service.
Anglo-Saxon	1715	iron screw 2-cyl simple	1856 Denny Dumbarton	1863 wrecked near Cape Race, Newfoundland Similar to *North American*.
Assyrian	3317	steel screw compound	1880 Earle Hull	Built as *Assyrian Monarch*, purchased by Allan Line 1887. Employed Glasgow, New York, Philadelphia, Boston Scrapped 1902
Australasian	3662	steel screw triple-exp.	1884 Napier Glasgow	Built for G. Thompson & Co. Purchased by Allan Line in 1901 but disposed of after a few voyages.
Austrian	2458	iron screw 2-cyl simple	1867 Barclay Curle Glasgow	1875 fitted with compound machinery 1888 fitted with triple expansion machinery Employed on Canadian and South American service 1905 scrapped

Name	Tonnage	Machinery	Built	Notes
Bavarian	10376	steel twin-screw triple-exp.	1899 Denny Dumbarton	Liverpool to Montreal service Trooping to South Africa 1899-1902 Stranded in the River St. Lawrence in 1905, without loss of life, and had to be broken up as she lay.
Belgian	2259	iron screw 2-cyl simple	1855 Caird Greenock	Built as the *Hammonia* for Hamburg America Line and purchased by Allan Line in 1864. Sold in 1872 and wrecked in 1873 as the Dominion Liner *Missouri*. Had the old-fashioned geared oscillating engine.
Bohemian	2200	iron screw 2-cyl simple	1859 Denny Dumbarton	Employed Liverpool to Portland. Wrecked off Cape Elizabeth 1864
Brazilian	3204	steel screw triple-exp.	1891 Henderson Glasgow	Employed London to Montreal with occasional voyage to South America. Sold to Brazil 1910.
Buenos Ayrean	4005	steel screw compound	1880 Denny Dumbarton	The first steel steamer on the North Atlantic. 1896 fitted with quadruple expansion machinery. Employed from Glasgow to Canada and U.S. with annual voyage to South America. Scrapped 1910.
Calgarian	17515	steel turbine quad-screw	1914 Fairfield Glasgow	Generally similar to *Alsatian* 1914 armed merchant cruiser 1917 taken over by CPOS 1918 torpedoed by U-boat
Californian				See *State of California*
Canadian (1)	1764	iron screw 2-cyl simple	1854 Denny Dumbarton	The first steamship of the Company. Similar to *Indian* 1855-56 trooping to the Crimea 1856 wrecked below Quebec.

Appendix IV (Cont)
(b) Steamships

Name	Tons	Description	Date and builder	Remarks
Canadian (2)	1926	iron screw 2-cyl simple	1860 Steele Greenock	Employed Liverpool-Portland or Quebec 1861 sank after striking an iceberg near Belle Isle.
Canadian (3)	2911	iron screw compound	1873 Roydon Liverpool	Employed Liverpool and Glasgow to Canada, from 1892 to South America mostly. 1903 scrapped
Carthaginian	4444	steel screw compound	1884 Govan S/B Co Glasgow	Employed on Glasgow and Liverpool service New boilers 1901 1917 mined near Inishtrahull
Caspian	2728	iron screw 2-cyl simple	1870 London & Glasgow Co. Glasgow	Employed mainly Liverpool - Baltimore Fitted with compound engine 1882 1897 scrapped
Castilian	7441	steel screw triple-exp.	1899 Workman Clark Belfast	Wrecked in the Bay of Fundy while returning from Portland on her maiden voyage from Liverpool.
Circassian	3211	iron screw 2-cyl simple	1873 Steele Greenock	1875 lengthened from 375 to 415 feet and fitted with compound engine. Employed Liverpool to Montreal until scrapped in 1896
Corean	3488	iron screw compound	1881 Doxford Sunderland	Employed on Glasgow and London routes. 1908 scrapped

Name	Year	Builder	Tonnage	Construction	Notes
Corinthian (1)	1856	Denny Dumbarton	1213	iron screw 2-cyl simple	Built as the *G.Lanza* for Italian owners, purchased by Cunard in 1860 and renamed *Damascus*; purchased by Allan Line in 1863 after chartering. Placed on Liverpool service until 1870 when lengthened from 253 to 288 feet and renamed *Corinthian*; compound engine also fitted. Employed on Glasgow service until 1881 when sold. Scrapped in 1912 when under the Turkish flag.
Corinthian (2)	1900	Workman Clark Belfast	6227	steel screw triple-exp.	Employed in succession on Liverpool, Glasgow and London service. 1917 taken over by CPOS and converted from passenger and cargo to cargo only. Wrecked in Bay of Fundy 1918.
Corsican	1907	Barclay Curle Glasgow	11419	steel twin screw triple-exp	In 1912 collided with an iceberg but only slightly damaged. Mostly on Glasgow service. 1917 taken over by CPOS. 1922 renamed *Marvale*. 1923 wrecked near Cape Race.
Damascus					See *Corinthian (1)*
European	1866	Malcolmson Waterford	2629	iron screw simple	Built as the *William Penn* and purchased by the Allan Line in 1869 for the Liverpool service, she was renamed *European* in 1872. In 1875 she broke her back on entering drydock and was lengthened from 316 to 327 feet and compounded. Re-engined 1884. Sold 1889 and scrapped 1894.
Gallia	1879	Thomson Glasgow	4809	iron screw 3-cyl compound	Built for Cunard 1896 became *Don Alvado de Bazan* of Compagna Transatlantica 1897 became *Gallia*, Beaver Line 1899 purchased by Allan Line. Stranded at Sorel that year and was subsequently scrapped.

Appendix IV (Cont)
(b) Steamships

Name	Tons	Description	Date and Builder	Remarks
Germany	3244	iron screw 2-cyl simple	1868 Pearse Stockton	1868-72 employed on Liverpool-Montreal service. 1872 wrecked near Bordeaux while on her second voyage to New Orleans, a service which was then abandoned.
Grampian	10955	steel twin screw triple-exp	1907 Stephen Glasgow	On Glasgow to Montreal service. 1917 taken over by CPOS 1926 scrapped.
Grecian	3613	iron screw compound	1880 Doxford Sunderland	On Glasgow service to Canada and U.S. 1898 picked up survivors of *Cromartyshire/La Bourgogne* collision. 1902 wrecked near Halifax.
Hanoverian	3603	iron screw compound	1882 Doxford Sunderland	1882 Glasgow to Montreal service, 1883 to U.S. 1885 wrecked off Newfoundland
Hesperian	10920	steel twin screw triple-exp	1908 Stephen Glasgow	Similar to *Grampian*, on Glasgow service 1915 torpedoed off the Fastnet
Hibernian	1888	iron screw 2-cyl simple	1861 Denny Dumbarton	Reputed the first liner to have flush spar deck. 1871 lengthened, 1884 fitted with compound machinery Liverpool and Glasgow service. Scrapped 1901

Name	Tonnage	Construction	Built	Notes
Hungarian	2200	iron screw 2-cyl simple	1859 Denny Dumbarton	Liverpool to Montreal service. 1861 wrecked off Cape Sable Island with all on board
Huronian	6550	steel screw triple-exp	1901 Palmer Newcastle	Liverpool service 1902 disappeared in the Atlantic without trace
Indian	1764	iron screw 2-cyl simple	1856 Denny Dumbarton	On completion when trooping to the Crimea. 1856 Liverpool to Quebec service 1859 wrecked off Nova Scotia coast
Ionian	8268	steel twin screw triple-exp	1901 Workman Clark Belfast	Glasgow, Liverpool and London to Canada and U.S. Taken over by CPOS in 1917 and subsequently torpedoed.
Jura	2241	iron screw 2-cyl simple	1854 Thomson Glasgow	Built for Cunard. Had a geared beam engine. 1860 chartered by Allan Line and purchased in the following year. 1864 wrecked in the Mersey
John Bell				See *Saint Patrick*
Lake Erie	7550	steel twin screw triple-exp	1900 Barclay Curle Glasgow	Built for Elder Dempster, acquired by Canadian Pacific in 1903. Chartered by the Allan Line 1910–1912 for London to Montreal service. Scrapped in 1925
Laurentian				See *Polynesian*
Livonian	4162	steel twin screw compound	1881 Dobie Glasgow	Built as the *Ludgate Hill* for the Twin Screw Line, purchased by Allan Line and renamed *Livonian* in 1897 Employed on Glasgow to U.S. service 1900 fitted with triple expansion machinery 1914 sold to Admiralty and sunk as a blockship at Dover

Appendix IV (Cont)
(b) Steamships

Name	Tons	Description	Date and builder	Remarks
Lucerne	1925	iron screw compound	1878 Laird Liverpool	Employed on all services including South America. 1898 sold to U.S. Government
Manitoban	1810	iron screw 2-cyl simple	1865 Laird Liverpool	Built as the *Ottawa* and purchased by Allan Line about 1868 when renamed *Manitoban*. 1872 lengthened from 287 to 339 feet and compounded, On Glasgow and U.S. service. Scrapped in 1899.
Mongolian	4838	steel screw triple-exp	1891 Henderson Glasgow	Employed on all services except South America 1900 trooping to South Africa 1914 sold to Admiralty 1918 torpedoed
Monte Videan	3076	steel screw triple-exp	1887 Henderson Glasgow	Employed on Glasgow to South America service. From 1888 also on London to Montreal run. 1910 scrapped
Moravian	2481	iron screw 2-cyl simple	1864 Steele Greenock	Employed on Liverpool to Portland service 1874 lengthened from 320 to 389 feet and fitted with compound machinery 1881 wrecked on Nova Scotia Coast
Nestorian	2466	iron screw 2-cyl simple	1867 Barclay Curle Glasgow	Employed on all Canadian U.S. services 1878 fitted with compound machinery 1897 scrapped

Name	Tonnage		Year	Builder	Notes
North American	1715	iron screw 2-cyl simple	1856	Denny Dumbarton	Similar to the *Anglo-Saxon*. Liverpool to Montreal service until 1871, thereafter to Baltimore. 1874 engines removed, sold.
North Briton	2187	iron screw 2-cyl simple	1858	Denny Dumbarton	Liverpool to Montreal service. Similar to *Nova Scotian*. 1861 wrecked on Mingan Island near Antigosti
Norwegian (1)	1888	iron screw 2-cyl simple	1861	Denny Dumbarton	Similar to *Hibernian* Employed Liverpool to Montreal 1863 wrecked on St. Paul's Island
Norwegian (2)	3523	iron screw compound	1865	Tod & McGregor Glasgow	Built for the Inman Line as *City of New York* Purchased by Allan Line 1884 Employed Glasgow to Canada and U.S. 1903 scrapped
Nova Scotian	2108	iron screw 2-cyl simple	1858	Denny Dumbarton	Liverpool service to Canada and U.S. 1873 lengthened from 298 to 366 feet and compounded 1893 scrapped
Numidian	4836	steel screw triple-exp	1891	Henderson Glasgow	Employed on Liverpool and Glasgow services 1914 sold to Admiralty for sinking as a blockship Similar to *Mongolian*
Ontarian	4078	steel screw triple-exp	1900	Duncan Port Glasgow	Cargo only 1913 sold to Donaldson Line
Palestine	1800	iron screw 2-cyl simple	1858	Steele Greenock	Built for Cunard and chartered by Allan Line in 1860 for temporary service liverpool to Montreal

Appendix IV (Cont)
(b) Steamships

Name	Tons	Description	Date and builder	Remarks
Parisian	5359	steel screw 3-cyl compound	1881 Napier Glasgow	Liverpool service to Canada and U.S. Originally fitted with 4 masts and 2 funnels, the fore and main masts carrying yards. After a brief period the main yards were removed. In 1899 rebuilt and fitted with triple-exp machinery with one funnel and 4 pole masts 1902 fitted with wireless 1914 scrapped after a remarkably successful career.
Peruvian	2549	iron screw 2-cyl simple	1864 Steele Greenock	Liverpool service mostly, Glasgow later Like the *Parisian* her appearance changed with refits 1891 compounded and a second funnel added 1905 scrapped
Phoenician				See *Saint David*
Polynesian	3983	iron screw 4-cyl compound	1872 Steele Greenock	Known as the *Rolling Poly* because of her propensity to roll at sea. 1893 refitted with triple-expansion engine and renamed *Laurentian*. Employed Liverpool and Glasgow to Canada & U.S. 1909 wrecked near Cape Race.
Pomeranian	4364	iron screw compound	1882 Earle Hull	Built as *Grecian Monarch* and purchased by Allan Line 1887. 1893 severely damaged in heavy weather 1902 refitted with triple expansion engine Taken over by CPOS in 1917, torpedoed 1918

Name	Tonnage	Year / Builder	Construction	History
Pretorian	6948	1901 Furness Withy West Hartlepool	steel screw triple-exp	Liverpool and Glasgow services 1917 taken over by CPOS 1925 scrapped
Prussian	2794	1869 Inglis Glasgow	iron screw 2-cyl simple	Liverpool and Glasgow services 1879 refitted with compound engine 1898 scrapped
Rosarian	3077	1887 Henderson Glasgow	steel screw triple-exp.	Employed on Atlantic and South American services 1910 scrapped
Roumanian	4225	1883 Murray Dumbarton	steel twin screw compound	Built for the Twin Screw Line as *Richmond Hill* 1897 purchased by Allan Line and renamed *Roumanian* 1898 sold
Saint Andrew	1432	1861 Barclay Curle Glasgow	iron screw 2-cyl simple	1861 opened the Glasgow service to Montreal 1874 lengthened from 253 to 322 feet, compounded and renamed *Waldensian* for Glasgow to U.S. service 1888 fitted with triple-expansion machinery and placed on South American run 1903 scrapped
Saint David	1516	1864 Barclay Curle Glasgow	iron screw 2-cyl simple	Served from Liverpool and Glasgow to Canada 1873 lengthened from 272 to 335 feet and compounded and renamed *Phoenician* 1888 refitted with quadruple expansion machinery - the first Atlantic liner to be so equipped. After South American service was scrapped in 1905
Saint George	1468	1861 Steele Greenock	iron screw 2-cyl simple	With *St. Andrew* opened the Glasgow service in 1861 1869 wrecked off Nova Scotia, near Seal Island.

207

Appendix IV (Cont)
(b) Steamships

Name	Tons	Description	Date and builder	Remarks
Saint Patrick	1101	iron screw 2-cyl simple	1854 Stephen Glasgow	Built as the full rigged sailing ship *John Bell* 1856 bought by Anchor Line and machinery fitted 1862 bought by the Allan Line for the Glasgow to Montreal service and renamed *Saint Patrick* in 1863 1875 machinery removed and went back into service with the Allan Line as a sailing ship. Subsequently sold and became the Italian *Diamant*. Scrapped about 1905.
Sarmatian	3647	iron screw 4-cyl compound	1871 Steele Greenock	Served on all North Atlantic routes. Trooping in 1874 1890 refitted with triple-expansion machinery 1908 scrapped
Sardinian	4349	iron screw compound	1875 Steele Greenock	1897 fitted with triple-expansion machinery Taken over by CPOS in 1917 and scrapped about 1920
Scandinavian (1)	2840	iron screw 2-cyl simple	1870 Steele Greenock	Liverpool and Glasgow services 1879 compounded 1899 scrapped
Scandinavian (2)	12099	steel twin screw triple-exp	1898 Harland & Wolff Belfast	Built as the *New England* and later became the White Star liner *Romanic*. 1912 purchased by Allan Line and renamed *Scandinavian* 1917 taken over by CPOS 1923 scrapped

Ship	Tonnage	Material / Type	Year	Builder	History
Scotian	10322	steel twin-screw triple-exp	1898	Harland & Wolff Belfast	Built as the *Statendam* for Holland America Line. Bought by the Allan Line in 1911 and renamed *Scotian*. Taken over by CPOS in 1917 and renamed *Marglen* in 1922. 1927 scrapped
Siberian	3904	steel screw compound	1884	Govan S/B Co Glasgow	Sailed Glasgow to Canada and U.S. 1912 scrapped
Sicilian	6224	steel twin screw triple-exp.	1899	Workman Clark Belfast	Trooping to South Africa until 1901. Liverpool, Glasgow and London services. 1917 taken over by CPOS, renamed *Bruton* in 1922. 1925 scrapped
State of California	4244	steel screw triple-exp	1891	Stephen Glasgow	Built for the State Line and purchased by the Allan Line for Glasgow to New York run. Renamed *Californian* in 1898. Sold in 1901 and scrapped in 1925
State of Georgia	2490	iron screw compound	1873	London & Glasgow Glasgow	Built as the *Georgia* and renamed in 1873. 1891 purchased by the Allan Line for New York service. 1893 sold to Aberdeen Line. 1896 disappeared at sea
State of Indiana	2528	iron screw compound	1874	Wingate Glasgow	Built for the State Line and purchased by Allan Line in 1891 for Glasgow to New York service. Sold to Turkey in 1893 and became *Ismir*
State of Nebraska	3986	iron screw compound	1880	London & Glasgow Glasgow	Built for State Line and purchased by Allan Line in 1891. Scrapped in 1902

Appendix IV (Cont)
(b) Steamships

Name	Tons	Description	Date and builder	Remarks
State of Nevada	2488	iron screw compound	1874 London & Glasgow Glasgow	Built for State Line and purchased by Allan Line in 1891 for Glasgow to New York service Sold to Turkey in 1893 and became *Mekke*
Sweden	908	–	1869 Barclay Curle Glasgow	Built for the Scandinavian feeder service carrying emigrants from Sweden to Hull for train to Liverpool Made a few Atlantic voyages in 1872
Tainui	5086	steel screw triple-exp	1884 Denny Dumbarton	Built for the Shaw Savill Line and after various changes was chartered by the Allan Line in 1899 for the Liverpool to Montreal service. After a few voyages became the *Astoria* of the Anchor Line and was scrapped in 1911
Tunisian	10576	steel twin screw triple-exp	1900 Stephen Glasgow	On Liverpool service to Canada 1917 taken over by CPOS 1922 renamed *Marburn* 1928 scrapped
Turanian	4021	steel twin screw compound	1881 Dobie Glasgow	Built for the Twin Screw Line as *Tower Hill* 1897 purchased by Allan Line for Glasgow to New York run and renamed *Turanian* 1899 placed on South America service and wrecked on Cape Verde Islands. Salvaged and sold for scrap

Name	Tons	Description	Date and builder	Remarks
Victorian	10635	steel triple screw turbine	1905 Workman Clark Belfast	First turbine liner on North Atlantic 1914 became armed merchant cruiser 1917 taken over by CPOS 1922 renamed *Marloch* and fitted with geared turbines 1929 scrapped
Virginian	10757	steel triple screw turbine	1905 Stephen Glasgow	Liverpool to Canada service 1914 taken over as armed merchant cruiser 1917 taken over by CPOS 1920 sold to Swedish America Line as *Drottningholm* 1948 renamed *Brasil* for Home Line and in 1951 renamed *Homeland* 1955 scrapped after a career which is probably a record of continuous service for an Atlantic liner.

Appendix IV (Cont)
(c) Coastal and inland water vessels and yachts.

Name	Tons	Description	Date and builder	Remarks
Arawa	220	steel schooner	1890 Henderson Glasgow	Employed for lightering at River plate. Towed from the Clyde to South America by Allan liner.
Avispa	220	steel schooner	1890 Henderson Glasgow	As *Arawa*
Bay of Kandy	–	iron paddle	1855 Stephen Glasgow	176 feet in length
Chicarra	220	steel schooner	1890 Blackwood & Gordon Glasgow	As *Arawa*

Appendix IV (Cont)
(c) Coastal and inland water vessels and yachts

Name	Tons	Description	Date and builder	Remarks
Herminga	220	steel schooner	1890 Henderson Glasgow	As *Arawa*
Hermione	320	steel screw quad-exp	1891 Fleming & Ferguson Paisley	Steam yacht designed by G.L. Watson. Fleming & Ferguson fitted their patent quadruple-expansion engine which had two pairs of cylinders driving a two-throw crankshaft by means of triangular frame connecting rods. Purchased by U.S. Navy in 1898 for the Spanish American War where she sunk the enemy ship *Alphonso XII* in action. Remained in the USN from 1898 as the USS *Hawk* until she was broken up in 1940 at Michigan City. For much of her career she was employed as a Reserve training ship on the Lakes.
Lady of the Lake	369	iron paddle	1867 Magog Que.	152-foot passenger steamer on Lake Memphremagog between Magog and Newport. Fabricated in Scotland, erected at site on Lake Memphremagog. Scrapped 1917
Lake Ontario	–	iron paddle	1864 Stephen Glasgow	180-feet in length
Meteor	252	wood	1866 Sorel Que.,	130-foot paddle tug owned by Hugh Allan between 1873–80 for service between Quebec and Montreal, including passengers. In 1900 became the passenger and freight steamer *City of Owen Sound* on the upper lakes. 1906 renamed *Erindale.*

Name	Tonnage	Type	Year	Builder	Notes
Mosquito	220	steel schooner	1890	Henderson Glasgow	As *Arawa*
Newfoundland	919	wood screw compound	1872	Baldwin Quebec	Machinery built by Ouseburn of Newcastle-on-Tyne. Rigged as as a brig. Employed on Halifax to Newfoundland feeder service 1872-1892. Sold to Nova Scotia and in 1904 to St. John's where she became one of the sealing fleet. Registry closed 1915.
Nora	60	wood paddle	1866	Knowlton's Landing Que.,	Owned by Hugh Allan 1873-80 and employed as a tug on Lake Memphremagog.
Ormond					Small steam yacht belonging to Sir Hugh Allan for use at Belmere on Lake Memphremagog.
Rocket	386	wood paddle	1866	Sorel Que.	Owned by Hugh Allan 1873-89 and employed on passenger and tug service between Montreal and the Gulf. 149 feet in length. 1900 renamed *Britannic*.
Topsy	—	iron paddle	1866	Stephen Glasgow	130 feet in length

BIBLIOGRAPHY

Allan Brothers & Company:
Practical Hints and Directions to Intending Emigrants to Canada and United States.
Liverpool, Allan Line, 1872 – Public Archives of Canada.

Allan Brothers & Company:
The Allan Line Handbook – every intending emigrant to Canada and United States should read this.
Liverpool, Allan Line, 1904 – Public Archives of Ottawa.

Allan Line:
Logbooks of brig *Favourite,* 1829 – 30 and 1836; ship *Canada,* 1831 – 35 and 1837 – 41; ship *Caledonia,* 1841 – 44; ship *Albion,* 1845 – 47.
Microfilm, Public Archives of Canada.

Allan Line Steamship Company Limited:
General Regulations and Regulations for the Navigation of the Company's Ships.
London, A.C. Fowler, 1910.

Allan, Sir Hugh:
"Some Sketches of Events in an Active Life".
Address to the Young Men's Association of St. Andrew's Church, Montreal, about 1880 – Public Archives of Canada.

Atherton William Henry:
History of Montreal, 1534-1914.
Montreal, City Improvement League, 1915

Atherton, William Henry:
History of the Harbour Front of Montreal, 1535-1935.
Montreal, City Improvement League, 1935.

Benstead, C.R.:
Atlantic Ferry.
London, Methuen, 1936.

Berton, Pierre:
The National Dream.
Toronto, McClelland & Stewart, 1970.

Bonar, James C:
"History of Canadian Pacific Ocean Steamship Services".
Montreal, unpublished, 1950.

Bonsor, N.R.P:
North Atlantic Seaway
Prescot, Lancs., T. Stephenson & Sons Ltd, 1955.

Bowen, Frank C:
A Century of Atlantic Travel, 1830-1930.
London, Sampson, Low, Marston & Co., 1930.

Bowen, Frank C:
History of the Canadian Pacific Line.
London, Sampson, Low, Marston & Co., 1930.

Burns, Robert:
Poems and Songs.
London, Oxford University Press, 1969.

Bush, Edward Forbes:
"The Canadian Fast Line on the North Atlantic, 1886-1915"
Ottawa, unpublished, 1970.

Cleghorn, R.A:
The History of Ravenscrag.
Montreal, McGill University, Department of Psychiatry, 1968.

Croil, James:
Steam Navigation and its Relation to the Commerce of Canada and the United States.
Toronto, William Briggs, 1898.

Fry, Henry:
The History of North Atlantic Steam Navigation.
London, Sampson, Low, Marston & Co., 1896.

Gibbs, C. Vernon:
Passenger Liners of the Western Ocean.
London, Staples Press Limited, 1957.

Gilbert, Heather:
*Awakening Continent; The life of Lord
Mountstephen:*
Aberdeen, University Press, 1965.

Hocking Charles:
*Dictionary of Disasters at Sea during the
age of Steam, 1824-1962.*
London, Lloyds Register of
Shipping, 1970.

Hunter, John Kelso:
The Retrospect of an Artist's Life.
Scotland, about 1867.

Hunter, John Kelso:
Life Studies of Character.
Scotland, about 1867.

Innis, Harold A:
A History of the Canadian Pacific Railway.
Toronto, McClelland & Stewart,
1923.

Jones, Clement:
Lives of Pioneer Shipowners.
Liverpool, Journal of Commerce,
1934.

Kelly, Owen.
"The Story of Saltcoats Harbour"
*Ardrossan and Saltcoats Herald, 22
January 1971.*

Lamb, W. Kaye:
"Empress to the Orient".
British Columbia Historical Quarterly,
Vol. IV., No. 1 and Vol. IV., No. 2.

Lamb, W. Kaye:
"Empress Odyssey".
British Columbia Historical Quarterly,
Vol. XII., No. 1.

Lindsay, Maurice:
Burns Encyclopedia.
Second edition, 1970.

Lloyd's Register of Shipping.
London.

Lubbock, Basil:
The Last of the Windjammers.
Glasgow, Brown, Son & Ferguson.

Maclehose, James and Sons:
*Memoirs and Portraits of One Hundred
Glasgow Men.*
Glasgow, James Maclehose and
Sons, 1886.

Maginnis, Arthur J:
*The Atlantic Ferry, Its ships, men and
working.*
London, Whittaker & Co., 1900.

McDougal, Lorne:
Canadian Pacific, a brief history.
Montreal, McGill University Press,
1968.

McJannet, Arnold F:
The Royal Burgh of Irvine.
Irvine, 1938.

McKnaught, D:
"Burns Topography, Kilmarnock and
its vicinity".
Burns Chronicle, 1892.

Montreal Board of Trade:
Semi-Centennial Report.
Montreal, 1892.

Musk, George:
*A Short History and Fleet List of the
Canadian Pacific Steamships, 1891-1961.*
London, Canadian Pacific and World
Ship Society, 1968.

Myers, Gustavus Adolphus:
A History of Canadian Wealth.
Toronto, Lewis & Samuel, 1972.

Notman, W and Taylor, Fenning:
*Portraits of British Americans with
Biographical Sketches.*
Montreal, Notman, 1867.

"One who knows";
"The Allan Family. Facts not
fiction."
Ardrossan and Saltcoats Herald,
8 October, 1886.

Ramsay, Robert:
Rough and Tumble on Old Clipper Ships:
New York, D. Appleton & Co.,
1930.

Reford, Eric:
The Robert Reford Company Limited,
1866-1966.
Montreal, Reford, 1966.

Sea Breezes,
Liverpool, periodical:
  Hughes, T.E.:
  "The 10th Cruiser Squadron",
  Vol. 12, July-December, 1951.

  Isherwood, J.H:
  "Allan Liners *Victorian* and *Virginian,*" Vol. 12, July-December, 1951.
  "Allan Liners *Alsatian* and *Calgarian,*" Vol. 23, January-June, 1957.
  "Allan Liners *Bavarian* and *Tunisian,*" Vol. 43, July-December, 1969.

  Lamont, R.C.W:
  "Laurentian crossings", Vol. 26, July-December, 1958.

Sessional Papers, Canada:

  Department of Public Works, Annual Report:
  1856,   pps. 27-28, 'Ocean Steamers';
  1857,   pps. 25-26, 'Ocean Steamers';
  1866-7, pps. 264-7, 'Grosse-Ile Quarantine Station';
  1866-7, Appendix No. 48, 'Port of Quebec – Statement of the number of
        vessels and their aggregate tonnage which have arrived at
        Quebec from sea in each year from 1764 to 1866 inclusive,
        distinguishing steamers from sailing vessels from 1831 to 1866
        inclusive, and the number of men employed etc.'
  1867,   Appendix No. 54, 'Return of passages, number of passengers,
        and cargoes of the steamships of the Montreal Ocean Steamship
        Company under contract for the conveyance of the mails from
        Liverpool to Quebec and Portland, from 9th November 1865 to
        4th December 1866.

  Department of Marine and Fisheries, Annual Report:
  1870,   Appendix No. 14 (1) 'Return of passages, number of passengers,
        and cargoes of the Montreal Ocean Steamship Company under
        contract for the conveyance of mails from Liverpool to Quebec
        and from Quebec to Liverpool from April 14th 1870 to
        November 26th 1870.'

(2) 'Return of passengers and cargoes of the Allan Glasgow Line from Glasgow to Quebec and from Quebec to Glasgow from April 13th 1870 to November 24th 1870'.

(3) 'Return of number of passages and cargoes of the steamships of the Allan Line from Liverpool to Quebec and Quebec to Liverpool from April 15th 1870 to November 22nd 1870.'

(4) 'Statement of the passengers and cargoes carried by the steamships and sailing vessels of the Allan Line during the season of St. Lawrence navigation 1870.'

1875,   Report of Chief Engineer, Montreal Harbour Commissioners, on the operations of the chain tug in St. Mary's current. This report gives names of Allan ships towed. (pps. 150-156)

1879,   pps. 194-6, Report by the Harbour Master, Montreal – first vessels from sea being Allan Liners *Circassian* from Liverpool and *Waldensian* from Glasgow.

1879,   pps. 223-5, Lightened cargoes, Allan Line inwards and outwards. Appendix No. 40, Report of the Port Warden, Montreal; grounding of the Allan Liner *Peruvian.*

1881,   p.1, Grounding of the Allan Liner *Moravian.* Appendix No. 33, Report of the Montreal Harbour Police. Pps. 323-7 contains narrative of Montreal dock strike.

1902,   pps. 27-8, Report on Casualties in the St. Lawrence.

1905,   pps. 78-82, St. Lawrence casualties, grounding of the *Victorian.*

1913,   Sessional Paper No. 21, 'Atlantic Emigrant Traffic'.

Young, Brian J:
"The defeat of George-Etienne Cartier in Montreal East in 1872."*Canadian Historical Review,* Vol. LI, No. 4, December 1970.

INDEX

For Allan family and business relationships see Appendices I and II. See Appendix III for chronology and Appendix IV for details of ships. Italicised entries refer to ships unless otherwise indicated.